JOHN CAGE

MESSIAEN'S LANGUAGE OF MYSTICAL LOVE
edited by Siglind Bruhn

EXPRESSION IN POP-ROCK MUSIC
A Collection of Critical and Analytical Essays
edited by Walter Everett

JOHN CAGE
Music, Philosophy, and Intention, 1933–1950
edited by David W. Patterson

JOHN CAGE

MUSIC, PHILOSOPHY, AND INTENTION, 1933–1950

EDITED BY
DAVID W. PATTERSON

ROUTLEDGE

NEW YORK   LONDON

Published in 2002 by
Routledge Publishing, Inc.
29 West 35th Street
New York, New York 10001

Published in Great Britain by
Routledge
11 New Fetter Lane
London EC4P 4EE

10 9 8 7 6 5 4 3 2 1

Library of Congress Cataloging-in-Publication Data

John Cage : music, philosophy, and intention, 1933–1950 / edited by David W. Patterson.
    p. cm.— (Studies in contemporary music and culture ; v. 3) (Garland reference library of the humanities ; vol. 2088)
    Includes bibliographical references and index.
    Contents: John Cage, Arnold Schoenberg, and the musical idea / David W. Bernstein — Cultural intersections : John Cage in Seattle (1938-1940) / Leta E. Miller — No ear for music : timbre in the early percussion music of John Cage / Christopher Shultis — John Cage's Imaginary landscape no. 1 : through the looking glass / Susan Key — "A therapeutic value for city dwellers" : the development of John Cage's early avant-garde aesthetic position / Branden Joseph — The picture that is not in the colors : Cage and Coomaraswamy, the impact of India / David W. Patterson — An imaginary grid : rhythmic structure in Cage's music up to circa 1950 / Paul van Emmerik — Structure vs. form in the Sonatas and interludes for prepared piano / Chadwick Jenkins
    ISBN 0-8153-2995-4 (alk. paper)
    1. Cage, John—Criticism and interpretation. I. Patterson, David Wayne. II. Series. III. Series: Garland reference library of the humanities ; vol.2088

ML410.C24 J625 2000
780'.92—dc21
                                                                00-042996

Printed on acid-free, 250-year-life paper
Manufactured in the United States of America

Contents

Series Editor's Foreword

Studies in Contemporary Music and Culture

Joseph Auner

Now that we have entered a new century, many of the established historical narratives of twentieth-century music are being questioned or reconfigured. New approaches from cultural studies and feminist theory, methodologies adapted from such disciplines as literary theory, philosophy, and anthropology, and debates about the canon, postmodernism, globalization, and multiculturalism are profoundly transforming our sense of both what the repertoire of twentieth- and twenty-first-century music is and how it should be understood. "Studies in Contemporary Music and Culture" provides a forum for research into topics that have been neglected by existing scholarship, as well as for new critical approaches to well-known composers, movements, and styles.

Volumes in the series will include studies of popular and rock music; gender and sexuality; institutions; the audience and reception; performance and the media; music and technology; and cross-cultural music and the whole range of the crossover phenomenon. By presenting innovative and provocative musical scholarship concerning all aspects of culture and society, it is our aim to stimulate new ways to listen to, study, teach, and perform the music of our time.

Introduction

Charles Hamm

These essays, written mostly by musicologists, deal with the early
life and music of John Cage. What follows is intended to place the
present volume in the perspective of previous Cage scholarship, and
in doing so, to underline its uniqueness.

Words and music by Cage

Throughout his career, John Cage wrote about his own work from the
perspectives of technique and aesthetics. Beginning in 1939, he contributed dozens of articles and essays to such publications as *Dance
Observer*, *New Music*, *The Village Voice*, *Art News*, and *Dance
Perspectives*. From 1959, when he began attracting international
attention, he wrote for similar journals in Germany, Sweden, Italy,
Japan, England, and elsewhere. He brought many of these pieces
together in a series of book-length volumes published by Wesleyan
University Press:

Silence (1961)	writings 1939–61
A Year from Monday (1967)	writings 1963–67
M (1973)	writings 1967–72
Empty Words (1979)	writings 1973–78
X (1983)	writings 1979–82

When one adds *I-VI*, the Charles Eliot Norton Lectures delivered
by Cage at Harvard University in 1988–89 and published by Harvard
University Press in 1990, one sees that virtually his entire career as
composer, poet, and visual artist was counterpointed by his own
words.[1]

Cage's writings are fundamental to research and writing on his music. Among them are such indispensable items as "The Future of Music: Credo," "To Describe the Process of Composition Used in *Music of Changes* and *Imaginary Landscape no. 4*," "Indeterminacy," "Diary: How to Improve the World (You Will Only Make Matters Worse)," "Empty Words," "Writing for the Second Time through *Finnegans Wake*," and various sets of mesostics.

Cage's words are available in another form as well, as interviews and "conversations with." As he achieved notoriety and then fame, a flood of interviews, far too numerous to be listed here, appeared in newspapers and journals all over the world. There were also book-length collections, including *For the Birds: John Cage in Conversation with Daniel Charles*,[2] *Conversing with Cage*,[3] and *Musicage: Cage Muses on Words Art Music*.[4] It must be kept in mind that in each case the interviewer mediated Cage's words to a greater or lesser extent to fit his or her own agenda, by selection of questions, omissions, translation, insertion of other material, and the like. As Leta Miller puts it in her essay in the present volume, "the oral interview [is] a powerful tool in the reconstruction of recent history, but [it] demands rigorous cross-examination to counteract the necessarily biased subjectivity of memory."

Cage's compositions remained less accessible than his writings for some time, with few of them available in published form before the early 1960s. But a combination of the upswing of interest in his music in the wake of a twenty-fifth anniversary concert given at Town Hall in May of 1958, the release of an LP of that event making a substantial sampling of his music available in recorded form for the first time, and Cage's successful forays into the European avant-garde scene at Darmstadt and elsewhere, persuaded the C. F. Peters Corporation to bring out many of his compositions. "Published" is a somewhat misleading term for what happened; Cage furnished fair copies of his compositions in his own distinctive hand to Peters, which then advertised and sold photocopies of these pieces through a subsidiary, Henmar Press. A catalogue listing and describing 101 of Cage's compositions written before 1961, available through Henmar, was published by Peters in 1962.[5] As Cage himself says in the foreword to the booklet, many of his compositions were not mentioned for one reason or another, including some that he felt were "inferior in quality." Peters continued to add new compositions by Cage to its catalogue on a selective basis for the remainder of his life.

It was not until 1970 that a comprehensive listing of Cage's compositions was attempted, by Richard Kostelanetz (with the assistance of Cage himself), in *John Cage*.[6] A decade later I compiled an expanded list to accompany my entry on Cage in *The New Grove Dictionary of Music and Musicians*.[6] Though both Cage and his editor at Peters cooperated with me on this list, it was still far from complete, since much of Cage's unpublished early music was scattered in various locations, and some was believed to be lost. Many pieces were in the process of being revised or reworked, and it was not always clear whether certain events in which he had been involved in the late 1960s and early 1970s—the *Musicircus*, for instance—should be listed as "compositions." A more complete list was published in 1982.[7]

During the winter of 1992–93 a number of scholars, including Paul van Emmerik, Martin Erdmann, James Pritchett, and Laura Kuhn, sorted and inventoried the materials in Cage's possession at the time of his death, and in the process they located some compositions believed to be lost and others that had been unknown. The collection was deposited in the New York Public Library, where it was catalogued by Robert Kosovsky.[8] Van Emmerik included a definitive list of Cage's compositions in his dissertation (1996), mentioned below.

Words by others

Most of the earliest writing on Cage took the form of brief journalistic pieces: reviews of performances of his music and of the audience's reaction to it; interviews with Cage and the performers of his music; descriptions of the unusual percussion instruments and the prepared piano used in his compositions. Though written for the mainstream press, often by persons with no particular knowledge of music, some of these pieces have been useful in chronicling the events of his early career, though they have little to say about the compositional and aesthetic issues with which Cage was wrestling.

In the early 1960s, Cage and his music began to be discussed in a more "serious" fashion, often in scholarly journals and books. Much of this writing was the work of composers and performers—Christian Wolff, Ellsworth Snyder, Morton Feldman, William Brooks, William Duckworth, Margaret Leng Tan, Tom Johnson, Roger Reynolds, James Tenney, Paul Zukofsky—and some of it was the work of critics and historians of the avant-garde who were supportive of Cage's music and aesthetics; prominent among them were Richard Kostelanetz and Peter Yates. Most of these authors were closely involved in one way or another with Cage and his music in the 1950s, '60s, and '70s, when he was still a highly controversial figure and when aligning oneself with him was not a wise career choice. These writers had a limited grasp of his overall compositional output, however, since little of his music had been published or recorded at that time. Most of what they had to say was concerned with whatever music Cage was currently writing. Likewise, their grasp of his musical and aesthetic thinking was based almost entirely on what Cage himself said or wrote about these things, since there was virtually no serious critical writing about him. Many of them thought of themselves as having been in the trenches with Cage, battling the Philistines who dominated the concert, academic, and critical worlds of that period. As a result, much of what they wrote was passionately supportive, defending Cage not only against widespread ignorance on the part of so many musicians and non-musicians, but also against what they took to be the misinterpretation of his music and his writings by a handful of authors who criticized or ridiculed him. This body of writing about Cage was recently characterized as "the usual 'insider' treatment (anecdote, personal reminiscence, hagiography, exposition of particular works according to the artist's own prescriptions)."[9]

The first attempt at a chronologically organized overview of Cage's life and works was my article for the *New Groves*, mentioned above. The first complete book on Cage, organized in roughly the same way, was Paul Griffiths' *Cage*.[10] Both drew heavily on Cage's own writings, and their discussions of the music were limited to compositions available through Peters or on recordings. Another decade passed before the next book-length biography appeared, David Revill's *The Roaring Silence: John Cage, A Life*.[11]

Beginning also in the 1960s, writers from fields other than music began to be drawn to Cage's music and aesthetics. Literary scholar John Hollander reviewed Cage's first book, *Silence*, in *Perspectives of New Music*,[12] and Calvin Tomkins, a noted critic of modern art, devoted a chapter to Cage in his book *The Bride and the Bachelors*, discussing him in the context of the American avant-garde at mid-century and also pointing out his artistic indebtedness to Satie.[13]

The literature on Cage by non-musicians proliferated to such an extent in the 1970s and '80s that it became the dominant stream, helped by the fact that Cage devoted much of his time and energy to writing poetry and creating visual works of art in the last decades of his life. An anthology of writings about Cage in celebration of his 70th birthday, "examines the almost alarming breadth of Cage's interests and accomplishments in music, theatre, literature, the visual arts, mycology, and even macrobiotic cookery;"[14] among the contributors, composers and performers are outnumbered by the likes of Norman O. Brown (humanities), Daniel Charles (philosophy and aesthetics), Anne D'Harnoncourt (art history) and Jill Johnston (dance criticism). A decade later the introduction to a somewhat similar anthology remarks that "none of [the contributors] is a composer or musician;" three of the ten are philosophers, one is a musicologist who "chose to examine . . . a verbal rather than a musical text," one is a poet, one is a cultural and architectural historian, one is a literary theorist, and the remainder "come to Cage from what is loosely called Comparative Literature."[15]

As scholars from the realms outside of music began to dominate the literature on Cage, the focus shifted to an investigation of "how Cage's aesthetic . . . accord[s] with the other philosophical discourses of our time,"[16] for example, the loose constellation of critical approaches to scholarship—literary theory, cultural studies, post-Marxist criticism, postmodern theory, postcolonialism, feminist theory—that came to dominate the academic world in the 1980s and '90s. As a result, issues never raised before, such as Cage's sexuality and its effect (if any) on his work, have been explored by Thomas S. Hines[17] and by Jill Johnston in her recent book on Jasper Johns.[18]

Cage and musicology

Though the literature on Cage was dominated more and more throughout the 1960s, '70s, and '80s by writers with scholarly credentials, few musicologists were among them. A striking exception is Leonard Meyer, whose essay "The End of the Renaissance?"[19] was the first extended piece of critical (as opposed to journalistic, biographical or anecdotal) writing on Cage. In addition, a number of histories of American and/or twentieth-century music written by musicologists devoted space to Cage and his music. Among these were Gilbert Chase's *America's Music: From the Pilgrims to the Present* (New York: McGraw-Hill, 1955), Wilfred Mellers' *Music in a New Found Land* (London: Barrie and Rockliff, 1964), Peter Hansen's *An Introduction to Twentieth Century Music* (Boston: Allyn & Bacon, 1967), William Austin's *Music in the Twentieth Century* (New York: W.W. Norton & Co., 1966), H. Wiley Hitchcock's *Music in the United States* (Englewood Cliffs, NJ: Prentice-Hall, Inc., 1969), and my *Music in the New World* (New York: W.W. Norton & Co., 1983).[20] Written as trade books and textbooks, their coverage of Cage's music was consequently quite general and not at all musicological.

The suspicion and caution with which most musicologists regarded Cage was reflected by the almost total absence of doctoral dissertations undertaken on his music during this period. Ellsworth Snyder's "John Cage and Music since World War II: A Study in Applied Aesthetics," written in 1970 at the University of Wisconsin at Madison, was a lonely first of its kind; next were John Francis's "Structure in the Solo Piano Music of John Cage" (Florida State University, 1976) and Monika Fürst-Heidtmann's "Das präparierte Klavier des John Cage" (Cologne, 1978).[21] It would be almost a decade before the next. But strangely enough, it was within the very discipline of musicology that a new phase of Cage scholarship emerged in the last decade and a half, beginning with a succession of dissertations, among them:

> Deborah Campana. "Form and Structure in the Music of John Cage." Northwestern University, 1985.

> James Pritchett. "The Development of Chance Techniques in the Music of John Cage." New York University, 1988.

> Laura Kuhn. "John Cage's 'Europeras 1 & 2': The Musical Means of Revolution." University of California at Los Angeles, 1992.

> Christopher Shultis. "Silencing the Sounded Self: John Cage and the Experimental Tradition in Twentieth-Century American Poetry and Music." University of New Mexico, 1993.

> Martin Erdmann. "Untersuchung zum Gesamtwerk von John Cage." Rheinische Friedrich-Wilhelms-Universität Bonn, 1993.

> Johann Rivest. "Le 'Concert for Piano and Orchestra' de John Cage, ou les limites de l'indétermination." Université de Montréal, 1996.

> David Patterson. "Appraising the Catchwords, c. 1942–1959: John Cage's Asian-Derived Rhetoric and the Historical Reference of Black Mountain College." Columbia University, 1996.

> Paul van Emmerik. "Thema's en Variaties: Systematische Tendensen in de Compositietechnieken van John Cage." University of Amsterdam, 1996.

Musicologists, especially in the United States, have traditionally relied on historical/positivist methodology.[22] They have been concerned with finding, cataloguing, evaluating, writing about, editing, and otherwise interpreting primary musical sources (holograph scores, sketches, copies, published editions of compositions, period phonograph recordings if available) and also with locating and utilizing written documents composed of letters to, from, and about composers, performers, and others involved with the music in question. Also included are performance reviews and other contemporary journalistic writings, official documents yielding information on births, deaths, education, employment, and other vital matters. In addition, musicologists are expected to be able to deal with "the music itself" through structural, tonal, harmonic, and melodic analysis.[23]

A "musicological" approach to Cage would involve the recovery and interpretation of primary documents pertaining to the events of his life and of his music (as in the dissertations by Patterson, Shultis, and Erdmann), detailed formal, structural, and rhythmic analyses of his music (Campana, Kuhn, and Pritchett), or a combination of these two (Rivest and van Emmerik).

The vast majority of this new musicological literature has focused on Cage's early music and the events of his early career. There are several reasons for this. As noted above, many of his earliest compositions, including some believed to be lost, are now published or otherwise available for study. Since these pieces are more or less conventionally notated, they are susceptible to systematic musical analysis, more so than many of Cage's later compositions. And since most of the events of Cage's early career were known only from his own recollections (and his memory was not always accurate, as he admitted himself), this period was in particular need of a thorough investigation based on documentary and primary evidence.

The work of James Pritchett and David Patterson demonstrates these two musicological approaches. In his dissertation, and even more strikingly in his book *The Music of John Cage*,[24] Pritchett demolishes the notion that Cage wasn't a composer but rather an inventor and manipulator whose music could not and should not be subjected to analysis.[25] Examining the full chronological range of Cage's music, Pritchett constructs a chronology of the compositional techniques used at various stages of his career, offering close analyses of key works to establish his points.[26] Patterson's dissertation, a chapter of which is included in the present volume, is based on an exhaustive examination and interpretation of primary documents bearing on two critical phases of Cage's early career: his involvement with Asian philosophy and aesthetics, and his activities during two summers at Black Mountain College in North Carolina. Patterson augments and enriches the conventional wisdom that Cage was influenced by Zen Buddhism and the *I Ching* by assembling a dazzling array of evidence clarifying when, where, and through whom Cage came into contact with Eastern thought, as well as which texts he read and how he paraphrased some of this material in his own writings. One of Patterson's most important findings is that writings by Indians, particularly Ananda Coomaraswamy, played as persuasive a role in Cage's evolving aesthetic thought as did his contact with Japanese and Chinese material. The second section of the dissertation likewise assembles a mass of documentary evidence bearing on a hitherto obscure but highly critical episode in Cage's career, which yielded, among other things, the first "happening."

Most of the essays in the present volume expand and refine this two-pronged musicological approach—analytical and documentary—to Cage and his music. Several deal with the seminal years at the Cornish School in Seattle (1938–1940), where he was first involved intimately with dance, where he wrote his first pieces for prepared piano, and where he met his long-time companion and artistic collaborator, Merce Cunningham. Leta Miller constructs a detailed chronology of events of this period from primary documents, weighs this information against Cage's often faulty recollections, then interprets these events in the context of the music he wrote in Seattle. Among other things, she discovers that the intellectual and political climate at the Cornish School, and in Seattle, was more liberal and radical than had been thought, and that Cage's seminal essay, "The Future of Music: Credo," doesn't date from 1937, as Cage remembered, but from 1940, when it was given as a lecture before the Seattle Artists League. According to Miller it is thus "a culmination, rather than a precursor, of this formative period, its ideas honed from Cage's interactions with the Seattle artistic community, and reflecting influences both within and outside of music." Also, Cage's *Imaginary Landscape No. 2* was written for a dance recital in Seattle, but it was withdrawn after a first performance, and the title was subsequently used for an altogether different composition written in Chicago.

Susan Key discusses Cage's *Imaginary Landscape No. 1*, written for performance at the Cornish School's then state-of-the-art radio studio, in the context of the early history of radio. Examining the composition itself and then a mass of contemporary writing on the implications of radio for "serious" music, she concludes that Cage was one of "a few isolated individuals [who] looked beyond these parameters, investigating the means by which radio's decontextualized sounds raised both new aesthetic issues and creative possibilities," and that Cage "transforms the radio studio itself into an instrument" in this composition, which together with Varèse's *Espace* represents "the most original musical response to radio in Depression-era America."

In his wide-ranging essay bridging Cage's stay in Seattle with his subsequent years in Chicago, New York, and Black Mountain College, Branden Joseph traces the development of Cage's advocacy of "a utopian social totality initially modeled in a universal aesthetic form, but which protected within its philosophy individual difference," a phase that culminated with the *Concerto for Prepared Piano and Chamber Orchestra* (1951), the "first work in which [Cage] made use of chance procedures." According to Joseph, this prolonged aesthetic odyssey began with Cage's contact with the painter Mark Tobey in Seattle. This interaction sensitized the young composer to the "energy and dynamism" of the urban landscape, and then continued as Cage came to know, in person or through their writings, such figures of the avant-garde as Russolo, Moholy-Nagy, William Carlos Williams, Eugene Jolas, George Antheil, and Carl Jung. Like Patterson, Joseph has read what Cage read, and he measures Cage's words against those by others which attracted him. Particular attention is paid to the avant-garde literary journal *transition* and the theory of Verticalism put forward therein by Jolas, its chief ideologue, which called for "disruptive assaults upon outworn linguistic and artistic rules." As Joseph sums it up, "*transition's* emphasis on the dialectical sublation of fragmentation—on both the aesthetic and social level—strongly resonates with Cage's own understanding of the interdependence of the therapeutic and aesthetic functions of music." In the course of this decade-long intellectual journey, Cage came to understand that the "idealization of individual expressive genius," so rampant in Romantic and Modern music had been a factor in the "social fragmentation" of contemporary society, and as a result (among other things), he completely reversed his attitude toward Arnold Schoenberg.

Paul van Emmerik, as are most of the authors represented in this volume, is interested in Cage's concept of "rhythmic structure," wherein "a musical form [is created] based on numerical relationships between the durations of sections and of groups of measures of a composition in such a way that the durations of both levels were governed by a single series of proportions." Unlike other writers who have assumed that such structures are rigidly imposed on the sonic materials of a piece, van Emmerik stresses Cage's flexibility in their application, finding that "in actual compositional practice Cage frequently compromised with himself over a precompositionally defined rhythmic structure, or he reached agreements with others about a structure mandated by the choreography, stage play, radio play, or film." He calls attention to numerous pieces in which Cage deviates from the precise application of the rhythmic structure governing a given piece, suggesting pragmatic and aesthetic reasons for these departures, and he also argues that contrary to what others have suggested, Cage's rhythmic structures "did affect the audible musical continuity."

Starting from Cage's idiosyncratic use of the terms "structure" and "form," Chadwick Jenkins offers an exhaustive analysis of Cage's *Sonatas and Interludes for Prepared Piano*, concluding that the composer's experiments with micro-macrocosmic form attained their highest peak of creative manipulation in these twenty pieces. Like van Emmerik he is alert to the many deviations from precompositionally-determined rhythmic structures, demonstrating through his analyses that:

> In *Sonatas and Interludes*, [Cage] manipulated the micro-macrocosmic Structure in such a wide variety of ways that . . . [they] are a virtual textbook on his techniques in the manipulation of Structure.

Challenging Cage's assertion, "I don't have an ear for music," Christopher Shultis examines a number of Cage's early compositions for percussion, finding that Cage's sensitivity to the timbre of non-pitched instruments increases over time, reaching a peak with the *Third Construction* (1941). Suggesting that these pieces should be performed "in relation to their historical past," that is, played by the instruments the composer intended rather than whatever instruments are readily available, Shultis painstakingly sifts through documentary evidence, including photographs of Cage's performing ensembles, to identify the precise types of rattles, tom-toms, gongs, and so on, used in early performances under Cage's direction. When these pieces are performed with "proper" instruments, Shultis finds that they are "not only more historically accurate, but actually sound better," and that the resulting timbres help articulate Cage's formal structures. Shultis concludes that Cage not only had an ear for timbre, but he also "had an exceptional ear for music, regardless of what he himself had to say;" this should not surprise anyone who has heard Cage performing his own music, Shultis adds.

David Bernstein discusses Cage's relationship with Arnold Schoenberg, a subject explored earlier by musicologists Robert Stevenson[27] and Michael Hicks.[28] After examining some of Cage's early compositions, he argues that his "emphasis on motivic integration as well as other forms of pitch relationships . . . betray Schoenberg's continuing influence," and that even after Cage lost interest in the manipulation of pitch relationships, "the underlying aesthetic assumptions behind [his] chance music correspond to Schoenberg's notion of a musical idea [i.e., the emancipation of the dissonance]."

● ● ●

The present volume is the first extensive collection of writings from the third, "musicological" stage of Cage scholarship, a phase that has yielded close musical analyses of pieces written in the first decades of his career and a reevaluation of these years based on previously unused documentary sources.

Many—but certainly not all—of the writers represented here knew Cage and benefited from his friendship and advice. But rather than the "not-yet Cage" of the 1940s and 1950s lurking on the fringes of the musical and intellectual worlds, the Cage they knew was generally acknowledged to be a genius in all but the most reactionary circles, and his work was celebrated all over the world in performances, recordings, commissions for new compositions, conferences, and other honors. There was no longer a need for writers to defend his words and music against the hostile and the ignorant, and there was no fear that critical investigation—in the sense of close examination—might diminish his work, even if it uncovered flaws. His own words are still used as a prime source of information, but they are now examined critically as opposed to being taken at face value. Inconsistencies in the application of his compositional techniques can be revealed without fear of invalidating his work. His frequent and critical paraphrasing of the words of other authors can be ferreted out, acknowledged, and placed in the context of his own unique intellectual development without tarring him as a plagiarist.

As is the case with so much musicological work, striking revelations and dramatic reevaluations are not necessarily the goal of the essays offered here, but instead a careful, thorough investigation, analysis, and evaluation of materials pertaining to his work. As they put the details of Cage's music and life in better order, musicologists are constructing a larger, more accurate picture.

Notes

1.   To supplement Cage's own collections of his writings, Richard Kostelanetz has published many pieces not included in these, in his *John Cage* (New York: Praeger Publishers, 1970) revised and expanded as *John Cage: An Anthology* (New York: Da Capo, 1991), and *John Cage: Writer* (New York: Limelight Editions, 1993).

2.   John Cage and Daniel Charles, *For the Birds: John Cage in Conversation with Daniel Charles* (Salem, NH: M. Boyars, 1981). First published in French as *Pour les Oiseaux* (Paris: Editions Pierre Belfond, 1976).

3.   Richard Kostelanetz, ed., *Conversing with Cage* (New York: Limelight Editions, 1988).

4.   John Cage and Joan Retallack, *Musicage: Cage Muses on Words Art Music* (Hanover, NH: Wesleyan University Press, 1996).

5.   Robert Dunn, ed., *John Cage* (New York: Henmar Press, 1962).

6.   *The New Grove Dictionary of Music and Musicians* (London: Macmillan, 1980), s.v. "Cage, John," by Charles Hamm.   Reprinted and revised for *The New Grove Dictionary of American Music*.

7.   n.a., "Chronological Listing of Musical Works Through the Summer of 1982" in Peter Gena and Jonathan Brent, eds., *A John Cage Reader: In Celebration of His 70th Birthday* (New York: C.F. Peters Corporation, 1982), 195–207.

8.   A detailed descriptive catalogue is available on the internet at http://catnyp.nypl.org.

9.   Marjorie Perloff and Charles Junkerman, eds., *John Cage: Composed In America* (Chicago and London: University of Chicago Press, 1994), 2.

10.   Paul Griffiths, *Cage* (Oxford and New York: Oxford University Press, 1981). Richard Kostelanetz's *John Cage* contained a selection of Cage's own

writings, brief pieces about Cage by other writers, lists of his compositions, a chronological list of the events of his life compiled by Ellsworth Snyder, a list of recordings of his music, bibliographies of his writings and those of other authors, etc. Though an innovative and useful book, it did not attempt to give an overview of his life or compositions.

11. David Revill, *The Roaring Silence: John Cage, A Life* (New York: Arcade Publishing, 1992).

12. John Hollander, review of *Silence: Lectures and Writings* by John Cage, *Perspectives of New Music* 1, no. 2 (Spring 1963): 137–41.

13. Calvin Tomkins, "Profiles: John Cage—Figure in an Imaginary Landscape," *The New Yorker* 40, no. 1 (November 28, 1964), 64–6, 68, 71–4, 77–8, 80, 83–4, 86, 88, 90, 93–4, 96, 99–100, 102, 104, 106, 111–12, 116, 118, 121–22, 126, 128. Reprinted in *The Bride and the Bachelors* (New York: Viking Press, 1965).

14. Gena and Brent, eds., xii.

15. Perloff and Junkerman, eds., 4.

16. Ibid., 2.

17. Thomas Hines, "Then Not Yet 'Cage'": The Los Angeles Years, 1912–1938," in Perloff and Junkerman, eds., 65–99.

18. Jill Johnston, *Jasper Johns: Privileged Information* (New York: Thames & Hudson, Inc., 1996).

19. Leonard Meyer, "The End of the Renaissance?" in *Music, The Arts, and Ideas* (Chicago: The University of Chicago Press, 1967), 68–84. First published in *Hudson Review* 6, no. 2 (Summer 1963).

20. The dates given are for the first editions of these books. Later editions expand the coverage of Cage.

21. William Duckworth's "Expanding Notational Parameters in the Music of John Cage" was submitted for a doctoral degree in music education, not musicology, at the University of Illinois in 1972.

22. This point is discussed at length in Joseph Kerman, *Contemplating Music: Challenges to Musicology* (Cambridge: Harvard University Press, 1985).

23. There has never been a distinction between these two approaches in European musicology. In the United States, on the other hand, abstract analysis (i.e., in isolation from historical and cultural considerations) was considered the discipline of music theory/analysis, until recently.

24. James Pritchett, *The Music of John Cage* (Cambridge: Cambridge University Press, 1993).

25. Roger Maren, reviewing *A Year From Monday*, characterizes Cage as being "didactic and not very interested in music," complains that he has "quit composing and begun indeterminate production of sound," and contends that the "devices" he was turning out were intended only "to help people behave so as to have a better world." (*Perspectives of New Music* 6, no. 2 (Spring–Summer 1968): 182–84).

26. For an analytical approach to Cage's music by another musicologist, see David Nicholls, *American Experimental Music, 1890–1940* (Cambridge: Cambridge University Press, 1990).

27. Robert Stevenson, "John Cage on his Seventieth Birthday," *Inter–American Music Review* 5 (Fall 1982), 34–17.

28. Michael Hicks, "John Cage's Studies with Schoenberg," *American Music* 8, no. 2 (Summer 1990), 125–40.

1. John Cage, Arnold Schoenberg, and the Musical Idea

David W. Bernstein

In memory of Patricia Carpenter

Throughout his life, John Cage was fond of telling stories about his studies with Arnold Schoenberg. One well-known anecdote dates back to 1934 when Schoenberg was teaching in Hollywood and Cage approached him regarding the possibility of composition lessons. As Cage recounted, Schoenberg asked if he had enough money to pay his fee:

> I told him that there wasn't any question of affording it, because I couldn't pay him anything at all. He then asked me whether I was willing to devote my life to music, and I said I was. "In that case, I will teach you free of charge."[1]

Similar references to Cage's studies with Schoenberg appear throughout Cage's writings. Cage held Schoenberg in high esteem, considering him "an extraordinary musical mind, one that was greater and more perceptive than the others,"[2] and this estimation of his former teacher continued to the last years of his life.[3] He was even studying Schoenberg's *Harmonielehre* just before his death; its principles for harmonic connection may well have inspired the "anarchic harmony" of Cage's late works.[4]

Cage's interactions with Schoenberg are now well documented.[5] But to what extent did Cage's classes with Schoenberg affect his development as a composer? The two figures seem to represent diverging paths in the history of twentieth-century music, especially in light of Cage's work after 1950. Indeed, in many ways, Cage turned his back on the past, rejecting compositional choice through his use of chance operations, seeking instead a musical continuity that avoided relationships between sounds. Schoenberg's music and theories draw upon nineteenth-century traditions, expressing a quintessential organicism articulated by "relationships between tones," which seems to be in direct opposition to Cage's aesthetic goals. Given this basic aesthetic incompatibility and the two composers' obviously disparate musical styles, it is not surprising that many scholars have downplayed Schoenberg's impact upon Cage.[6] James Pritchett, for example, states that while Schoenberg did not influence the development of Cage's actual compositional style, his dedication to music was a more abstract and meaningful model for Cage.[7] Michael Hicks suggests that Cage self-consciously referred to his ties with Schoenberg in order to "legitimize" his own work by demonstrating its roots in the past, just as Schoenberg had done for himself with the music of the previous century.[8] Catherine Parsons Smith takes a far harsher stance, cynically maintaining that Cage skillfully "constructed" his relationship with Schoenberg in order to further his own career.[9]

This essay examines the extent of Schoenberg's compositional influence on Cage. Beginning with Cage's earliest exposure to Schoenberg's work, it reconstructs the contents of Schoenberg's courses at USC and UCLA, in part through the recollections and extant class notes of several of his students. It also takes into account Schoenberg's theoretical writings from this period, which provide particular insight into the nature of his teachings, since what is arguably his most important theoretical writing occurred while he was teaching in Los Angeles. The essay then examines how Schoenberg influenced Cage's early compositional techniques both directly and indirectly through the work of the American "ultramodernist" school. Finally, it proposes that the two composers' approaches to musical form are not as far apart as one might expect, and that Cage's early studies with Schoenberg had a profound impact on the development of his compositional thinking that lasted his entire career.

i

Cage's youthful encounters with modern art and music in Paris included works by Schoenberg. In 1930 he met pianist John Kirkpatrick, who gave a concert of works by Stravinsky and Scriabin, and subsequently Cage was inspired to purchase a collection entitled *Das neue Klavierbuch* that included short, easy pieces by Schoenberg, Stravinsky, Satie, and others.[10] Upon his return to Los Angeles in 1931, Cage saw the musical landscape in terms of two camps: followers of Schoenberg were on the one hand and disciples of Stravinsky were on the other. It is at this point that his interest in Schoenberg took root:

> I came to think that it was fairly clear from a survey of contemporary music that the important figures then were Schoenberg and Stravinsky, and that you could go in one direction or the other. I myself preferred Schoenberg.[11]

Undoubtedly, Cage was also influenced by Henry Cowell, who numbered among Schoenberg's most loyal American supporters. Under the auspices of the New Music Society, Cowell organized concerts featuring Schoenberg's music and also published Schoenberg's *Klavierstück*, Op. 33b in the *New Music Quarterly*.[12]

While Cage's own recollections are unreliable and there are no official records of his studies with Schoenberg, Michael Hicks has reconstructed the details of these studies through correspondence between Cage and Adolph Weiss and recollections of students who attended Schoenberg's classes. On the advice of Henry Cowell, Cage began composition studies with Weiss in New York in 1934. Weiss, who had studied with Schoenberg, was an acknowledged expert on his music and theories.[13] Cage also continued his studies with Cowell, attending his classes in contemporary and world music at the New School for Social Research.[14]

Cage returned to Los Angeles in December 1934.[15] Schoenberg, who had arrived in California in the fall, had begun teaching a private class consisting of theory instructors from local high schools and the University of Southern California. Members of the class included Julia Howell and Pauline Alderman, both of whom were members of the advisory committee for the Alchin Chair of Composition at USC.[16] The class was a success, and Schoenberg was asked to teach during USC's summer session in 1935.

Meanwhile, Schoenberg's private classes continued. In the spring of 1935 he attracted twenty-five students among whom, according to Alderman, was John Cage.[17] The course that Cage attended was essentially an analysis class in which the students studied eighteenth- and nineteenth-century works. As an instructor, Schoenberg emphasized the expression of musical ideas and not any particular compositional style. This is a constant theme in both his classroom pedagogy and his writings. As he explained several years later, "please do not expect modernistic music. If students tell me they want me to teach them to write modern music I always answer, I teach only music."[18] Composer Gerald Strang, who was among Schoenberg's students at both USC and UCLA, reinforced this notion, stating:

> Schoenberg didn't care much what the style was; he was concerned with the technique, the integrity, the expressiveness, and

the meaningfulness, and things of this kind. He was concerned with the compositional organization. But he never attempted to influence people with respect to style, or to convert them or persuade them to write in the twelve-tone manner.[19]

Analysis also helped Schoenberg's students to understand universal compositional principles applicable to their own music. To this end, as Alderman recalls, Schoenberg constantly focused on "the musical logic of every motivic usage."[20] Many of Schoenberg's students had enrolled hoping to study his twelve-tone system, and at their request his class did include lectures on his *Third String Quartet*. There were also several open rehearsals and a performance by the Abas String Quartet who were visiting USC at that time.[21] These lectures and performances must have piqued Cage's curiosity, fueling what was his own marked interest in twelve-tone techniques.

Schoenberg taught two composition classes during the 1935 USC summer session. The first was essentially an analysis course focusing on the Beethoven piano sonatas; the second was a more traditional composition class in which each student wrote a movement of a string quartet. He continued to teach part-time at USC through the summer of 1936, offering such courses as "The Art of Contrapuntal Instruction" and "Thematic Construction." He also presented two public lectures titled, "The Elements of Musical Forms as Discovered by Means of Analysis" and "The Evaluation of Musical Works."[22] The faculty at USC wanted Schoenberg to continue teaching in the fall semester of 1936, but he left for a full-time position at UCLA where he remained until February 1944.[23]

Despite Cage's claims that he attended "all" of Schoenberg's courses at USC and UCLA, Hicks explains that it is difficult to ascertain exactly which of Schoenberg's classes Cage actually attended since there are no extant enrollment records.[24] He believes that Cage attended at least one semester of Schoenberg's classes in analysis, composition and harmony and two sessions of his counterpoint class.[25] From Aldermann's account we know that Cage was a member of Schoenberg's private class in the spring of 1935. Hicks suggests that Cage's last class with Schoenberg may have been the latter's first harmony course at UCLA.[26] Documents exist indicating that Cage studied with Schoenberg during the spring and fall of 1936. A page from Gerald Strang's notes dated January 13, 1936 from Schoenberg's spring semester counterpoint class indicates that Strang planned to get the notes from Cage for a missed class the following week.[27] Other documents show that Cage was enrolled in Schoenberg's counterpoint class in the fall of 1936. These include Cage's copies of several pages of musical examples from this class dated October and November 1936,[28] and a page from Leonard Stein's notes from the same class dated September 9, 1936, that bears the telling annotation, "Cage at board" (Example 1-1). Apparently, Cage was an active and well-respected member of the class; a conclusion supported by an earlier page from Strang's notes from December 3, 1935 describing a discussion between Cage, Strang, and Schoenberg during which Cage correctly identifies the motive for the Rondo from Beethoven's *Piano Sonata in D major*, Op. 10, No. 3. Cage may have attended Schoenberg's classes through the spring of 1938, just before he left Los Angeles for a position at the Cornish School in Seattle.[29]

Example 1-1. Leonard Stein's notes, September 9, 1936.

II

Schoenberg was engaged in important theoretical work around the time that Cage was attending his classes, and this work undoubtedly had an impact upon his teaching. An examination of Schoenberg's theoretical writings from this period may thus shed light on what Cage gleaned from his studies with Schoenberg. Although Schoenberg taught a variety of classes during his tenure at USC and UCLA—Composition, Analysis, Counterpoint, and "Structural Functions of

Harmony"—it is crucial to note that he believed these disparate disciplines should constitute a unified whole:

> At present, the theory of harmony, counterpoint, and the theory of form mainly serve pedagogical purposes. With the exception of the theory of harmony, the individual disciplines completely lack even a truly theoretical basis emanating from external criteria. On the whole, the consequence is that three different disciplines, which together should constitute the theory of composition, in reality fall apart because they lack a common point of view. [30]

Schoenberg contemplated writing a comprehensive theory of composition as early as 1911.[31] He never finished this project, but he did work on a series of manuscripts between 1917 and 1936 hoping to complete a unified theory of music.[32] The most mature and complete discussion of his theory appears in the manuscript, *Die musikalische Gedanke und die Logik, Technik, und Kunst seiner Darstellung* (The Musical Idea and the Logic, Technique, and Art of Its Presentation). Schoenberg worked on this manuscript between June and August 1934 and from September to October 1936; during this latter period Cage was attending his classes.

The foundation of Schoenberg's theory is his concept of the "musical idea." He departed from the traditional meaning of the term as "melody" or "theme," positing instead several interrelated meanings. A musical idea is all at once the work itself, the dynamic process through which the composition unfolds and the potential for imbalance inherent in the opening material. According to Schoenberg, the composer initially perceives a musical idea in an instant as "an unnamable sense of a sounding and moving space, of a form with characteristic relationships."[33] After receiving this image of the work as a whole, as inspiration—"a lightning-like appearance of extraordinary duration"[34]—the composer is then faced with the task of making it concrete, a project that at best can only lead to an approximation of the ideal image. As Schoenberg explained:

> [Composition] is a gamble. As when a dice-thrower relies on throwing the highest stakes. Certainly you must play well, but do you win at bridge with bad cards and without luck? Only one stroke of luck can help the chess player—a mistake by his opponent; everything else he must be able to do himself. The composer is better off: nine tenths luck, but only if he knows how to do the remaining tenth and has tried hard for eleven tenths. Then God gives his blessing if the composer deserves luck.[35]

In this sense, at least, Schoenberg overtly acknowledged the role that chance plays in the compositional process, an acknowledgement of particular relevance to the study of Cage's response to Schoenberg's aesthetic.

Schoenberg called the initial concrete articulation of a musical idea a *Grundgestalt* which consists of striking intervallic and/or rhythmic motives stated at the beginning of a composition.[36] He defined the term "coherence" as the capacity to connect related or similar things with one another.[37] A motive is the smallest musical unit used to create coherence:

> In this way, the smallest musical gestalt fulfills the *laws of coher-ence*: the motive, the greatest common denominator of all musi-cal phenomena. Musical art, after all, consists of producing large and small images, which cohere by means of this motive, which in their individual contents likewise cohere with it, and which are assembled so that the *logic* of the total image is as apparent as that of its single parts and of their combination.[38]

Schoenberg strays notably from the conventional metaphor that equates a motive with a seed from which a composition evolves, even going as far as to state that a given motive may yield more than a sin-gle piece[39]:

> It will be noted that this departs from the usual understanding of the *motive as germ* of the piece out of which it grows. For if this conception were correct, *only one single piece* could arise from one motive. As is well known, such is not the case. I consider the motive the *building material* that can assume and realize all forms.[40]

He noted that although a motive "stands in a certain relationship to what is presented," it has the potential for more than a single compo-sitional realization. This approach is a significant departure from the determinism often associated with organicist aesthetics, and it became an important point of aesthetic convergence between Schoenberg and Cage.

As Schoenberg warned in a poignant reference to the German political situation at that time, tones cohere through repetition, but literal repetition is uninteresting since it does not yield new gestalten: "The joining of like kinds is unfruitful (racial purity). We shall see how far the Germans get with this."[41] Similarly, since musical "coherence" resulting from literal repetition is undesirable, this uni-fying concept must accept inherently the notion of "variation." Simply put, variation occurs when certain features of a gestalt are maintained, while others are not.[42] Schoenberg understood variation as a special approach to the gradual process of change:

> In a change, that which is to be altered is partly maintained; oth-erwise, it would be something different and not something

changed. I can cut off pieces from an apple, I can hollow it out and stuff it with other things, but I cannot make a pear out of it. (I can give it the shape of a pear, but I can write no piece "in the form of a pear" as the good joke by Satie pretends to do.)

Changing thus means repeating, but repeating only in part. The parts that are not repeated can be replaced by something else.[43]

Schoenberg outlined several different types of variation, including "developing variation," which produces new gestalten from the old,[44] as exemplified by the emergence of the second theme from the first in a sonata form movement.

It is reasonable to infer that Cage was familiar with the principles presented in Schoenberg's manuscript on the musical idea, since concepts such as the musical idea and developing variation were at the core of his teaching. Gerald Strang's class notes from the 1935 summer session document that Schoenberg began the course by teaching that a composition should be perceived as a unified whole, the expression of a single idea. He used the metaphor of a "picture book" to explain this concept; like a "picture book," Schoenberg explained, a musical work is:

> . . . a group of separate entities (ideas) [existing] effectively as a group, not solely as units. [The units are] distinct, complete in themselves, organized, but parts of a whole.[45]

His students learned that while composing they should "have the end in view, as a whole, clearly," and should understand the developmental potentials of the materials (themes, phrases, and motives) as well as the necessity for variety and variation to sustain interest.[46] According to Strang, Schoenberg differentiated between several types of repetition, such as repetition that was achieved without change, with variation (i.e., by changing the "setting" [range], harmony, or rhythm), and through developing variation.[47] Similarly, Leonard Stein's UCLA class notes record Schoenberg's classroom focus upon principles articulated in his manuscript on the musical idea. Variation is defined as "chang[ing] some features of a model, but preserv[ing] some others. . . . Variation and repetition [are] the foremost tools for coherence and comprehensibility."[48] Stein's notes also contain Schoenberg's clear distinction between "motive" and "idea:"

> Motive: composed number of features of rhythm and interval becomes motive in manner in which it is used. Manner of use: varied or unvaried repetition. ("Motive idea of a piece": misunderstanding), [a motive is] an element which is *used to express* [a] musical idea, not [the] "germ" of [the] piece—as composer does

not compose from germ—[he or she] must know [the] length of [the] piece.[49]

Schoenberg's students received a rigorous training in counterpoint, ranging from species counterpoint to the composition of chorale preludes and fugues, and in harmony. The latter included a study of the structural functions of harmony. In this advanced analysis course, students examined works from the traditional repertory (as well as some of Schoenberg's early tonal music), identified tonal structure in terms of regions and analyzed sections of "roving" harmony and motivic/thematic material.[50] According to Cage, it was during this course that his famous exchange with Schoenberg about his poor ear for harmony took place:

> Schoenberg was a magnificent teacher, who always gave the impression that he was putting us in touch with the musical principles. I studied counterpoint at his home and attended all his courses at USC and later UCLA when he moved there. I also took his course on harmony, for which I had no gift. Several times I tried to explain to Schoenberg that I had no feeling for harmony. He told me without a feeling for harmony I would always encounter an obstacle, a wall through which I wouldn't be able to pass. My reply was that in that case I would devote my life to beating my head against that wall.[51]

III

The foregoing commentary describes the contents of Schoenberg's classes; a subsequent examination of Cage's musical development from his earliest works through the time that he was studying with Schoenberg shows how he adapted Schoenberg's theories to his own compositional style. It is important to point out that Cage's first experiences of Schoenberg's music and ideas were limited, and further, that these were mostly through an exposure to the work of others. Indeed, Cage was not the only American for whom Schoenberg was a compositional inspiration. As mentioned above, Henry Cowell was an active Schoenberg advocate, and the musical milieu that Cage joined after returning from Europe owed much to Schoenberg's influence. In fact, while many composers in the American ultramodernist school— Cowell, Ruth Crawford, Charles Seeger, Carl Ruggles, Johanna Beyer, among others—sought to break their ties to European musical traditions, their dissonant harmonies and experiments with serialism nonetheless attest to the impact of Schoenberg's atonal and twelve-tone techniques. Like Schoenberg, both Cowell and Seeger looked beyond traditional distinctions between consonance and dissonance.

While Schoenberg's notion of the "emancipation of dissonance" established dissonance and consonance as equivalent (differing only in degree), these Americans formulated a new hierarchy under the rubric of what they termed "dissonant counterpoint." As Cowell commented:

> Let us, however, meet the question of what would result if we were frankly to shift the center of musical gravity from consonance, on the edge of which it has long been poised, to seeming dissonance, on the edge of which it now rests. The difference might not be, any more than in Bach's practice, a matter of numerical proportion between consonant and dissonant effects, but rather an essential dissonant basis, the consonance being felt to rely on dissonance for resolution. An examination in fact would reveal that all the rules of Bach would seem to have been reversed, not with the result of substituting chaos, but with that of substituting a new order. The first and last chords would be now not consonant, but dissonant; and although consonant chords were admitted, it would be found that conditions were in turn applied to them, on the basis of the essential legitimacy of dissonances as independent intervals.[52]

Seeger's short article entitled "On Dissonant Counterpoint" openly acknowledges Schoenberg's importance in the development of this new musical language, but it explains that the previous use of dissonant harmony and melodic writing was merely an "elaboration and extension of the old diatonic harmony rather than a revolutionary reversal of it."[53] He ultimately criticized Schoenberg not for his treatment of dissonance but for his use of consonance:

> The chief fault of the Schoenberg school, as of all the others, seemed to lie not in the handling of dissonance, but of consonance. All went well as long as a thoroughly dissonant structure was maintained, but upon first introduction of consonance, a feeling of disappointment, of defeat, frequently occurred. It was as if there were holes in the fabric.[54]

As an alternative, Seeger offered his own ideas concerning the application of "dissonance" to rhythm, melody, harmony, as well as counterpoint, even speculating that categories of "dissonant dynamics" and "dissonant tone colors" might develop in the future. "Dissonant melody," for example, consisted of rapidly differentiated rhythmic values and/or meters, in which dissonant intervals were more common than consonant intervals, the latter most often resolving by a dissonant leap. Similarly, in dissonant counterpoint, vertical consonance is resolved by dissonance. Rhythmic dissonance could be achieved through unaligned syncopations and cross rhythms ranging from 3 against 2 or 4 against 3 to 7 against 4. Seeger began developing his theories around 1914 or 1915 while teaching composition to Cowell.[55] Cowell's *New Musical Resources* mentions dissonant counterpoint, and it was with Cowell that Cage eventually studied this technique.[56]

Cage's early compositions not only drew upon his studies of dissonant counterpoint, but they also demonstrated a rudimentary knowledge of Schoenberg's twelve-tone and atonal music. Around the time that he first met Cowell, Cage had been studying with Richard Buhlig, a pianist who had performed Schoenberg's *Drei Klavierstücke*, Op. 11 in Berlin.[57] He first approached Buhlig seeking help with a lecture—one of many that he presented to Santa Monica housewives during that period—on Schoenberg's *Piano Suite*, Op. 25. Buhlig refused Cage's offer, but agreed to take him on as a student of composition. Although Cage's lessons with Buhlig lasted only a few months, it is reasonable to assume that they included aspects of Schoenberg's twelve-tone techniques.

This is musically confirmed in Cage's *Solo for Clarinet* (1933), which he described as "an unaccompanied chromatic work in three movements, the last of which, though not rhythmically, is a retrograde canon of the first."[58] The first movement is clearly the work of an American ultramodernist writing what Seeger would have called "dissonated melody." Within the first eight bars (Example 1-2a)[59] dissonant intervals far outnumber consonant ones, and there are very few instances in which a consonant leap is not resolved by a dissonance. The rhythm is also "dissonated" through syncopation and changing beat divisions. The second movement, however, points more obviously to the techniques of Schoenberg, using a twelve-tone row, with its inversion, retrograde, and retrograde inversion.[60] The outer movements are not "freely" chromatic; they have a serial structure based upon melodic segments and their retrogrades.[61] In the first movement, measures 1–2 and 4–5 reappear in retrograde form in measures 20–21 and 23–24 (compare Example 1-2a: **a** and **b** with Example 1-2b: **a'** and **b'**). Phrases **a** and **a'** have the same rhythm;[62] **b** and **b'** are retrogrades both in pitch and duration. Measure 6 reappears in measure 25, although not in literal retrograde (compare Example 1-2a: **c** with Example 1-2b: **c'**). The last two sixteenth notes in measure 5 and all of measure 6 (Example 1-2a: **d**) as well as most of bars 7 and 8 (Example 1-2a: **e**) return either in retrograde or in their original form in the middle of the movement (Example 1-2c: **d** and Example 1-2d: **d'** and **e**). There are also similar correspondences between the middle and end of the movement. (Compare Example 1-2c: **f**, **g**, and **h** with Example 1-2d: **f'**, **g**, and **h'**).

Example 1-2a. Cage, *Solo for Clarinet*, 1933, I. mm. 1–8.

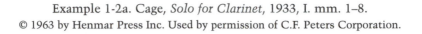

Example 1-2b. mm. 20–25.

Example 1-2c. mm. 9–12.

Example 1-2d. mm. 13–19.

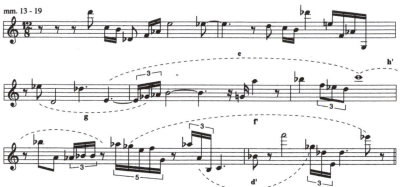

Cage quickly turned away from the relatively systematic writing of his *Solo for Clarinet*. His next works—the *Sonata for Two Voices* (1933), *Composition for Three Voices* (1934), and the *Solo with Obbligato Accompaniment for Two Voices in Canon, and Six Short Inventions on the Subject of the Solo* (1934)—take a much freer approach to serial technique.[63] In these works each voice is not fixed within a twelve-tone row but within a two-octave span. While the 25 pitches of this two-octave range are neither ordered into a row nor subjected to classic serial treatment, each voice is nonetheless obliged to state every one of the pitches before any is repeated. The first ten bars of Cage's *Sonata for Two Voices* (Example 1-3) illustrate this technique. (The composer marked the completion of the twenty-five tones in each voice with a double-bar.) For the most part, this work adheres to the rigors of dissonant counterpoint. Melodic consonances rarely appear and are most often followed by dissonant "resolutions." This applies to harmonic consonance as well. The counterpoint in the first three bars is properly "dissonated:" the consonant major sixth (C-A) in measure 2 is resolved by a major seventh (C-B), the consonant sixth (D-B) by a major seventh (D♭-C), and the major sixth (D♭-B♭) by an augmented sixth (D♭-B). In measure three, the minor tenth (A-C) is resolved by a major ninth (B♭-C). As the piece progresses, however, it becomes increasingly difficult for Cage to adhere to the guidelines of dissonant counterpoint; as the twenty-five tones in each of the voices are exhausted, his choices become more and more limited, and ultimately many of the melodic and intervallic consonances are left unresolved.[64]

Example 1-3. Cage, *Sonata for Two Voices*, 1933. mm. 1–10.

© 1979 by Henmar Press Inc. Used by permission of C.F. Peters Corporation.

Although he continued to develop his own idiosyncratic approach, Cage's work between 1935 and 1938 shows a continued focus on the twelve-tone system and bears closer resemblance to Schoenberg's serial music. One representative work from this period is *Metamorphosis* (1938), a five-movement piano piece which Cage described as "a twelve-tone piece [for piano] wholly composed of row fragments never subjected to variation. The transpositions of these fragments were chosen according to the intervals of the series."[65]

The opening of the first movement illustrates his technique (see Example 1-4). This passage consists entirely of transpositions of a three-note motive in the right hand (A-G-G♭) and a five-note motive in the left hand (D-E-B-B♭-A♭). These motives are clearly related, the right-hand motive constituting the retrograde inversion of the last three notes in the left-hand motive. Both motives also begin with a major second or its octave equivalent, which is an important melodic idea throughout the work. (See, for example, the opening of movements four and five.) Cage never states his row in *Metamorphosis* and it seems impossible to reconstruct it in its entirety. However, since the motives were transposed according to the notes of the row,[66] some of its linear adjacencies quickly become apparent. For example, the initial appearance of the five-note motive ends on A♭; a transposition beginning with C follows; A♭ and C are therefore identifiable adjacencies in one of the row forms. The following dyads result from remaining transpositions of the five-note motive in Example 1-4:

A♭—C
G♭—E♭
A—G
C—D♭
D♭—A
E♭—F
B—B♭
E—B
B♭—A♭
D—E
D—F
G♭—G

The transpositions of the three-note motive, beginning in measure four proceed according to the same dyads; the first instance of the motive is joined to the second by G and G♭, the second to the third by E and D, the third to the fourth by A♭ and B♭, and so on.

The rhythm in both hands remains constant throughout the passage, and aside from octave displacements the motives do not change. In fact, much of the work's five movements consists of literal or quasi-literal repetitions such as those in Example 1-4. This absence of motivic development marks an important break from Schoenberg. Cage learned from Schoenberg that variation, and in particular developing variation, was an important means for creating continuity:

> The things that Schoenberg emphasized in his teaching were repetition and variation, which would tend to what we call relationships. And then he said—to simplify it—he said that everything was a repetition. Even a variation was a repetition, with some things changed and some things not.[67]

This particular premise, had important implications for Cage; since repetition and variation were equivalent, he did not see the necessity for variation:

> In all of my pieces coming between 1935 and 1940, I had Schoenberg's lessons in mind; since he had taught me that a variation was in fact a repetition, I hardly saw the usefulness of variation, and I accumulated repetitions. All of my early works for percussion, and also my compositions for piano, contain systematically repeated groups of sounds or durations.[68]

Example 1-4. Cage, *Metamorphosis*, 1938; I. mm. 1–6.

Later on in his career, Cage criticized his own incessant repetitions in
Metamorphosis.[69] But, this criticism notwithstanding, these repetitions had profound ramifications in facilitating the construction of
the work according to sections of predetermined time lengths. In fact,
as David Nicholls demonstrates,[70] this composition is an early example of Cage's work with rhythmic structure. "Structure," for Cage, is
based on time. Although he learned from Schoenberg that musical
structure entails the division of a work into parts, Cage's own structures did not depend on tonal or thematic articulation;[71] instead they
relied on pre-compositionally determined temporal divisions. Cage
perceived this approach to structure as a necessary improvement on
Schoenberg's theory,[72] since time is the *a priori* phenomenon within
which pitch, harmony, noise, and silence may exist.

Example 1-5. Cage, *Metamorphosis*, 1938; I. mm. 7–10.

© 1961 by Henmar Press Inc. Used by permission of C.F. Peters Corporation.

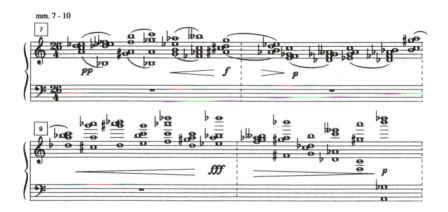

These differences aside, one passage from *Metamorphosis* initi-
ates a development that seems particularly "Schoenbergian" (see
Example 1-5, mm. 7-10). On the surface, the slow-moving chordal texture of this section contrasts with the previous measures. Closer
examination reveals that the first chord in measure seven contains the
same trichord (in this case C-D-E♭) shared by both the three-note and
the five-note motive discussed in Example 1-4. Each tone in the initial tetrachord in Example 1-5 moves by half step, or its octave equivalent. The harmony thereby is constant until the third tetrachord,
which occurs when each note in the second tetrachord moves according to one of the row's linear adjacencies listed above: E goes to B, E♭

to F, D♭ to A, and B♭ to A♭, and the entire passage proceeds in this manner. (See Example 1-6 for an illustration of the voice-leading.) Through this developmental process, Cage was able to transform his material without losing sight of his row; as new tetrachordal harmonies emerge, each one nonetheless derives from the series.

Example 1-6. Voice leading in *Metamorphosis*.

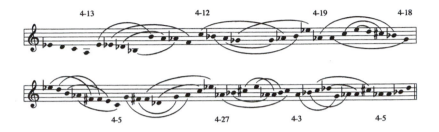

This procedure continues in the bass part (see Example 1-7, mm. 11–13). Each vertical dyad is transposed by a minor second and the resultant pitches move via row-form adjacencies. For example, the second dyad, E-A♭, becomes B♭-D: the adjacencies are E-D and A♭-B♭. The treble introduces a new motive: a major second and its octave displacements, taken from the initial interval of the five-note figure which opens the movement. Once again, a series of melodic major seconds, major ninths, and minor sevenths is linked by row adjacencies: A-B becomes E-F♯ (B connects with E), E-F♯ becomes G-A (F♯ connects to G), and G-A becomes D♭-E♭ (A connects with D♭).

Cage's idiosyncratic interpretation of the twelve-tone system and the general style of *Metamorphosis* point to Schoenberg. The degree of its motivic proliferation is perhaps the most convincing evidence in light of Schoenberg's own concern with this sort of motivic unity. This work even suggests that Cage may have been aware of the type of associations between unordered collections characteristic of Schoenberg's non-tonal music. The opening subject of the fugue-like third movement, marked by a dotted slur, is actually a transposed re-ordering of the pitch-class set (5-28) which opens the first movement (see Example 1-8).

After *Metamorphosis*, Cage's interest in the twelve-tone system continued in his *Five Songs for Contralto* (1938) and *Music for Wind Instruments* (1938). By this time he had also written a few percussion

Example 1-7. Cage, *Metamorphosis*, 1938; I. mm. 11–13.

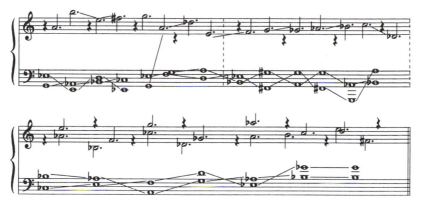

Example 1-8. Cage, *Metamorphosis*, 1938; III, opening.

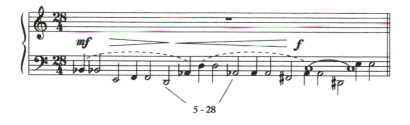

works,[73] and by the late 1930s his attentions had shifted noticeably and were increasingly focused on this medium and on the musical potential of noise—a preoccupation that would last his entire career. Cage equated the arbitrary distinction between noise and "musical" sounds in the same light as the historical distinction between consonance and dissonance. In a lecture entitled "The Future Of Music: Credo" (c. 1940), he explained that "whereas, in the past, the point of disagreement has been between dissonance and consonance, it will be, in the immediate future, between noise and so-called musical sounds."[74] It is likely that Cage had recently finished Schoenberg's harmony course at UCLA in which the *Harmonielehre* was used as a text.[75] In this historical context, the parallels between Schoenberg's notion of the "emancipation of dissonance" and Cage's insistence on the elimination of the distinction between noise and so-called musical sounds are even more striking.

Cage's works from the late 1930s and 1940s initiated his career as a professional composer, and after 1938 he abandoned the twelve-tone system, pursuing instead his explorations for new sounds. Yet by the mid-1940s, his work still bore overt connections to the Schoenberg "school" in the minds of some musicians. As composer-critic Virgil Thomson remarked in the *New York Herald Tribune*:

> Mr. Cage has carried Schoenberg's twelve-tone maneuvers to their logical conclusion. . . . His continuity devices are chiefly those of the Schoenberg school. There are themes and sometimes melodies, even though these are limited, when they have real pitch, to the range of a fourth, thus avoiding the tonal effect of dominant and tonic. All these appear in augmentation, diminution, inversion, fragmentation, backward movement, and the various forms of canon.[76]

Five years later Thomson refined this assessment, noting the stylistic elements that differentiated Cage from the European "atonalists:"

> John Cage employs a numerical ratio in any piece between the phrase, the period, and the whole, the phrase occupying a time measure which is the square root of the whole time and the periods occupying times proportional to those of the rhythmic motifs within the phrase. This procedure, though it allows for asymmetry within the phrase and period, produces a tight symmetry in the whole composition and is therefore not quite the rendering of spontaneous emotion that the European atonalists hope to achieve.[77]

Indeed, some of Cage's post-1938 works are still dressed with remnants of Schoenberg's thought. His *First Construction (in Metal)* (1939), for example has a certain motivic coherence, based on sixteen systematically deployed rhythmic motives.[78] As Cage himself admitted, despite its innovations, the *First Construction* is in a certain sense a nineteenth-century work "with exposition and development (without recapitulation) and with the form (climax, apotheosis (?)) etc."[79] Perhaps most striking is the persistence of dodecaphonic thinking even in Cage's *Music of Changes*—a work that marked a decisive break from his earlier style into the realm of chance techniques. In describing the charts used for selecting the sounds for this work Cage explained:

> The thirty-two sounds, thirty-two silences were arranged in two squares one above the other, each four by four. Whether the charts were mobile or immobile, all twelve tones were present in any four elements of a given chart, whether a line of the chart was read

horizontally or vertically. Once this dodecaphonic requirement was satisfied, noises and repetitions of tones were used with freedom.[80]

IV

Cage seemed to diverge most from Schoenberg in his evolving concept of musical "form," which he defined as "the morphological line of the sound-continuity."[81] Prior to 1950, he understood this continuity in a traditional sense, as the connection between sounds. As he had learned from Schoenberg:

> One of the ways to compose is to go over what you are doing and see if it still works as you add something else to it. Just go over it again and see how it continues, how it flows . . . so as to make something that flows.[82]

Although there are exceptions, a sense of linear continuity characterizes many of Cage's early works. Progression from one sound to another is prevalent in the first movement of *Metamorphosis*, a continuity achieved through its motoric rhythm and web of motivic repetitions. In the *Sonatas and Interludes* (1946–48), there is often a subtle interplay between degrees of harmonic tension and relaxation; Cage often plays with our sense of tonal "closure." (See for example, the centricity around B in the Sonata VI.) Progression also results from motivic associations, reinforced by Cage's extraordinary gamut of piano preparations. In the first half of Sonata I, the sound of the F♯ (with a screw inserted between strings two and three) in the upper voice in measure 1 continues into the next phrase (Example 1-9).[83] After the first phrase reappears in measure 3, it is followed by new material, but the F♯ remains in bars 5 and 6, thus retaining a connection with the opening. The sonority beginning in measure 5 recurs in measures 6 and 7. Its top note, an E with rubber inserted between strings one, two, and three, becomes a central sonority in measure 8. (Note that the F♯ remains, both at the beginning of the measure and as part of both the three-note cluster in the left hand and the dyad in the right hand.) Continuity here is a consequence of development in the "Schoenbergian" sense; some elements change, while others do not.

Cage's understanding of form as continuity changed radically by 1950. As he related to Pierre Boulez: "I keep, of course, the means of rhythmic structure feeling that that is the 'espace sonore' in which [each] of these sounds may exist and change. Composition becomes 'throwing sound into silence' and rhythm, which in my *Sonatas* had been one of breathing, becomes now one of a flow of sound and sil-

Example 1-9. Cage, *Sonatas and Interludes*, 1946–48; Sonata I. mm. 1–8.

© 1960 by Henmar Press Inc. Used by permission of C.F. Peters Corporation.

ence."[84] While still thinking of form in terms of continuity, Cage's method for controlling this continuity became less and less a matter of conscious compositional choice. For example, in the first two movements of his *Concerto for Prepared Piano and Chamber Orchestra* (1951), the composition proceeds according to systematic moves within a pre-determined chart of sonorities. In the third movement of the *Concerto* and in the *Music of Changes* (1951) the sounds were selected by chance operations.

As a result of Cage's apparent withdrawal of compositional control, continuity no longer occurs in the traditional sense by means of intentional relationships between sounds. As Cage explained:

> It is thus possible to make a musical composition the continuity of which is free of individual taste and memory (psychology) and also of the literature and "traditions" of art. The sounds enter the time-space centered within themselves, unimpeded by service to any abstraction, their 360 degrees of circumference free for an infinite play of interpenetration.[85]

On the surface, this break with "tradition" seems yet another step further away from Schoenberg. However, while Cage had established a musical style with its own unique terrain, its underlying aesthetic principles remained consistent with that of Schoenberg. Cage often told a story about a counterpoint class with Schoenberg during which the students were asked to provide every possible solution for a given *cantus firmus*. After the task was completed, Schoenberg then asked, "what is the principle underlying all of the solutions?" Although Cage was unable to answer the question, the problem that it posed had a significant impact on his compositional thinking:

> I couldn't answer his question; but I had always worshipped the man, and at that point I did even more. I spent the rest of my life, until recently, hearing him ask that question over and over. And then it occurred to me through the direction that my work has taken, which is the renunciation of choices and the substitution of asking questions, that the principle underlying all of the solutions that I had given him was the question that he had asked, because they certainly didn't come from any other point. He would have liked the answer, I think. The answers have the question in common. Therefore the question underlies the answers.[86]

For Schoenberg, the "principle underlying the solutions" was the musical idea, which according to his theory of composition is the essence of a work, an abstract conception that becomes concrete through the process of composition. Just as a counterpoint exercise could have several solutions, Schoenberg's musical idea could result in more than one compositional realization.[87] For Schoenberg as well as for Cage, composition was a "gamble."

With the *Music of Changes*, Cage's compositional focus shifted from making choices to asking questions. The pre-compositional materials for this work consisted of charts containing sounds, silences, attacks, durations, and densities; the answers to the questions concerning which of these materials should appear in the finished score were determined by the *I Ching*. Although Cage composed the *Music of Changes* using chance operations, its underlying creative process is closer to Schoenberg's own methods than it first seems. Ultimately, the carefully structured arena in which Cage applied his chance operations did not entirely eliminate the causal link between his questions and answers. Like Schoenberg, Cage began a composition with a musical idea; the fundamental difference is that Cage did not express his ideas in terms of organically integrated compositions.

Schoenberg's theories, and in particular his concept of the musical idea, may shed light on Cage's compositional process and may even help establish the groundwork for an analytical methodology applicable to Cage's music composed with chance operations. They may facilitate a "way into" Cage's chance works by examining the questions that he formulated and by considering the musical potential of the materials he selected. After all, the fact that Cage employed chance operations in his music did not mean that he completely gave up compositional control, as he recently explained:

> If you use, as I do chance operations, you don't have control except in the way of designing the questions which you ask. That you can control. I mean you can decide to ask certain questions and not others. But if you use chance operations, you have no control over the answers, except the limits within which they operate.[88]

A careful examination of the musical ideas behind Cage's chance works—the questions which he posed before applying chance operations—may provide a basis for the critical evaluation of his work. Cage was the first to point this out:

> I'm arguing on the other side of the fence from critics who say that my work is trivial since it can't really be analyzed in the conventional sense. What can be analyzed in my work, or criticized, are the questions that I ask. But most of the critics don't trouble to find out what those questions were. And that would make the difference between one composition made with chance operations and another. That is, the principle underlying the results of those chance operations is the questions. The things which should be criticized, if one wants to criticize, are the questions that are asked.[89]

V

During a panel discussion entitled "Cage's Influence," Christian Wolff suggested that "influence" was not a subject that seemed to interest John Cage.[90] Wolff noted that this word rarely appeared in Cage's writings, except for the famous quote borrowed from Willem de Kooning: "The past doesn't influence me, I influence the past."[91] Indeed, Cage's work affected the way we view the past; as Wolff observed, he profoundly influenced the way we perceive the work of Erik Satie and Henry David Thoreau. On the other hand, we tend to underestimate the relationship of Cage's own creative output to the past, finding it much easier to concentrate on his innovations and breaks with tradition. This attitude is as much a result of his own iconoclasm and unique creative output as it is a tendency of criticism in general. As T. S. Eliot explained in reference to poetry, criticism tends to "dwell with satisfaction on the poet's difference from his predecessors, especially his immediate predecessors; we endeavor to find something that can be isolated in order to be enjoyed."[92] Considering Cage solely in terms of his radical break with the past, however, can limit our understanding of his music. Focus on his use of chance operations in the compositional process, for example, has led critics to underestimate

Cage's skill as a composer and to the conclusion that his primary contribution to twentieth-century music was his work as a philosopher and aesthetician.[93]

In fact, Cage often acknowledged the importance of others to his own work, and his list of "influences" included many luminaries, such as Norman O. Brown, Buckminster Fuller, Marshall McLuhan, Marcel Duchamp, and Arnold Schoenberg. Rather than dismissing this as an attempt by Cage to establish his own "legitimacy," it is more fruitful to explore how these "influences" helped shape Cage's aesthetic philosophy and compositional style. This is especially true in the case of Cage's relationship with Schoenberg. As described in this essay, Cage's initial exposures to new music took place at a time when Schoenberg exerted a strong influence upon the American musical landscape, through both his own activities in Los Angeles and the dissemination of his ideas and works through supporters such as Henry Cowell, Richard Buhlig, and Adolph Weiss. Cage's earliest works are the products of this milieu; his experiments with atonality and serialism are either directly or indirectly inspired by Schoenberg's music.

Ironically, Cage's *Solo for Clarinet*—a composition written before his classes with Schoenberg—is his most conventional twelve-tone work. The order relations in the *Solo* also appear in Cage's twenty-five tone works, but the twenty-five tone technique necessitated a "loosening" of serial control (in addition to the above-mentioned limitations that it imposed on Cage's dissonant counterpoint). In general, the obligation to state every pitch in a pre-determined two-octave span before a repetition limited the possibilities for motivic connections of any sort; this may have led Cage to abandon this system rather quickly. Cage continued to develop his own singular approach to twelve-tone music during the time that he was studying with Schoenberg. Perhaps his most striking departure from Schoenbergian twelve-tone technique during this period involves the absence of twelve-tone themes. In works such as his *Two Pieces for Piano* (1935) and *Metamorphosis*, the row operates only as a part of Cage's pre-compositional process; it never appears in the finished work. The distinction between a pre-compositional activity and its manifestation in the final score anticipated a crucial feature of Cage's later music, as preparing a written score increasingly became the least important step in Cage's compositional process. Instead, the bulk of the actual composing took place through creating gamuts, charts, and other collections of sounds that, by means of chance operations, eventually yielded finished works.

These differences between Cage's early works and Schoenberg's twelve-tone music notwithstanding, Cage's emphasis on motivic integration as well as other forms of pitch relationships in compositions such as *Metamorphosis* betray Schoenberg's continuing influence. After 1938, Cage's stylistic development seems to take him farther and farther away from his former teacher, but beyond matters of musical style and compositional technique his evolving philosophy and aesthetics maintained some substantial connections with Schoenberg's teachings. This essay has noted the parallels between Schoenberg's notion of the "emancipation of dissonance" and Cage's elimination of the distinction between noise and so-called "musical sounds," Cage's reaction to Schoenberg's definitions of repetition and variation, and, above all, the correspondence of the underlying aesthetic assumptions behind Cage's chance music to Schoenberg's notion of a musical idea. In their final estimation, Cage's often cited references to his studies with Schoenberg were sincere acknowledgments of the debt he owed to his former teacher. Ultimately, Schoenberg not only provided Cage with a solid grounding in the past, he also played an essential role in shaping the younger composer's vision for the future.

Notes

1.   Calvin Tompkins, *The Bride and the Bachelors* (New York: Penguin Books, 1968), 84-85. Originally cited in "John Cage Interviewed by Jeff Goldberg," *Transatlantic Review* 55/56 (1976): 103–4.

2.   John Cage, interview with Paul Hertelendy (1982), as excerpted in *Conversing with Cage*, ed. Richard Kostelanetz (New York: Limelight Editions, 1994), 5.

3.   See, for example, the fascinating references to Cage's studies with Schoenberg in John Cage and Joan Retallack, *Musicage: Cage Muses on Words Art and Music* (Hanover, NH: University Press of New England, 1996), 2, 61, 63, 65, 83–84, 87–88, 94, 99, 159, 175–76, 297.

4.   For an enlightening article on Cage's evolving concept of harmony, see Eric de Visscher, "John Cage and the Idea of Harmony," *Musicworks* 52 (Spring 1992): 50–59. This article was inspired by James Tenney's seminal essay "John Cage and the Theory of Harmony," reprinted in *Writings about John Cage*, ed., Richard Kostelanetz (Ann Arbor, Michigan: The University Press of Michigan, 1996), 136–61.

5.   Michael Hicks, "John Cage's Studies with Arnold Schoenberg," *American Music* 8, no. 2 (Summer 1990): 125-40. Hicks' article contains the most detailed account of Cage's studies with Schoenberg. For an unprecedently thorough discussion of the cultural and social milieu in Los Angeles surrounding Cage during the 1930s, see Thomas S. Hines, "Then Not Yet 'Cage': The Los Angeles Years, 1912–38," in *John Cage: Composed in America*, ed. Marjorie Perloff and Charles Junkerman (Chicago: The University of Chicago Press, 1994), 65-99.

6. A noteworthy exception is David Nicholls, who observes that Cage learned from Schoenberg that "structure is a fundamental necessity for musical composition." See David Nicholls, *American Experimental Music, 1890–1940* (New York: Cambridge University Press, 1990), 217.

7. James Pritchett, *The Music of John Cage* (New York: Cambridge University Press, 1993), 6.

8. Hicks, 135.

9. Catherine Parsons Smith, "Athena at the Manuscript Club: John Cage and Mary Carr Moore," *Musical Quarterly* 79 (Summer 1995): 354ff.

10. Retallack, 84.

11. Ibid., 88.

12. For a detailed description of these concerts and additional information regarding Cowell's interactions with Schoenberg, see Rita Mead, *Henry Cowell's New Music 1925–36: The Society, the Music Editions, and the Recordings* (Ann Arbor, Michigan: UMI Research Press, 1981).

13. Hicks points out that Weiss translated Schoenberg's important essay "Problems of Harmony" and that he was working on a translation of Schoenberg's *Harmonielehre* during the time that Cage was his student. See Hicks, 126.

14. John Cage, interview with Cole Gagne and Tracy Caras (1975), as excerpted in Kostelanetz, 7.

15. There remains some confusion regarding the chronology of Cage's activities during 1933–34. Both Tompkins (p. 84) and Hines (pp. 91–2) claim that Cage left for New York in the spring of 1933, staying there until the fall of 1934 when he returned to Los Angeles to begin his studies with Schoenberg. However, according to the inscription in the score, Cage's *Solo with Obbligato Accompaniment of Two Voices in Canon* and *Six Short Inventions on the Subject of the Solo* were completed in Carmel, California on April 5, 1934.

16. This information, also cited by Hicks, appears in Pauline Alderman, "Reminiscences: Arnold Schoenberg at USC," *Journal of the Arnold Schoenberg Institute* 5 (1981): 203–10.

17. Ibid., 206.

18. Arnold Schoenberg, unpublished draft of introductory remarks prepared for a concert of music by Schoenberg's composition students, on February 18, 1940 on deposit at the Arnold Schönberg Center, Vienna, Austria.

19. Leonard Stein, "Gerald Strang (1908–83)," *Journal of the Arnold Schoenberg Institute* 7 (1983): 257.

20. Alderman, 204.

21. Ibid., 206.

22. Brochure, the Gerald Strang Collection, at the Arnold Schönberg Center.

23. H. H. Stuckenschmidt, *Arnold Schoenberg: His Life, World, and Work*, trans. Humphrey Searle (New York: Schirmer Books, 1977), 462.

24. Hicks, 128.

25. Ibid., 128–29.

26. Ibid., 130.

27.   Gerald Strang's and Leonard Stein's class notes (cited below), formerly housed at the Arnold Schoenberg Institute in Los Angeles, are now located at the Arnold Schönberg Center. I am grateful to Severine Neff for providing me with copies of the pages from Strang's notes dated December 3, 1935 and January 13, 1936.

28.   These materials are now part of the David Tudor Archives at the Getty Research Institute for the History of Art and the Humanities, box 7, folder 4. It appears that Cage wrote his name in the upper left-hand corner of one of the sheets of examples.

29.   There are conflicting dates for Cage's arrival in Seattle. Ellsworth Snyder ("A Chronological Table of John Cage's Life," in *Rolywholyover, John Cage, A Circus,* ed. Russell Ferguson [New York: Rizzoli, 1993]) places Cage in Seattle in the summer of 1938; an earlier account states that Cage was in Seattle beginning in 1937 (Peter Gena and Jonathan Brent, eds., *A John Cage Reader* [New York: C. F. Peters, 1982], 185). For a detailed chronology of Cage's activities from 1938 to 1954, see David W. Patterson, "Appraising the Catchwords, c. 1942-1959: John Cage's Asian-Derived Rhetoric and the Historical Reference of Black Mountain College," (Ph.D. diss., Columbia University, 1996), 249ff. Patterson lists Cage as employed at the Cornish School from 1938–40. See also Leta Miller's essay in this collection.

30.   Arnold Schoenberg, Manuscript No. 4, *Der musikalische Gedanke und seine Darstellung und Durchführung* (c. 1929). Translated in Arnold Schoenberg, *The Musical Idea and the Logic, Technique, and Art of Its Presentation,* edited, translated, and with a commentary by Patricia Carpenter and Severine Neff (New York: Columbia University Press, 1995), 428, note 4. The translation of this passage is by Charlotte M. Cross.

31.   Schoenberg described his plans in a letter to publisher Emil Hertzka dated July 23, 1911. Bryan Simms has translated this letter (from the Vienna Stadt- und Landesbibliothek) in his review of Arnold Schoenberg, *Theory of Harmony,* trans. Roy E. Carter in *Music Theory Spectrum* 4 (1982): 156–57.

32.   The manuscripts are listed in Schoenberg, *The Musical Idea,* xv-xvi.

33.   Ibid., 21. The quotation is from Willi Reich, *Schoenberg: A Critical Biography,* trans. Leo Black (New York: Praeger, 1971), 238.

34.   Wayne R. Shoaf, "From the Archives; The Felix Greissle Collection," *Journal of the Arnold Schoenberg Institute* 10, no. 1 (1987): 81-82. Cited in Schoenberg, *The Musical Idea,* 375.

35.   Schoenberg, *The Musical Idea,* 91.

36.   Ibid., 169–71.

37.   Ibid., 147.

38.   Ibid.

39.   Ibid., 151.

40.   Ibid.

41.   Ibid., 149.

42.   Schoenberg discussed these matters in detail in his 1917 manuscript, *Zussamenhang, Kontrapunkt, Instrumentation, Formenlehre,* 4–63. For a translation of this manuscript see Arnold Schoenberg, *Coherence, Counterpoint, Instrumentation, Instruction in Form,* edited with an intro-

duction by Severine Neff and Charlotte M. Cross (Lincoln, Nebraska: University of Nebraska Press, 1994).

43.   Schoenberg, *The Musical Idea*, 227–29.

44.   Ibid., 231.

45.   Strang's class notes dated June 19, 1935.

46.   Ibid.

47.   Strang's class notes dated June 20, 1935.

48.   Stein's class notes dated June 30, 1936.

49.   Ibid.

50.   There exist several assignments and examinations from this class in the Clara Silvers Steuermann Collection at the Arnold Schönberg Center.

51.   Tompkins, 85.

52.   Henry Cowell, *New Musical Resources* (New York: Something Else Press, 1969), 38–9.

53.   Charles Seeger, "On Dissonant Counterpoint," *Modern Music* 7 (June/July, 1929): 25. This quotation also appears in Nicholls (p. 90). His text includes a fine discussion of Seeger's technique and music.

54.   Seeger, 26.

55.   Nicholls, 90.

56.   Henry Cowell, "Current Chronicle," *Musical Quarterly* 38 (January 1952): 152. "When I first met John Cage about 1932, he was writing strange little piano pieces with an unusual sense of sound-interest created by odd tonal combinations. . . . He studied dissonant counterpoint and composition with me in California."

57.   Stuckenschmidt, 464.

58.   John Cage, "Notes on Compositions I (1933-48)," in *John Cage: Writer*, ed. Richard Kostelanetz (New York: Limelight Editions, 1993), 6.

59.   In this and subsequent examples, an accidental applies only to the note it precedes.

60.   Nicholls analyzes this movement (p. 176) and other early works by Cage.

61.   Paul van Emmerik mentions this aspect of Cage's *Solo for Clarinet* in his doctoral dissertation, "Thema's en Variaties: systematische tendensen in de compositietechnieken van John Cage," (Ph.D. diss., University of Amsterdam, 1996), 31.

62.   Ibid. This leads van Emmerik to label measures 20ff. a "varied reprise."

63.   For a detailed discussion of these works see, Nicholls, 177–82.

64.   Nicholls (p. 178) also notes the limitations of Cage's twenty-five tone technique.

65.   Cage, "Notes on Compositions I (1933–48)," 6.

66.   "I took those groups of tones, and at the end of each group, I arranged things so that I could begin any other of the remaining groups from the following or preceding degree of the row. This could be done following either the form of the original or the inversion, or its retrograde or retrograde inversion." John Cage and Daniel Charles, *For the Birds: John Cage in Conversation with Daniel Charles* (London: Marion Boyars, 1981), 72.

67.   Cage and Retallack, 176.

68.   Cage and Charles, 75.

69.   "D.C.: Would *Metamorphosis* then be an exaggeratedly intellectual work? Would you agree to recognizing in it what you later called a 'Frankenstein' monster. J.C.: Yes indeed! And the repeated cells are boring as hell! (Laughter)." Ibid., 37.

70.   Nicholls, 192ff.

71.   Cage and Charles, 35.

72.   This point is also discussed in Hicks, 131ff.

73.   He had already composed a *Quartet* (1935) and a *Trio* (1936) for percussion.

74.   John Cage, "The Future of Music: Credo" [c. 1940], in *Silence: Lectures and Writings* (Middletown, CT: Wesleyan University Press, 1961), 4.

75.   Hicks, 130.

76.   Virgil Thomson, "Expressive Percussion," *New York Herald Tribune,* January 22, 1945. Reprinted in *A Virgil Thomson Reader* (Boston: Houghton Mifflin Company, 1981), 263.

77.   Ibid., 340. The quotation was first published in the *New York Herald Tribune* on February 5, 1950.

78.   For an analysis of this work, see David W. Bernstein, "In Order to Thicken the Plot: Toward a Critical Reception of Cage's Music," *Writings through John Cage's Music, Poetry, and Art*, ed. David W. Bernstein and Christopher Hatch (Chicago: University of Chicago Press, 2001), 22ff.

79.   Jean-Jacques Nattiez et al., ed., *The Boulez-Cage Correspondence* (New York: Cambridge University Press, 1990), 50.

80.   Cage, "Composition as Process" [1958], *Silence*, 26.

81.   Cage, "Defense of Satie" [1948], *John Cage: An Anthology*, ed. Richard Kostelanetz (New York: Da Capo, 1991), 79.

82.   Cage and Retallack, 61.

83.   The movement's rhythmic structure consists of asymmetrical phrases arranged according to the proportion $1\frac{1}{4}$: $\frac{3}{4}$: $1\frac{1}{4}$: $\frac{3}{4}$: $1\frac{1}{2}$: $1\frac{1}{2}$ which form a larger unit seven measures long that is repeated seven times.

84.   Nattiez et al., ed. 78.

85.   Cage, "Composition: To Describe the Process of Composition used in *Music of Changes* and *Imaginary Landscape No. 4*" [1952], *Silence*, 59.

86.   John Cage, interview with David Cope (1980), as excerpted in Kostelanetz, ed., *Conversing with Cage*, 215.

87.   Schoenberg, *Coherence, Counterpoint, Instrumentation, Instruction in Form*, lv.

88.   Cage and Retallack, 124.

89.   John Cage, interview with David Cope (1980), as excerpted in Kostelanetz, ed., *Conversing with Cage*, 85.

90.   The panel took place at Mills College (Oakland, California) at a festival/conference entitled "'Here Comes Everybody': The Music, Poetry, and Art of John Cage," November 15-19, 1995. A transcript of this panel appears in Bernstein and Hatch, 167–89.

91.   Cage, "History of Experimental Music in the United States"[1959] in *Silence*, 67.

92.   T. S. Eliot, "Tradition and the Individual Talent," in *Selected Prose of T. S. Eliot*, ed. with an introduction by Frank Kermode (New York: Harcourt Brace Jovanovich, 1975), 38.

93.   See, for example, Rose Rosengard Subotnick, *Deconstructive Variations: Music and Reason in Western Society* (Minneapolis, MN: University of Minnesota Press, 1996), xx. James Pritchett's monograph on Cage addresses this issue, focusing on the development of Cage's compositional style.

2. Cultural Intersections: John Cage in Seattle (1938–1940)

Leta E. Miller[1]

Although John Cage taught at Seattle's Cornish School for only two years (1938–1940), he often cited this period as seminal to his later work. At Cornish Cage first had access to a large repository of percussion instruments, prompting him to form an ensemble that presented concerts throughout the Northwest; among these was the first all-percussion concert in the nation. The school also housed a recording studio, where Cage conducted experiments resulting in his first electronic compositions. In addition, his interaction with the Seattle dance community prompted experiments with timbre that led directly to the prepared piano. In a series of public lectures, Cage expounded his evolving ideas on the relation of music and noise, which took shape within the Cornish School's interdisciplinary environment; the most influential of these talks, "The Future of Music: Credo," was later published as the opening essay in *Silence* (with an incorrect date).

Despite the importance of this period and the extensive (and ever-growing) literature by and about Cage, information on these years is minimal and even, on occasion, erroneous. In part, the problem stems from Cage himself, for while he often spoke of his Cornish School period in interviews and wrote about it in essays, he provided little help in clarifying details, frequently citing his bad memory. To a certain extent, however, the fault also lies with the privileging of the oral interview, a powerful tool in the reconstruction of recent history, but one that demands rigorous cross-examination to counteract the necessarily biased subjectivity of memory. Faulty information about Cage's Seattle years in general has been repeated so often that at times it has been considered "documented."

In 1982 Robert Stevenson helped rectify this situation with a small article in the *Inter-American Music Review*.[2] Characteristically thorough, Stevenson mined a wealth of information from periodicals, catalogues, brochures, and other sources. His research has since been supplemented by that of others, notably Thomas Hines and David Patterson.[3] Nevertheless errors and lacunae remain, which are addressed in this essay. More importantly, however, I hope to shed light on the sociocultural environment in which Cage worked and to highlight his interaction with a circle of artists whose impact on his development has not been adequately credited. A chronology of the events discussed herein appears at the end of the chapter.

How John Cage Came to Seattle

In the spring of 1938 Cage was living in Los Angeles with his wife Xenia Andreyevna Kashevaroff (daughter of a Russian-Orthodox priest from Alaska)[4], piecing together a precarious livelihood through odd jobs. Among these were teaching extension courses through UCLA and working with dancers.[5] At the end of the spring semester he decided to seek work in Northern California. He and Xenia first headed for Carmel where her sisters Sasha and Natalya were part of a lively intellectual circle that included, among others, the author John Steinbeck. From Carmel Cage drove on alone to San Francisco. On his agenda was to seek out Lou Harrison, a young composer who, according to Henry Cowell, shared Cage's interests in percussion and modern dance.[6] Cage appeared unannounced on Harrison's doorstep to find Lou composing at his upright piano. "Hello, my name is John Cage," said Cage matter-of-factly. "Henry Cowell sent me."[7] As Cowell anticipated, the two men soon discovered their common interests, and Harrison, who had been living and working in San Francisco since 1935, introduced Cage to his artistic circle. (Cage would later return the favor when Harrison moved to New York in the summer of 1943.)

During the previous three years Harrison had developed productive contacts in the San Francisco and East Bay dance communities, and in the fall of 1937 (at the age of 20), he was hired as dance accompanist by the Mills College Physical Education Department (which supervised the dance program until the 1941–42 academic year). Harrison's main task was to accompany the Mary Wigman-trained dancer Tina Flade in classes and recitals. Though the job could easily become tedious (Harrison recalls spending an entire day improvising over a single four-note motive), he used the assignment to hone his skills in improvisation on the piano and on various percussion instruments, becoming adept at translating the dancer's "counts" into a musical line that functioned as a counterpoint to the physical movement.

Under Rosalind Cassidy, the chairman of the Physical Education Department, Mills fostered innovative and experimental offerings in dance education and supplemented its regular academic program with an active summer session. For the summer of 1938 (Harrison's first as a Mills College staff member) the Lester Horton troupe from Los Angeles was in residence, as was Bonnie Bird, a young woman from Seattle who presented a two-week workshop in the Martha Graham technique.

Upon her graduation from the Seattle public schools in August 1931, Bird had received a scholarship to study with Graham in New York.[8] She spent more than five years in the East, first as a Graham student and then as a member of the professional company. Before taking a position on the faculty of Seattle's Cornish School in the fall of 1937, Bird had taught at the Graham studio in New York, at Sarah Lawrence and Bennington Colleges, and, for two summers (1936 and 1937) at the University of Washington. Energetic and enterprising, she leapt eagerly into the task of building a modern dance program at Cornish. Although there were but five dance majors that first year,[9] three proved to be exceptionally talented: Dorothy Herrmann (who soon after married drama student Cole Weston, youngest son of photographer Edward Weston), Syvilla Fort (who eventually became supervising director of the Katherine Dunham School in New York), and a young man from Centralia, Washington, named Mercier Cunningham (who, of course, would become one of the country's most noted dancers and choreographers, and would establish a half-century-long collaboration with John Cage).[10]

Bird immediately took on an active role in the community, presenting a series of lecture/demonstrations beginning in October 1937, in which she traced the history of dance forms.[11] Graham had all of her students take a course in "pre-classic dance forms" with composer Louis Horst (1884–1964), who served as music director for Ruth St. Denis, Ted Shawn, and the Denishawn dance company from 1915–1925, and then as accompanist and music director for Graham from 1926–1948. In this course, Horst described metric, rhythmic, affective, and temporal characteristics of Renaissance and Baroque dances, along with generalized descriptions of binary form and common dance steps. If his approach at times appears both teleological and reductionist (his concise book on the subject[12] makes some rather encompassing generalizations about music from the middle ages to the end of the Baroque), it is important to recall that his object was not historical re-creation, but rather contemporary interpretation of historical dance aesthetics.

During her first year on the faculty, Bird presented her Cornish dance troupe both at the school and in other venues in the city. The students demonstrated a broad repertoire ranging from interpretations of early court dances to a new suite she had composed depicting the history of Spain from the Inquisition to the then-current Civil War.[13] The music for Bird's "Dance for Spain" was written by her regular accompanist, Ralph Gilbert, who had studied piano at Cornish with Stephen Balogh. At the end of the 1937-38 year, however, Gilbert left for the East to work with Graham, supported by a scholarship from Seattle's Music and Art Foundation (founded in Spring 1923 to raise funds for cultural activities in the community).[14] In the capacity of staff pianist, Gilbert proved to be quite exceptional, as Graham herself attested when she brought her company to Seattle in March 1940.[15]

By the time Bird came to Mills College in Oakland, California, for their 1938 summer session, she had begun to build Cornish's modern dance program into a vibrant and visible force in the Seattle community. But with Gilbert off to New York, she faced a crisis for her second year: she needed a skilled accompanist. At Mills she met Lou Harrison and offered him the job, but he declined. Instead he recommended his new friend, John Cage.

Cage recalled the Seattle offer as one of several he received through his contact with Harrison. He chose the job at Cornish in large part because Bird described a closet at the school filled with percussion instruments.[16]

Cage had been focusing on the possibilities of percussion music since writing his first trio and quartet for percussion ensemble in Los Angeles in 1935–36. He saw the expansion of the traditional instrumentarium as "part of the attempt to liberate all audible sound from the limitations of musical prejudice," just as "modern music in general may be said to have been the history of the liberation of the dissonance."[17] Yet he found greater interest in his percussion music among dancers than among musicians:

> While I was studying with Adolph Weiss in the early 1930's, I became aware of his unhappiness in face of the fact that his music was rarely performed. I too had experienced difficulty in arranging performances of my compositions, so I determined to consider a piece of music only half done when I completed a manuscript. It was my responsibility to finish it by getting it played.
>
> It was evident that musicians interested in new music were rare. It was equally evident that modern dancers were grateful for any sounds or noises that could be produced for their recitals . . .

> Very soon I was earning a livelihood accompanying dance classes
> and occasionally writing music for performances.[18]

Cage even wrote music for an aquatic ballet, during which he discovered the possibilities of the "water gong." Lowering a gong into the water so the swimmers could hear it, he was delighted by the resulting glissando.

The instrument collection that Bonnie Bird described to Cage included a set of Chinese gongs, cymbals, tom-toms, and woodblocks that belonged to the German dancer Lore Deja, a "fiery little redhead"[19] who joined the Cornish School faculty in Fall 1930. Deja had acted as assistant to Mary Wigman in Dresden and had drawn rave reviews for her performance of "Totenmal" in Munich (choreography by Albert Talhof). She was "the only graduate of the Mary Wigman School in the country," boasted the Cornish brochure for the summer session of 1931. "The Wigman School is considered the most active and progressive center of the Modern German Dance Movement, and it is interesting to note that Seattle was ahead of New York in seeing a recital of the Wigman School of dancing . . . "[20] At Cornish, Deja taught dance technique and composition as well as eurythmics. "An unusual feature" of her course of study was "the use of gongs and primitive instruments . . . for dance accompaniment."[21] By 1932 Deja's summer session course offerings included "Teaching Methods and Materials," "Dance Technique and Composition," "Exercises in Creative Imagination," and "Instruction in the Use of Primitive Instruments."

By the time Cage came to Cornish for the fall semester 1938, Deja had left Seattle. But her percussion collection remained (temporarily) at the school. A year later, she requested that her instruments be shipped to New York, forcing Cage to seek funding for replacements during his second year in Seattle.[22]

Lectures, Demonstrations, and the Seattle Artists League

By the beginning of the fall semester, John and Xenia Cage were settled in Seattle and collaboration with Bird began in earnest.[23] On October 7, less than a month after the term began,[24] Bird was featured in the opening event of the school's "Three Arts Series," a set of programs instigated in 1924 by Nellie Cornish (1876–1956) to introduce outstanding faculty and students to the Seattle public.[25] Bird presented a lecture-demonstration on modern dance, assisted by students Dorothy Herrmann and Merce Cunningham, and by "composer and accompanist" John Cage. What, if anything, Cage composed for this concert is unclear. The first part of the program consisted of a "demonstration of modern dance technique as developed by Martha Graham" (music, if any, unspecified), while the second portion contained "examples of some of the compositions that have been built in study of pre-classic dance forms." Listed in this part of the program are a pavane and galliard by [Thoinot] Arbeau, a sarabande and rigaudon by [Gregorio] Lambranzi, a courante by Loeillet, an allemande by François Couperin, a gigue by Durante, and a chaconne by Louis Couperin. Whether Cage harmonized the monophonic tunes from Arbeau's *Orchésographie* (1588) and Lambranzi's *Neue und curieuse theatrialische Tantz-Schul* (1716) or whether he played harmonizations by Horst is unclear. (The Arbeau pavane was most likely "Belle qui tiens ma vie," which appeared in the 1588 treatise in a four-part version, but all the galliards in Arbeau's book are monophonic, as are the Lambranzi examples.) Several of the works on the recital seem to correspond to those included or cited in Horst's *Pre-Classic Dance Forms* of 1937, which appeared in installments in his journal, the *Dance Observer*, from 1934–37. "Belle qui tiens ma vie" was included in the second installment, and the opening phrase of a courante by Loeillet was printed in November 1935.[26] An allemande by François Couperin, a chaconne by Louis Couperin, and the Loeillet courante are all listed in an addenda of "suggested music" at the end of Horst's book. A sarabande by Lambranzi, reproduced from the 1716 treatise along with the accompanying dance illustration, appeared in the *Dance Observer* in its monophonic form,[27] but Horst included his own harmonization of the tune in his book. As an example of his adaptation of early dance music for use in the modern dance, his keyboard setting shows rather distinctive (and sometimes decidedly un-Baroque) voicings and harmonic language—an interesting study in musical as well as choreographic adaptations of early music. Other settings of monophonic tunes do not appear in Horst's book, but Cage may well have had access to them through Bird or from Horst himself.

That Cage and Horst were in direct contact during these years is evident from a series of six articles on "Percussion Music and its Relation to the Modern Dance" that appeared in Horst's journal between October 1939 and March 1940. Cage wrote the lead article ("Introduction") and the well-known essay "Goal: New Music, New Dance," which later appeared in *Silence*. Other contributors to the series included Henry Cowell, Lou Harrison, William Russell, and Franziska Boas.[28]

The Cornish School's promotion of Bird's lecture-demonstration as one of a series of programs in its October 1938 "Three Arts Series" reflects the interdisciplinary focus of both the school and the dancer.[29] Programs and news articles from Cage's years in Seattle suggest frequent collaboration among the faculty in theatrical presentations,

arts festivals, and music-dance programs. Cooperation in the class
was encouraged as well; Cage not only accompanied Bird's classes,
even took over her course in dance composition for two weeks durin
1939–40 academic year while Bird was in New York.[30] This philosop
close interaction among diverse artforms was central to the Co
School; founder Nellie Cornish—who was trained as a pianist but dev
her life to indisciplinary arts education both traditional and emergin
kept her eye on this interactive goal throughout her years as head of
institution. She traced her practical educational philosophy to the p
gressive teachings of her father:

> Father believed that education was fundamentally the stimulation
> of true thinking—how to think, rather than what to think. . . . He
> felt that children shouldn't be burdened with textbooks, but
> should first be made aware of what was going on around them, be
> acquainted with the things they used. . . . Together we read
> unbowdlerized stories of Greek mythology. He made arithmetic
> interesting by giving us problems which were part of our daily life.
> . . . Geography dealt with lakes, mountains, and rivers that were
> familiar. . . . We spelled by rote. . . . Original thinking was encour-
> aged. Father believed that direct personal experiences were . . .
> more useful than textbooks and memorizing.[31]

The Cornish School's catalog for 1938–39 lists twenty-five faculty, with
music instruction concentrated in piano, voice, and strings (Table 1). Cage
apparently accepted the Cornish position too late to be included in this
catalogue; he is listed only the following year.

Table 1. Cornish School's "Outline of Courses" for 1938–39.

Disciplines	Number of Faculty
Piano:	6
Voice:	2
Harp:	1
Violin/viola:	2
Cello:	1
Music education:	1
Eurythmics:	1
Art:	3
Theater:	2
Costume design and stagecraft:	3 (two of whom are also listed under "art"
Dance:	3
Language:	2 (French and Italian)
Radio:	TBA [Donald MacLean]

Several of the music faculty also taught theory, composition, counterpoint, or conducting. Among the dance faculty, responsibilities were divided among Bird (modern dance), Dorothy Fisher (ballet and tap dance), and Frances Ryan (Hawaiian dance).

Three days after Bird's October 7 lecture-demonstration, Cage presented his own lecture-recital on "Some Aspects of Modern Music" at the annual dinner of the Seattle chapter of Pro Musica, Inc., an organization devoted to "the modern and unusual in music and musical interpretation."[32] His talk centered on percussion music and problems of rhythm; he illustrated with his own piano piece, *Metamorphosis*, and other contemporary works, including music by George McKay, who had joined the University of Washington faculty in 1927.[33]

The Pro Musica talk was but one of several such lectures Cage gave during his years in Seattle. On at least two other occasions, he spoke at the Seattle Artists League, the first time soon after he came to the city ("New Directions in Music," December 11, 1938) and the second shortly before he returned to California ("What Next in American Art?" February 18, 1940).[34] Cage's well-known essay, "The Future of Music: Credo," originated as one of these lectures. In his introduction to the published version in *Silence*, he wrote, "The following text was delivered as a talk at a meeting of a Seattle arts society organized by Bonnie Bird in 1937." The 1937 date published in this source has continually posed a quandary for scholars since Cage's residency in Seattle could only be dated to 1938. In fact, as we have already seen, he did not meet Bonnie Bird until the summer of 1938 and moved to the northwest thereafter. Furthermore, the Seattle Artists League, of which Bonnie Bird was indeed a founding member, was not even envisioned until the spring of 1938; its first meeting was the December event at which Cage spoke[35] (see Figure 2-1). Some scholars have skirted the date issue by suggesting 1937-38 for Cage's presentation while others have merely repeated the questionable information without comment.[36]

How did this erroneous date find its way with such authority into the introductory remarks in *Silence*? "The Future of Music: Credo," which opens Cage's 1961 volume of essays, was actually taken from an earlier published source: an elaborate program booklet issued in conjunction with a 25-year retrospective concert of his music at Town Hall, New York, on May 15, 1958. (The booklet is included in the published recording of the concert.)[37] Cage's essay appears there under the heading, "The Future of Music: Credo. Seattle, 1937." George Avakian, producer of this recording—and, incidentally, husband of violinist Anahid Ajemian, who worked closely with Cage and Harrison for many years—kindly confirmed my suspicion that the

Figure 2-1. Anouncement for the first meeting of the Seattle Artists League, December 11, 1938. The year is confirmed by the day of the week. A copy of this document can be found in the John Cage Archive at Northwestern University. Reprinted by permission of the John Cage Trust.

THE SEATTLE ARTISTS LEAGUE

presents its opening program

Sunday, December 11

8:30 P. M.

THE REPERTORY PLAYHOUSE

41st and University Way

TICKETS—25 CENTS

DRAMA: The Repertory Players
"RED HEAD BAKER"
By Albert Maltz
An experimental modern drama

MUSIC: JOHN CAGE, composer-pianist, discussing, and illustrating at the piano, trends and developments in modern music.

PAINTING: An exhibition of paintings by representative Seattle artists, including Raymond Hill, Kenneth Callahan, Earl T. Fields, James Houston, Robert Iglehart and others.

DR. MELVIN RADER will discuss the relationship of the modern arts to the past.

The Artists' League has been established to assist in making the arts a more integral part of civic life. Membership in the League is open to practicing artists in all fields, teachers and students of the arts, and anyone wishing to further the purposes of the organization.

Address inquiries to BONNIE BIRD, *Secretary*
226 33rd N., Seattle

1937 date in the program came solely from Cage's memory (as Avakian put it, "in conversation").[38] A manuscript of the lecture's basic text at Northwestern University not only confirms that "The Future of Music" dates after 1937, but also situates it clearly at the *later* Seattle Artists League meeting at which Cage spoke (February 1940), since the manuscript bears at its head the notation 1940 (without month or day).[39]

Why, one might ask, should we be so concerned with the dating of this lecture? This talk, in which Cage bruited his concept of music as "the organization of sound,"[40] has often been seen as a foreshadowing of his work with electronic instruments and his search for organizational principles in percussion music. If, however, the lecture was not delivered until February 1940, the predictions and assertions in it actually postdate, rather than predate, most of Cage's work at Cornish—indeed they were shaped by his activities within the Seattle community. The proclamation that "the use of noise to make music will continue and increase until we reach a music produced through the aid of electrical instruments" *follows* the composition of *Imaginary Landscape No. 1*; the assertion that "new methods will be discovered, bearing a definite relation to . . . percussion music and any other methods which are free from the concept of a fundamental tone" *postdates* his Seattle percussion works; and his statement that "the principle of form will be our only constant connection with the past" comes *after*, not before, *First Construction (in Metal)*, the first work using micro-macrocosmic principles (often called his "square-root system"). In short, the redating of this lecture recasts it as a culmination, rather than a precursor, of this formative period, its ideas honed from Cage's interactions with the Seattle artistic community, and reflecting influences both within and outside of music.

The first meeting at which Cage spoke (December 11, 1938) was held at the Repertory Playhouse, a venue that figured prominently in his work in Seattle. The Playhouse was home to a theater company founded ten years earlier by Florence and Burton James, who had been hired by the Cornish School in 1923 to run the drama department. Five years later, they branched out into this new community-based venture.[41] Cage's lecture-demonstration, "New Directions in Music," opened the Seattle Artists League's first program, followed by a talk on "The Arts, Past and Present" by University of Washington philosophy professor Melvin Rader. At intermission, patrons were invited to view paintings by local artists displayed in the lounge, after which the Repertory Players presented Albert Maltz's 1937 radio play, *Red-Head Baker*.[42]

Despite the Seattle Artists League's focus on interdisciplinary collaboration, the activities and affiliations of several of its members suggest a more encompassing agenda. In fact, the organization seems to have had a decidedly political complexion. A number of League members—for example, Melvin Rader, the Jameses, Bonnie Bird and her husband (University of Washington psychology professor Ralph Gundlach), among others[43]—were heavily involved in leftist organizations during the 1930s, associations that came back to haunt them years later during the Cold War.[44]

After the second world war, both Rader and Gundlach were brought before the Committee on Un-American Activities of the Washington State Legislature (the Canwell Committee), along with more than two dozen other University of Washington faculty members and community activists. The two men were accused of having attended a secret Communist training school in New York during the summer of 1938, where they were allegedly indoctrinated with revolutionary philosophy aimed at overthrowing the U.S. government. Rader spent the better part of a year proving that he had never been a member of the Communist Party.[45] Gundlach, whose home was often at the center of social activism in the 1930s and 1940s (and who interacted closely with Cage, providing him, for instance, with the test-tone recordings that led to Cage's first electronic compositions), refused entirely to cooperate with the Canwell committee. He was fined $250 and spent a month in prison. In the fall of 1948, Gundlach, a tenured associate professor, was recommended by the Dean of the College of Arts and Sciences for dismissal from the University faculty, was tried by the Committee on Tenure and Academic Freedom, and was fired.[46] He and Bird subsequently moved to New York where they eked out a precarious living while Gundlach retrained for private practice.[47]

Florence and Burton James, founders of the Repertory Playhouse (whose small stage prompted Cage to write his first piece for prepared piano), were also repeatedly accused during the Canwell hearings of Communist ties. The theater company was branded "a Communist mouthpiece" and a "recruiting center" for Communist Party members among the students at the University of Washington.[48] The repertory company—which managed a 342-seat theater and depended heavily on ticket revenues for its operating expenses—was forced out of business after the hearings.[49]

The author of the play presented at the Artists League's first meeting in 1938 similarly ran afoul of post-war anti-Communist purges. Albert Maltz was one of the "Hollywood 10" called to testify at the House Un-American Activities Committee hearings in Washington, D.C. in 1947. He refused to discuss his political affiliations, was indicted for contempt of Congress, and served ten months in jail.[50]

While I have found no direct evidence of Cage's participation in the political organizations patronized by some of his colleagues, he clearly chose to associate closely with this coterie of left-wing artists. Indeed, his challenges to the traditional definition of "music" resonated with their own concerns. Cage's sometimes inflammatory rhetoric ("Percussion music is revolution," he proclaimed in 1939) laid down a gauntlet in his own field, stimulating a productive relationship with the members of the Artists League. Judging by their own activities, his words fell on sympathetic ears: "Sound and rhythm have too long been submissive to the restrictions of nineteenth-century music," he declared. "Today we are fighting for their emancipation. Tomorrow, with electronic music in our ears, we will hear freedom."[51]

Percussion Music

We do not know precisely what Cage said at the December 1938 meeting of the Artists League, but it is likely that he discussed his current work, just as he had at the Pro Musica meeting two months earlier: that work was percussion music, a term he used "not [to] mean that all the sounds . . . are obtained by the act of striking or hitting," but "in a loose sense to refer to sound inclusive of noise. . . . "[52]

Cage had begun to explore percussion music after becoming disillusioned with the exercises in serialism he was writing during his studies in Los Angeles with Schoenberg. "There were so many exercises to write, that I found little time to compose," he later recalled.

> What little that I did write was atonal, and based on 12-tone rows. At that time I admired the theory of 12-tone music, but I did not like its sound. . . . I was convinced . . . that although 12-tone music was excellent theoretically, in making use of the instruments which had been developed for tonal music, it had continually to be written negatively rather than straightforwardly: it had always to avoid the harmonic relationships which were natural to the tonal instruments, which instruments it did not so much use as usurp; I was convinced that for atonal music new instruments proper to it were required.[53]

Percussion music also solved another problem for the contemporary composer: mounting public performances became not only feasible but also practical. "I have met very many [American composers] who have grown bitter and lonely in their studios," Cage noted in 1948. "I solved this problem for myself by writing music which could be played by a group of literate amateur musicians, people who had not developed instrumental skills on a professional level and therefore still had time to enjoy playing music together with their friends."[54]

In Los Angeles Cage's first percussion pieces were played by a group of friends with whom he and Xenia were studying bookbinding. As soon as he arrived in Seattle, he assembled another such group at Cornish, including both musicians and non-musicians. At the core were Cage and Margaret Jansen (a member of the Cornish piano faculty) as well as two non-professionals (Xenia Cage, an artist, and Doris Dennison, instructor of eurythmics). For concerts at the school, the group was expanded to include students in various disciplines, a policy Cage maintained in his later percussion ensembles. For example, Merce Cunningham's friend Joyce Wike, an anthropology student at the University of Washington, played in Cage's ensemble and also danced in a performance at Cornish on April 26, 1939.[55] At a concert at Mills College in the summer of 1940, the seventeen "percussors" (as Cowell called them) were quite diverse, ranging from professional musicians to the consulting architect of the Golden Gate Bridge.[56] (Considering the personnel, the music played was surprisingly difficult.) Similarly, in a widely-publicized percussion concert at the Museum of Modern Art in New York in February 1943 dancer/choreographers Jean Erdman and Merce Cunningham were among the performing musicians. Such efforts to bring contemporary music out of its specialized and, as some saw it, elitist orientation, to appeal to a wider constituency of non-professionals harmonized with the educational and artistic philosophy advocated by many members of the Seattle Artists League.

During his two years in Seattle, Cage presented three all-percussion concerts at Cornish (December 9, 1938; May 19, 1939; and December 9, 1939) as well as additional performances in the surrounding area (for instance, a recital with Bonnie Bird in Tacoma in January 1939). By the third percussion concert Cage had built up an impressive ensemble of twelve players including, among others, Dorothy Fisher, the ballet and tap dance teacher, and Imogene Horsley, a young student who would later become a well-known musicologist specializing in Renaissance and Baroque music. (For a detailed account of Cage's percussion work in these years, see my article, "The Art of Noise: John Cage, Lou Harrison, and the West Coast Percussion Ensemble."[57]) The list of sponsors for Cage's third program is also impressive: twenty-three individuals or couples, including "Mr. John Steinbeck," presumably from Xenia's Carmel connections.

The printed program for this third percussion concert (see Figure 2-2) also featured a quotation from Henry Cowell that bears an uncanny resemblance to Cage's own essay, "The Future of Music." Cowell wrote: "I honestly believe and formally predict that the immediate *future of music* lies in the bringing of percussion on [the] one hand, and sliding tones on the other, to as great a state of perfection in construction of composition and flexibility of handling on instruments as older elements are now" (italics added). Indeed, Cage had kept in close contact with Cowell even during this period, when Cowell was in San Quentin prison on a morals charge.[58] Several months earlier, in preparation for his May 1939 performance, Cage had written to composers around the country soliciting new percussion works. Harrison sent *Fifth Simfony* and *Counterdance in the Spring*; Cowell responded with *Pulse* and *Return*.[59]

In January–February 1940, the core group from Cornish, who called themselves the "Cage Percussion Players" (John and Xenia Cage, Margaret Jansen, and Doris Dennison) went on tour to the University of Montana (Missoula), the University of Idaho (Moscow), Whitman College (Walla Walla, Washington), and Reed College (Portland).[60] At each of these performances, Cage spoke to the audience about the future of music. "Believing that music as it is commonly known is in the tottering stage," wrote the reviewer at the University of Montana, "the group played compositions comparable in spirit to surrealism. . . . Should this movement gain precedence over the present form[s of music] . . . the whole development of musical history, its emotional and intellectual meanings, vocabulary and form would be valuable to the world of the future only as an historical fact, John Cage, leader of the group, said."[61] The Missoula audience's reaction—"skepticism with an admixture of amusement and slight hysteria"—was nothing compared to that the previous night in Moscow, Idaho, which Cage claimed was downright "hysterical."

Cage's predictions were less apocalyptic in his program notes to the Reed College concert on February 14, 1940. "The sounds which have been accepted as musical are surprisingly few," he noted.

> Many variations of sound quality, amplitude, pitch and duration are yet to be found and used. In the realm of pitch, for example, we have yet to explore the possibilities of sliding tones. Some composers of percussion music have made use of sirens, slide whistles, gongs struck while being lowered into water, and the glissandi available on pedal timpani. Perhaps in the near future, we will have electrical instruments which, when dials are turned, buttons pushed, etc., will give us everything we want: free access to sound. Machines will be invented which will play rhythms which human beings could not.[62]

As we will see, Cage's own *Imaginary Landscape No. 1*, featuring electronically produced sliding tones, had already been performed nearly a year earlier.

Figure 2-2.
Program from Cage's third percussion concert,
Cornish Theatre, December 9, 1939.

PROGRAM

PULSE . . . . COWELL
    dragon's mouths, wood blocks, drums,
    tom toms, rice bowls, temple gongs,
    cymbals, gongs, pipe lengths, brake
    drums

FUGUE . . . . RUSSELL
    snare drum, xylophone, tympani, piano,
    cymbals, triangle, orchestral bells, bass
    drum

DIRGE . . . . COUPER
    two pianos, one of which is tuned a
    quarter tone higher than the other

RITMICAS, V and VI . . . ROLDAN
    claves, maracas, guiro, cow bells, qui-
    jadas, bongos, drums, marimbula
    EN TIEMPO DE SON
    EN TIEMPO DE RUMBA

INTERMISSION

CONSTRUCTION IN METAL . CAGE
    thundersheets, orchestral bells, string
    piano, sleigh bells, cow bells, temple
    gongs, brake drums, cymbals, anvils,
    gongs

RETURN . . . . COWELL
    dragon's mouths, wood blocks, tom
    toms, bells, cup gongs, gongs, wind
    bell, cymbal, lion's roar, wailer

3 DANCE MOVEMENTS . . RUSSELL
    dinner bell, steel bar, cymbals, drums,
    wood blocks, bottle, piano
    WALTZ
    MARCH
    FOXTROT

PLAYERS

MARIE BALAGNO
MARY ANN BIER
XENIA CAGE
DORIS DENNISON
DENISE FARWELL
DOROTHY FISHER
IMOGENE HORSLEY
LENORE HOVEY
MARGARET JANSEN
MARJORIE LIVINGOOD
LENORE THAYER
LENORE WARD

NOTES

"I honestly believe and formally predict that the immediate future of music lies in the bringing of percussion
on one hand, and sliding tones on the other, to as great
a state of perfection in construction of composition and
flexibility of handling on instruments as older elements
are now." **HENRY COWELL**

MILDRED COUPER lives in Santa Barbara, California.
Her "Dirge" is published in the New Music Quarterly.

AMADEO ROLDAN (1900-1939) was born of Cuban
parents in Paris. In 1932 he was appointed Conductor
of the Philharmonic Orchestra of Havana.

WILLIAM RUSSELL is at present in Los Angeles, where
he is engaged with the Chinese Shadow Play Company.

"I felt that noise, the unrelated noise of life, such as
this in the subway, had not been battered out as would
have been the case with Beethoven still warm in the
mind, but it had actually been mastered, subjugated.
The composer had taken this hated thing, life, and
rigged himself into power over it by his music. The
offense had not been held, cooled, varnished over, but
annihilated, and life itself made thereby triumphant.
This is an important difference. By hearing such music,
seemingly so much noise, when I actually came upon
noise in reality, I found that I had gone up over it."
W. C. WILLIAMS

SPONSORS

MR. THEODORE ABRAMS
MRS. AUGUSTUS AGNEW
MR. ALBERT M. BENDER
MR. HAROLD C. BLACK
MR. WILLIAM BOBBITT
MR. GLENN DEXTER
MR. AND MRS. HOLLIS FARWELL
MRS. MARGARET E. FULLER
DR. RICHARD E. FULLER
MISS JO GARRETSON
MRS. FREDERICK GLEASON
MRS. E. B. KLUCKHOHN
MR. GEORGE MANTOR
MRS. TOM MESDAG
MR. AND MRS. R. F. MILLER
MRS. H. F. OSTRANDER
MRS. CHARLES ROSS
MRS. HALLIE SAVERY
MR. JOHN SCHACK
MR. JOHN STEINBECK
MRS. THOMAS D. STIMSON
MR. MARK TOBEY
MR. C. B. WARREN

During the summer of 1939 Cage taught at the Cornish School Summer Session, designing courses for everyone from children to professionals. Building on his philosophy of creating music by and for those with a wide range of training, he offered classes directed at four constituencies. "Experimental Music" was designed for experienced composers, providing "advanced work in new materials." A course in composition, form, and analysis of music for modern dance was aimed at those "without special music experience." School teachers were encouraged to enroll in a course on "the use of percussion instruments and their application in the school room." Finally, Cage worked directly with the children in a "Creative Music" class (similar to one he had taught in Los Angeles) in which the students played "simple instruments" that they had built.[63] Bird enlisted Cage's help in other educational programs for children as well, including a production at the Helen Bush School on May 23, 1939. On this occasion grade-school students presented a Mexican fiesta with percussion music written by Cage and performed by the children on "water glasses of different pitches (played with sticks), automobile brake drums and blocks of wood," along with more conventional instruments.[64]

This same summer, Lou Harrison convinced Mills College to bring Cage to Oakland to stage a percussion concert at the end of July, an event that proved successful enough that Cage was invited to return the following summer. For the first program, on July 27, 1939, Cage joined forces with dancer and percussionist Franziska Boas and composer William Russell to present a program primarily of works from his first two concerts at Cornish (among them, Russell's *March Suite* and *Studies in Cuban Rhythms*, Harrison's *Counterdance in the Spring*, and selected movements from Cage's *Quartet* and Johanna Beyer's *Three Movements*).[65] Performers included dancer Merce Cunningham as well as Bonnie Bird's former accompanist Ralph Gilbert. The concert elicited a mixed review from the *San Francisco Chronicle*'s Alfred Frankenstein, who was normally very sympathetic to new music. The players "handled a vast assortment of instruments," reported Frankenstein:

> . . . ranging from the conventional piano, gongs and cymbals through various folk instruments to such crudely new contraptions as lengths of iron pipe and the theatrical lion's roar. The music ran a similar gamut. Sometimes it was monotonously mathematical. . . . But there was grand gusto and spirit in William Russell's "Cuban Rhythms" and "Three Dance Movements," and much good color and rhythmic counterpoint in Lou Harrison's "Counterdance in the Spring," the first movement of a quartet by John Cage and Franziska Boas' "Changing Tensions."

One suspects the whole thing will take on firmer outlines when dance accompanists acquire a genuine percussion technique. It doesn't take much skill to smash a beer bottle with a mighty heave, as was done once last night [ed: in the "March" from Russell's *Three Dance Movements*], but it does take a lot of skill to play the timpani, which were not in evidence.[66]

Experiments with Electronic Sounds and the Prepared Piano

By the end of August 1939, John and Xenia Cage were in the Carmel/Monterey area (presumably visiting Xenia's sisters), where Cage presented a lecture-demonstration on the "Art of Noise" at Margaret Lial's music shop.[67] He illustrated at the piano and played recordings of compositions by Beyer, Russell, Cowell, Harrison, and himself, made at the Cornish School's recording studio the previous year.

Indeed, for a small school Cornish offered innovative training in emerging technologies. Nellie Cornish, always eager to explore new ideas in the arts and willing to invest in or raise funds for cutting-edge enterprises that would benefit her students, had opened the nation's first radio school in April 1936. In preparation for this new area of study, "Aunt Nellie" visited Edward R. Murrow at CBS and John Royal at NBC in New York to educate herself in the new artform. She even had a building erected behind the main school to house a reception room, a broadcasting and recording studio, and an "engineer's little den."[68] The studio was equipped with the latest recording and broadcasting equipment and its opening was heralded by a national broadcast of a student-produced dramatic improvisation. This state-of-the-art facility not only enabled Cage to make recordings with his percussion ensemble but also provided a laboratory in which he could experiment with electronic sounds.

Like his percussion works, Cage's first efforts with electronics were closely allied to dance, and more specifically to Bonnie Bird and Ralph Gundlach. Though Gundlach was a psychologist, his early research centered on music, which had been a strong interest since his childhood. His mother Berta was a professional singer,[69] and Ralph himself sang and played the piano. His doctoral dissertation (University of Illinois, 1927), explored "The Dependence of Tonal Attributes upon Phase," a topic he pursued in several articles soon after he began teaching at the University of Washington. In a 1929 article Gundlach discussed the interrelationship of four aspects of sound (pitch, intensity, volume, and brightness), based on responses by trained subjects to controlled sound sources.[70] This article was followed a year later by a longer one in which he discussed the effect on these same four factors of changes in the sound's apparent location, simulated by phase differences in the sound signals fed to the two ears.[71] By the mid-1930s Gundlach was conducting experiments to determine whether emotional responses to music were sociological or inherent in rhythmic, dynamic, intervallic, and melodic patterns.[72] With these interests, it is hardly surprising that he found recordings of constant-frequency test-tones (which technicians in this period used to calibrate recording equipment) useful as sound sources for his research program. Gundlach gave some of these records to Cage, who discovered that changing the turntable speed while the record was playing produced intriguing electronic sliding tones.

Imaginary Landscape No. 1, the first of Cage's works to use the test-tone recordings, was designed to accompany a dance choreographed by Bird. The dance focused on arms and legs detached from their respective bodies, an effect she created by hiding the dancers' bodies behind triangular and rectangular stage props covered in black fabric (see figure 2–3). "Electrical music forms the background for the 'Imaginary Landscape [No. 1],' a sophisticated comment on surrealism," reported a pre-concert announcement in the *Seattle Post-Intelligencer*. "Sliding tones, associated with static, are employed in combination with an unusual use of the piano and cymbal."[73] (The "unusual use of the piano" involved muting several strings with the palm of the hand, and at times sweeping a gong beater across the bass strings.)

The program of March 24/25, 1939, which included *Imaginary Landscape No. 1*,[74] also featured Jean Cocteau's *Marriage at the Eiffel Tower* with choreography by Bird and a new score by Cage, Cowell, and George McKay (following the collaborative model of *Les Six*). Cunningham danced the part of the General; Syvilla Fort portrayed the lion, the ostrich, the bicycle girl, the art dealer, and the Trouville bathing-beauty. Wooden caricatures represented other characters, while Bird and Gundlach provided narration. Jane Givan from the art faculty constructed mobiles and Cage and Doris Dennison accompanied.[75] Cage composed the music for four scenes: "Wedding March—'Rubbish Music,'" "Toccata and Fuge [sic] and Subsequent Mow Down," "Sad Music in the Modern Minor," and "Quadrille that is a Barn Dance." He also wrote "Toy Orchestra Interludes." Cowell sent his contributions from San Quentin: "Hilarious Curtain Opener" and "Train Finale," as well as three *ritournelles* that were not used in the production.[76]

Figure 2-3. *Imaginary Landscape No. 1*, March 24/25, 1939.
The young man shown in the photo is Merce Cunningham.
Photo courtesy of Heidi Gundlach Smith. Photographer unknown.

Cage's first piece for prepared piano was also associated with dance, with Bonnie Bird, and, in this case, with the Seattle Artists League. He composed *Bacchanale* for a choreography by Bird's student Syvilla Fort, who premiered it on April 28, 1940 in a League-sponsored solo recital at the Repertory Playhouse. Cage had intended to score the music for percussion ensemble, but the Playhouse's stage had insufficient space in its wings to accommodate his group; he was restricted instead to a single piano. During one of Bird's dance classes, a metal rod rolled into the piano, leading Cage to experiment with inserting various objects into its strings. "Once he discovered these sounds in the class, we completely lost him for the rest of the hour," Bird recalled in later years.[77] Indeed, Cage had serendipitously discovered the prepared piano, by which he could transform the standard instrument into "a percussion orchestra of an original sound and the decibel range of a harpsichord directly under the control of a pianist's fingertips."[78]

Less than two weeks after Fort's recital, Bird presented a series of performances of her American Dance Theatre, which included Fort, Dorothy Herrmann, and sixteen high school students chosen the previous January from a pool of more than eighty applicants. (Cunningham had by this time moved to New York, enticed by an invitation from Martha Graham.) This set of recitals (May 7–11, 1940) featured another new work with electronic music by Cage: *Imaginary Landscape No. 2*, choreographed by Bird and danced by her along with Fort, Herrmann, and Cole Weston.[79]

Cage's music, recorded in a radio studio by four players, two assistants, and a technician, was later withdrawn. He subsequently reused the title for a different piece, which he composed in Chicago in 1942 and sent to Lou Harrison to premiere in San Francisco. Harrison programmed the 1942 work under the title *Fourth Construction*,[80] but Cage later renamed it *March* (*Imaginary Landscape No. 2*). The change of title may have reflected his ambivalence about the work's alliances both to his previous percussion compositions (*Constructions 1–3*) and to his experiments with electronic sounds (*Imaginary Landscape No. 1* and the rejected 1940 *Imaginary Landscape No. 2*). The 1942 work is indebted to both genres, calling for a battery of tin cans, ratchet, bass drum, buzzers, metal waste-basket, water gong, and lion's roar, along with a conch shell and an amplified coil of wire, which Harrison recalls assembling for the premiere.[81]

The rejected 1940 *Imaginary Landscape No. 2* not only built on Cage's previous work with test-tone recordings, but also combined electronic sliding tones with the prepared piano and percussion.[82] Of the four performers of this work, two played phonograph records, the third a tam-tam and large Chinese cymbal, and the fourth played a piano prepared with screws inserted between the strings of specified pitches. As in *Imaginary Landscape No. 1*, the players controlling the records changed the turntable speed from 33–1/3 rpm to 78 rpm at points precisely specified in the score. (See example 2-1; the symbol *x* indicates the speed shift.) Dynamics ranging from *ppp* to *fff* were controlled by assistants who adjusted the volume of two microphones; one picked up the sounds of players 1 and 2, and the other those of players 3 and 4. An assisting technician made a recording of the entire piece. Cage recommended a director as well, "placed that all participants may see him."

The dance that complemented this novel musical experience was "a humorous interpretation of 'Trees,' titled under the more formal caption of 'Imaginary Landscape No. 2,'" according to a review in the *Seattle Times*. "It was dance humor at its best and the audience loved it."[83] (The reviewer seems to have taken no notice whatsoever of the extraordinary musical background.) Cage provided music for other works on the program as well: *Spiritual*, choreographed and performed by Syvilla Fort; *Four Songs of the Moment*, choreographed and per-

Example 2-1. *Imaginary Landscape No. 2.* Reprinted by permission of the John Cage Trust.

formed by Dorothy Herrmann; and *America Was Promises*, choreographed by Bird and danced by the ensemble of sixteen students accompanied by music for piano four-hands and a recitation of Archibald MacLeish's new poem of the same name.

End of the Seattle Years

When Cage left Seattle after the Spring semester 1940, it was not to take up a position elsewhere. He and Xenia, along with Margaret Jansen and Doris Dennison, moved to San Francisco, where Cage continued his exploration of the percussion ensemble in collaboration with Lou Harrison. He also began a determined letter-writing campaign in search of an institution willing to invest in the establishment of a "Center of Experimental Music."[84]

The timing of Cage's departure from Cornish may have been prompted in part by changes in the school's faculty and administration. Nellie Cornish left Seattle in the spring of 1939 after years of struggle to finance various innovative projects and bring high-profile faculty and guest artists to the school.

Bonnie Bird submitted her own resignation the following year. Despite her persistent efforts, the dance program at Cornish had floundered. The class of five dance majors in her first year was reduced to three in the second and only one in the third. In a letter to the Friends of Cornish on November 2, 1939, Bird described the extraordinary efforts she had undertaken to build a successful dance program at the school despite a lack of publicity and financial support.[85] She proposed her American Dance Theatre as a last-ditch effort to revitalize the dance program. Despite its success, Bird became so discouraged that she not only left Cornish but even moved away from dance for several years.[86]

Cage, in any case, was impatient with his job as dance accompanist; he often found the work tedious, as he wrote to Harrison as early as April 1939. "I have the possibility of a job in Taos this summer," he reported. "Director of music, if you please; also cooperating with Alice Sherbon, dancer. I wouldn't get paid very much if at all; but it would be a step away from accompaniment—drudgery which I hate."[87] He perhaps hoped as well for Mills College's support for his Center for Experimental Music, in view of the warm reception he had received following his percussion concerts of 1939 and 1940. The 1940 event also provided the opportunity for collaboration with members of the Chicago School of Design, ultimately leading to Cage's move to Chicago in August 1941. In the year's time before this move, he and Harrison staged percussion ensemble concerts, recorded new works, and even composed a joint piece, the quartet *Double Music* (premiered May 14, 1941 at San Francisco's California Club), now a staple of the percussion ensemble repertoire.[88]

Though Cage's Seattle residency was short-lived, its long-range impact on his musical thought was profound. Had he remained in Los Angeles, the trajectory of his work might well have been similar, but the cultural environment was far less supportive. With some notable exceptions, the Los Angeles artistic community greeted Cage's experiments with considerable skepticism. Schoenberg, for example, was decidedly unimpressed by the concept of a percussion ensemble, as Calvin Tomkins reports:

> Outsiders began coming in to hear [his] percussion concerts, and Cage was so pleased with the results that he invited Schönberg to come. "Ah, so?" said Schönberg, when invited, but said he was busy that night. Cage said he would arrange a concert for any other night that Schönberg was free. Schönberg said he would not be free any other night either.[89]

In contrast, the Cornish School not only offered Cage a collection of percussion instruments, but also encouraged the development of his ensemble and provided venues without charge for its public performances. The school's emphasis on interdisciplinary collaboration and its openness to new ideas fostered Cage's experiments with the prepared piano and electronic sounds, developments enhanced by the ready availability of a recording studio. From the institution's earliest years, Nellie Cornish had been able to attract outstanding talent from as far away as New York and Europe by her enthusiasm, her broad-based approach to arts education, and her pedagogical philosophy: "once having engaged a faculty member, she left him—or her—strictly alone to work out his own teaching program within the School's elastic boundaries. She welcomed the interplay of dissimilar points of view."[90] In short, Cornish offered Cage facilities, an environment of open-minded inquiry, and a devotion to arts education that allowed him to experiment with new sonorities. Even the tedium of dance accompaniment may have been beneficial by encouraging him to search for novel solutions to sustain his interest.

Perhaps most importantly, however, Seattle was home, in that crucial period, to a group of artists and writers who actively pressed at the boundaries of their fields and who were willing to defy established traditions in their individual areas of inquiry. Among those artists who influenced Cage's work, none played a greater role than Bonnie Bird. Her impact on his compositional development extended far beyond her initial invitation for him to come to Seattle, for, as we have seen, she served as the catalyst for his most important innovations in this period. Bird involved Cage in the American Dance Theatre and encouraged his teaching of students from young children through college. Musical requirements for her choreographies led to many of his important percussion works, and during one of her dance classes he fortuitously discovered the possibilities of the prepared piano (in his role as accompanist for one of her most talented students). Through Bird's involvement with the Seattle Artists League, Cage met colleagues with complementary aesthetic ideas and was encouraged to articulate his own thoughts on the future of music in a series of public lectures. His inclusion of laypersons in the performance experience—not only as audience members but also as performers—accorded with the egalitarian ideals embraced by the League and other left-wing organizations of the 1930s (in which Bird and Gundlach played an active role). Cage's commitment to the amateur extended to his broad-based teaching activities as well, through which he could give equal attention and respect to children, non-professional adults, and music professionals. Finally, through his association with Bird and her husband Ralph Gundlach, he first obtained the test-tone recordings with which he experimented with electronic sounds.

It is no wonder, then, that Cage so often cited his two years in Seattle as central to the development of his thought. After his move to New York in 1942, the prepared piano and electronic instruments became increasingly prominent in his work, until ultimately his attempts to liberate sound from the "limitations of musical prejudice" led him to challenge even his own prior definitions of music. For these later developments, the environment of the Seattle arts community and the tiny Cornish School provided a supportive foundation.

Chronology of the Events Discussed in this Chapter

	1936
April	Cornish School opens the first radio school in the United States.

	1937
Fall	Bonnie Bird assumes faculty post at the Cornish School.

	1938
Spring	Seattle Artists League organized.
Late spring–early summer	John and Xenia Cage leave Los Angeles for northern California. Cage meets Lou Harrison in San Francisco.
June 26–Aug. 6	Mills College Summer Session: Bonnie Bird in residence for the first two weeks. Bird meets Harrison, who introduces her to Cage. Bird offers

the job at Cornish first to Harrison and then, when he declines, to Cage.

Before Oct. John and Xenia Cage move to Seattle.

Oct. 7 Bird presents lecture-demonstration as the opening program in Cornish's "Three Arts Series." Cage accompanies.

Oct. 10 Cage presents lecture-recital, "Some Aspects of Modern Music," at the annual dinner of the Seattle chapter of Pro Musica, Inc.

Dec. 9 Cage's First Percussion Concert at the Cornish School.

Dec. 11 First meeting of the Seattle Artists League; Cage talks on "New Directions in Music."

1939

Jan. 11 Tacoma Drama League: Bonnie Bird, the Cornish - dance group, and Cage's percussion ensemble.

Mar. 24/25 Performance of Cage's *Imaginary Landscape No. 1* (also Cocteau's *Marriage at the Eiffel Tower* with score by Cage, Cowell, and George McKay).

May 19 Cage's Second Percussion Concert at Cornish (includes works solicited from composers around the country, including Lou Harrison, Henry Cowell, Johanna Beyer, et al.).

May 23 Performance at the Helen Bush School with grade-school students playing percussion music composed by Cage.

Summer Cage teaches at the Cornish Summer School.

July 27 Percussion concert at Mills College, Oakland, California, arranged by Lou Harrison: Cage joins forces with Franziska Boas and William Russell.

Aug. 25 Cage presents lecture-recital on percussion music at the Lial Music Shop in Monterey, California.

Dec. 9	Cage's Third Percussion Concert at Cornish.

1940

Jan.	Tour by "Cage Percussion Players": Jan. 8, University of Idaho; Jan. 9, University of Montana; Jan. 11, Whitman College.
Feb. 14	Performance by the Cage Percussion Players at Reed College, Portland.
Feb. 18	Seattle Artists League meeting; Cage lectures on "What Next in American Art?" (Lecture later titled "The Future of Music: Credo" and published in the booklet accompanying the recording of the 1958 retrospective concert in Town Hall, New York, and in *Silence.*)
Apr. 28	Performance of *Bacchanale* by dancer Syvilla Fort with Cage using a prepared piano (Repertory Playhouse; sponsored by the Seattle Artists League).
May 7–11	American Dance Theatre performances, including Cage's *Imaginary Landscape No. 2* (later rejected; title reused for a different work composed in 1942).
Following the spring semester	John and Xenia Cage, Doris Dennison, and Margaret Jansen move to San Francisco.
July 18	Percussion concert by Harrison, Cage, and William Russell at Mills College, Oakland (in collaboration with artists from the Chicago School of Design).

1941

May 14	Premiere of *Double Music*, jointly composed by Cage and Harrison (California Club, San Francisco).

July 26	Concert of "Percussion, Quarter Tones, Dance, Electric Sound, " Mills College (in collaboration with dancer Marian Van Tuyl).

1942

May 7	Premiere of Cage's *Fourth Construction*, later retitled *March* (*Imaginary Landscape No. 2*) by Lou Harrison in San Francisco.

1948

July	Second hearing of the Washington State legislative committee on un-American activities (Canwell committee). Melvin Rader, Ralph Gundlach, Florence James, and Burton James accused of Communist affiliations.
Oct. 27	Hearings begin by the University of Washington's Committee on Tenure and Academic Freedom.

1949

Jan. 22	University of Washington Regents order firing of Gundlach and two other tenured faculty members.

Notes

1.   Many thanks to David Nicholls and David Patterson for their helpful comments on this article, and to Laura Kuhn of the John Cage Trust for providing scores.

2.   Robert Stevenson, "John Cage on his 70th Birthday: West Coast Background," *Inter-American Music Review* 5, no. 1 (Fall 1982): 3–17.

3.   Thomas S. Hines, "Then Not Yet 'Cage': The Los Angeles Years, 1912–1938," in *John Cage: Composed in America*, ed. Marjorie Perloff and Charles Junkerman (Chicago: University of Chicago Press, 1994), 65–99; David Wayne Patterson, "Appraising the Catchwords, c. 1942–1959: John Cage's Asian-Derived Rhetoric and the Historical Reference of Black Mountain College" (Ph.D. dissertation, Columbia University, 1996).

4.   John and Xenia Cage were married in Yuma, Arizona, at a sunrise service at 5 a.m. on June 7, 1935.

5.   Citations from the UCLA extension catalog are given by Stevenson. In addition to the Los Angeles activities described by Stevenson and Hines, a 1938 announcement for a lecture by Cage in Seattle mentions that he previously "accompanied a concert dance group under Martha Deane," who at the time taught dance in the department of physical education at UCLA.

6.   Cage had taken courses with Cowell in New York in 1934. Although previous studies reported that he spent 12–18 months in New York, recent

research supports a shorter residency. See Michael Hicks, "John Cage's Studies with Schoenberg," *American Music* 8, no. 2 (Summer 1990): 125–40.

7.   Lou Harrison, interview with the author. Cage and Harrison discussed this first meeting during a public panel discussion at the Cornish School in 1992. (A videotape by Bob Campbell was kindly made available to me by Jarrad Powell.)

8.   "Presents Bonnie Bird in Recital," *W. Woodland News*, Mar. 16, 1938. Bird had studied with Graham the previous summer when Graham taught in Seattle (Heidi Gundlach Smith, interview, June 20, 1998).

9.   Karen Bell-Kanner, *Frontiers: The Life and Times of Bonnie Bird, American Modern Dancer and Dance Educator* (Amsterdam: Harwood Academic Publishers, 1998), 99. Bell-Kanner's information apparently came from a letter from Bonnie Bird to Frances Hawkins, Jan. 19, 1938 (courtesy of Bird's daughter, Heidi Gundlach Smith).

10.   Cunningham entered Cornish as a theater student, but all theater majors were required to take dance classes as well. He soon became a dance major instead. See David Vaughan, *Merce Cunningham: Fifty Years* (N.P.: Aperture, 1997), 15.

11.   Bird's presentations are documented in a series of newspaper articles; for example: "Bonnie Bird Will Demonstrate Dance," *Seattle Post-Intelligencer*, Oct. 7, 1937 ("Miss Bonnie Bird will speak on the modern dance in the Cornish Theater tomorrow evening . . . , giving a demonstration of the Martha Graham technique"); "Bonnie Bird in New Dance Recital," *Seattle Star*, Jan. 25, 1938 ("Bonnie Bird . . . will present another in her series of dance demonstrations, Thursday evening. . . . The program will include a continuation of the study of pre-classic dance forms and a demonstration of modern dance technique"); "Teacher and Pupils to Show Dance Before Group," *Seattle Times*, Apr. 24, 1938 ("Miss Bonnie Bird . . . will discuss the modern dance [tomorrow afternoon] and will illustrate her subject with dances by her pupils").

12.   Louis Horst, *Pre-Classic Dance Forms* (Princeton: Princeton Book Company, 1987).

13.   "And Spain Sings," the final section of the complete suite, was premiered at the Sunset Club on Feb. 23, 1938. The full suite was presented at Cornish on March 18 and 19 (program and numerous news articles in the Cornish School scrapbooks at the University of Washington).

14.   On the Music and Art Foundation, see Nellie C. Cornish, *Miss Aunt Nellie: The Autobiography of Nellie C. Cornish* (Seattle: University of Washington Press, 1964), 150.

15.   "Ralph Gilbert is Lauded by Miss Graham," *Seattle Times*, Mar. 17, 1940; "Martha Graham Lauds Seattleite," *Seattle Post-Intelligencer*, Mar. 19, 1940.

16.   Panel discussion, Harrison and Cage, Cornish School, 1992 (videotape by Bob Campbell. Used by permission.)

17.   John Cage, "A Composer's Confessions (1948)," *Musicworks* 52 (Spring 1992): 9, reprinted in Richard Kostelanetz, ed., *John Cage: Writer* (New York: Limelight Editions, 1993), 32.

18.   John Cage, *Silence: Lectures and Writings* (Middletown, CT: Wesleyan University Press, 1961), 86. The incorrect 1937 date for "The Future of Music" essay is repeated here.

19.   Cornish, *Miss Aunt Nellie*, 208.

20.   Cornish School Summer Session brochure for 1931. There are two versions of this brochure with slightly different descriptions of Deja and with different photos of her. The brochure from which this quotation is taken lists the dates of the summer session as June 2–July 31. The other gives them (correctly) as June 22–July 31. Both announcements are found in the Cornish scrapbooks, University of Washington.

21.   Announcement of the Cornish School's seventeenth summer session, 1931 (Cornish School scrapbooks).

22.   Cage wrote to several people seeking funding to replace the instruments. For example, on Sept. 14, 1939 he wrote to Mr. and Mrs. John H. Ballinger, Seattle: "A few weeks ago I received a letter . . . to the effect that many of the instruments which I had used last year would not be available this coming year. These instruments were Chinese gongs, cymbals, tomtoms and woodblocks belonging to Lora [sic] Deja . . . In order to have the proper materials I have, heretofore, borrowed, constructed and invented instruments to supplement Miss Deja's collection. It is not, however, possible to *replace* her instruments in any other way than buying them" (John Cage Collection, Northwestern University Music Library; italics mine). Lore Deja taught at Cornish for three years (Cornish, *Miss Aunt Nellie*, 208).

23.   It is not clear exactly when the Cages arrived in Seattle. Cage's *Five Songs* is dated "Seattle, July 1938," but the word "Seattle" is in a different pen, and possibly a different hand, from the rest of the score (including the date), and thus may have been added later. Thanks to David Nicholls for the information on the *Five Songs* manuscript.

24.   The term opened Sept. 12 after a registration period from Sept. 1–10.

25.   Nellie Cornish, *Miss Aunt Nellie*, 155.

26.   *Dance Observer* 1, no. 2 (March 1934), 15; and 2, no. 8 (Nov. 1935), 87.

27.   *Dance Observer* 1, no. 4 (May 1934), 39.

28.   The individual contributions were as follows: Cage, "Introduction," and Russell, "Hot Jazz and Percussion Music" in the *Dance Observer* 6, no. 8 (Oct. 1939), 266, 274; Cowell, "East Indian Tala Music" and Cage, "Goal: New Music, New Dance," in volume 6, no. 10 (December 1939), 296–7; Boas, "Fundamental Concepts" in volume 7, no. 1 (February 1940), 6–7 and Harrison, "Statement" in volume 7, no. 3 (March 1940), 32.

29.   Other events included a talk on "modern radio and recording" and faculty recitals on violin and voice.

30.   Vaughan, *Merce Cunningham: Fifty Years*, 17.

31.   Cornish, *Miss Aunt Nellie*, 33–34. Nellie Cornish founded the Cornish School in 1914 and remained at its helm until Spring 1939.

32.   Letter of announcement, dated Oct. 4, 1938, from Floyd Oles, secretary (John Cage Archive, Northwestern University Music Library).

33.   McKay (1899–1970) studied at Eastman and taught at the University of Washington from 1927–1968. He composed orchestral works and concerti,

chamber music, and music for chorus and for band (*New Grove Dictionary of American Music*, s.v. "McKay, George Frederick," by Katherine K. Preston).

34.   Taken from programs and/or announcements among the materials in the John Cage Archive, Northwestern University Music Library.

35.   An announcement in the *Seattle Post-Intelligencer* on December 4, 1938 read: "The newly formed Seattle Artists' League will give its initial program Sunday evening in the Repertory Playhouse with drama, music and an exhibition of paintings on the bill . . . .John Cage, composer-pianist, will discuss and illustrate trends and developments in modern music." (The article is headlined "Artists on Program: Varied Show Planned by Group.") *The Seattle Times* noted on the same day: "The Seattle Artists League, which last spring announced its organization . . . , is announcing now the first in a series of Sunday evening programs of contemporary American art forms. First of these programs, a combined concert of music, drama and graphic arts, will be held . . . December 11." (Thanks to Kathy Harvey at the Seattle Public Library for her help in locating documents on the Seattle Artists League.)

36.   For example, James Pritchett, *The Music of John Cage* (Cambridge: Cambridge University Press, 1993) places the essay in 1937 or 1938; David Revill, *The Roaring Silence. John Cage: A Life* (New York: Arcade, 1992), presents the conflicting date information without comment.

37.   *The 25-year Retrospective Concert of The Music of John Cage* (New York: Distributed by George Avakian, 1959), matrix no. K08Y 1499–1504.

38.   Letter, George Avakian to Leta Miller, July 23, 1997. Other data in the program booklet similarly appear to have stemmed from casual recollection. The short biography of Cage, for instance, dates his faculty position at Cornish "from 1936 to 1938." David Patterson, "Appraising the Catchwords," encountered a similar problem regarding the dates of Cage's interaction with Daisetz Teitaro Suzuki. Cage situated Suzuki's Columbia lectures in the late 1940s, but again his estimate was too early, since Suzuki did not even come to New York until 1950 and did not lecture at Columbia before March 1951 (Patterson, 141–44).

39.   John Cage Archive, Northwestern University. (Thanks to Deborah Campana at Northwestern University for making this material available to me.) There are three versions of this text in the Cage archives at Northwestern: the manuscript copy cited here, a typed copy, and a copy written as part of a grant application. The extensive glosses on the basic text that appear in *Silence* are lacking in these sources.

40.   Cage claimed that he used this term prior to reading Varèse's December 1940 article in which Varèse called music "organized sound" (Edgard Varèse, "Organized Sound for the Sound Film," *The Commonweal*, Dec. 13, 1940: 204–05). However, David Nicholls has suggested that Cage may well have heard Varèse use the term when he met Varèse in Los Angeles in May 1938 (Nicholls, "Cage and the Ultra-Modernists," paper read at the American Musicological Society national meeting, October 1998).

41.   Cornish, *Miss Aunt Nellie*, 153. On the founding of the Repertory Playhouse, see Vern Countryman, *Un-American Activities in the State of Washington: The Work of the Canwell Committee* (Ithaca, New York:

Cornell University Press, 1951), 150–51. See also Sharon Boswell and Lorraine McConaghy, "Cultivating Culture," *Seattle Times*, June 9, 1996.

42.   The painters whose works were displayed include Kenneth Callahan, Earl T. Fields, Robert Lee, James Houston, Barney Nestor, Robert Iglehart, and Raymond Hill. On Maltz, see Jack Salzman, *Albert Maltz* (Boston: Twayne Publishers, 1978), preface, where the playwright is described as "one of the mainstays of the literary Left in the 1930s." *Red Head Baker* was produced by CBS radio in 1937. In this work, Maltz advocated a liberal, individually-oriented approach to education and described a success story: a rambunctious child, freed from a narrowly-defined, prescriptive curriculum and allowed to pursue his own interests at will, is stimulated to intellectual pursuits and discovers the need for the rigorous training he had previously rejected. It is tempting to conclude that the play was chosen in part because it reflected the pedagogical philosophy of members of the League such as Bird, Gundlach, and Rader.

43.   Bird and Gundlach were married on May 19, 1938.

44.   These organizations included support groups for the Spanish loyalists during the Civil War of 1936–39, a favorite cause for young liberals throughout the country. Bonnie Bird was but one among many artists nationally who supported the loyalists' resistance to Francisco Franco with works such as her "Dance for Spain." (Lou Harrison and his circle of friends in San Francisco were involved in similar activities, with the goal of raising much-needed funding for the republican movement. For a discussion and score of Harrison's sextet *France 1917—Spain 1937* see Leta E. Miller, *Lou Harrison: Selected Keyboard and Chamber Music, 1937–1994*, in *Music in the United States of America* [Madison, WI: A-R Editions, 1998]). Since the Soviet Union actively supported the loyalists with armaments and personnel (including international brigades such as the Lincoln Brigade), any association with these support groups came to have Communist implications in the post-war McCarthy era.

45.   Rader was further "tainted" by his legacy as the son of a lawyer who defended several victims of a red scare near the end of the First World War. Rader's book, *No Compromise*, a study of the conflict between democracy and fascism, appeared in 1939, shortly after the events under discussion in this article. During the post-war legislative hearings, a former vice-chairman of the King County Democratic Party (Sarah Eldredge) took Rader to task for statements in this 1939 book which, she claimed, extolled the constitution of the Soviet Union and in general "followed the Party line." Rader recounted in detail the story of his interactions with the Canwell Committee in *False Witness* (Seattle and London: University of Washington Press, 1969). Ed Guthman, a *Seattle Times* reporter who helped Rader document his whereabouts during the time in question and who publicly exposed the facts, won the Pulitzer Prize for this work in 1949. Albert Canwell, who continues adamantly to defend his actions, still lives in Spokane. The state legislature later determined that the FBI should have all of the committee's files, but could not locate them; Canwell later admitted burning much of this material.

46.   The committee considered the cases of six professors. Of the other five, three had previously been members of the Communist Party, but had resigned some years earlier. These three retained their jobs, but were subjected to a two-year probationary period. The two remaining faculty, Joseph Butterworth (professor of English and specialist in Chaucer) and Herbert Phillips (professor of philosophy), were current members of the Party. Both were fired despite a recommendation by a majority of the committee that they remain on the faculty. (Butterworth ended up on public assistance and died destitute in 1970. Phillips worked as a laborer on dairy farms in the Northwest and as a dockworker; he died in San Francisco in 1978.) Also fired from the University of Washington for his failure to cooperate with the Canwell committee was graduate student and veterans counselor Ted Astley. Gundlach's case was the most complicated of the six. In a meeting with University of Washington president Raymond Allen preceding the hearings, Gundlach had responded to questions about Communist Party affiliation with what Allen considered equivocal and evasive answers. Although the tenure committee found no proof that Gundlach was a member of the Communist Party, his prior response to Allen and his refusal to answer questions posed by the legislative committee led to a majority recommendation for dismissal. (Several committee members became convinced that even were he not a Communist, Gundlach's support of Communist-backed causes and his membership in numerous alleged Communist front organizations made him an effective mouthpiece for their agenda—perhaps even more so than if he had actually been a party member.) See Jane Sanders, *Cold War on the Campus: Academic Freedom at the University of Washington, 1946–64* (Seattle and London: University of Washington Press, 1979), 62–63 and Ellen W. Schrecker, *No Ivory Tower: McCarthyism and the Universities* (New York and Oxford: Oxford University Press, 1986), especially pp. 94–105. A detailed account of the Canwell legislative hearings is found in Countryman, *Un-American Activities*. The case at the University of Washington attracted national attention. See, for example, *The American Scholar* 18, no. 3 (Summer 1949), for a summary of findings, statements by the three dismissed professors, and a series of editorials on the advisability of employing communists on university faculties.

47.   Gundlach later worked as a research psychologist at the State University of New York Downstate Medical Center (see *American Men and Women of Science: The Social and Behavioral Sciences*, 12th ed., 1973). He died in August 1978. In 1994, sixteen years after his death, then president of the University of Washington, William Gerberding, issued a formal apology for the University's actions nearly a half century earlier.

48.   Countryman, 86, 89. When Florence James attempted to protest the manner in which the Canwell committee hearings were being conducted, she was forcibly evicted from the committee chamber. Both she and her husband were charged with contempt of the legislature along with Gundlach in 1949. Burton James received the same sentence as Gundlach. Florence James was found guilty, but given a suspended sentence and fined $125.

49.   The company's gross income, which was $40,000 in 1946–47, was reduced to $33,500 in 1947–48 and to $14,000 in 1948–49. See Countryman,

151. The following year, the University of Washington purchased the land and the theater building for use by the drama department at half of the property's appraised value. Burton James died of a heart attack shortly after these events. Florence James moved to Canada. Their role in the establishment of the Repertory Playhouse was for all practical purposes wiped from the records in Seattle. In 1998, however, on the fiftieth anniversary of the legislative hearings, the University of Washington presented a series of events including a restaging of portions of the hearings and the production of a play (part fact and part fiction) by faculty member Mark Jenkins, which was mounted in the old Repertory Playhouse. "All Powers Necessary and Convenient" played to sold-out audiences for eleven performances. On this occasion a plaque honoring Burton and Florence James was hung in the theater.

50.   *Contemporary Authors*, New Revision Series, vol. 5. His prison term ran from June 1950 to April 1951. During the 1930s Albert Maltz was a founding member of the executive board of the Theatre Union in New York, a "worker's theater" that presented plays on social issues at affordable prices. The Union distributed free tickets to organizations for the unemployed, and its productions (seven plays staged between 1933 and 1937) were the first in New York to open orchestra seating to African Americans. The Theatre Union's initial offering was by Maltz and George Sklar: an anti-war play entitled *Peace on Earth*. In the 1940s Maltz moved to Los Angeles, where he became a screenwriter for Hollywood films.

51.   John Cage, "Goal: New Music, New Dance," *Dance Observer* 6, no. 10 (December 1939): 296–97; reprinted in *Silence*, 87.

52.   Cage, "A Composer's Confessions," 9.

53.   Ibid.

54.   Ibid, 10.

55.   Vaughan, 19–20. Wike completed her master's thesis on "Modern Spirit Dancing of Northern Puget Sound" at the University of Washington in 1941 and her Ph.D. on "The Effect of the Maritime Fur Trade on Northwest Coast Indian Society" at Columbia in 1951. She taught at the University of Nebraska.

56.   Irving Morrow. See the *Report of the Chief Engineer to the Board of Directors of the Golden Gate Bridge and Highway District*, September 1937 (reprint: Golden Gate Bridge Highway and Transportation District, 1987), 36. Morrow also designed the San Francisco house of Henry Cowell's mother and stepfather.

57.   *Perspectives on American Music, 1900–1950* (New York: Garland, 2000), 215–63.

58.   For an in-depth account of Cowell's imprisonment, see Michael Hicks, "The Imprisonment of Henry Cowell," *Journal of the American Musicological Society* 44, no. 1 (Spring 1991): 92–119.

59.   *Pulse* was programmed by Cage on the May 19 concert. *Return*, which may have been sent later, was programmed on the third concert, December 9, 1939. For the May concert, Cage also received *Three Movements* by Johanna Beyer, which he programmed along with the Harrison and Cowell pieces, his own *Trio*, and several works by William Russell. For the score and

a discussion of Harrison's *Counterdance*, see Miller, *Lou Harrison: Selected Keyboard and Chamber Music.*

60.   The concerts were held on Jan. 8 1940, University of Idaho; Jan. 9 1940, University of Montana; Jan. 11 1940, Whitman College; and Feb. 14, Reed College. Documents concerning this tour in the Cage Archive, Northwestern University, are confusing, as some undated articles are misplaced and/or associated with unrelated publications. I reconstructed the dates of the performances, with some difficulty, from a comparison of many documents, including Cage's expense report for the trip.

61.   Review, Thursday Jan. 11, 1940, incorrectly identified in the scrapbook at the John Cage Archive, Northwestern University, as coming from the *Whitman College Pioneer*. The review situates the concert as having taken place on "Tuesday night," when the Cage Percussion Players performed at the University of Montana (program in the same scrapbook). The Whitman College Concert was on Thursday, January 11.

62.   A copy of the Reed College program may be found in the Cage Archive at Northwestern University.

63.   Cornish School brochure for Summer 1939 (copies in the Cornish School scrapbooks, University of Washington archives, and at the Northwestern University Cage archive).

64.   "Bush Pupils Practicing for Fiesta," *Seattle Times*, May 20, 1939. The article appears in the scrapbooks assembled by Cage's mother at the Cage Archive at Northwestern University, but the title of the paper, the headline, and the date erroneously appear over an unrelated article on the American Dance Theatre, which actually dates from May 1940.

65.   Boas's *Changing Tensions* was also included on the program. Boas, daughter of anthropologist and ethnomusicologist Franz Boas, studied with Hanya Holm and acted as her percussionist for six years. She was later head of dance at Bryn Mawr College and established a dance major at Shorter College in Georgia. (See Sali Ann Kriegsman, *Modern Dance in America: The Bennington Years* [Boston: G.K. Hal, 1981], 316). William Russell was involved in both jazz and Asian music. During the 1930s he served as musician with Pauline Benton's "Red Gate Players," who mounted Chinese shadow puppet plays. He moved to New Orleans in 1940 and eventually became jazz-archive curator at Tulane. For more information on his percussion music, see my article "The Art of Noise," in *Perspectives on American Music*. Boas and Russell were among the five authors who contributed to the series of articles on "Percussion Music and its Relation to the Modern Dance" published in the *Dance Observer* between October 1939 and March 1940.

66.   Alfred Frankenstein, "A Program of Percussion," *San Francisco Chronicle*, July 28, 1939.

67.   The lecture-recital took place on August 25. Various announcements about this event are found in the Cage Archive at Northwestern University.

68.   Cornish, *Miss Aunt Nellie*, 245.

69.   Berta Jean Richardson (later Gundlach) was trained in Chicago and New York, and sang professionally in Kansas City, Missouri, before she and her husband Stuart moved to Wallace, Idaho. According to Ralph Gundlach's sister Jean, their house was always filled with music, the family often singing

together around the dinner table. Stuart Gundlach "had a beautiful baritone voice" and was also trained in vocal technique, although he worked professionally as an attorney. (Telephone interview with Jean Gundlach, July 7, 1998.)

70.   Ralph Gundlach, "Tonal Attributes and Frequency Theories of Hearing," *Journal of Experimental Psychology* 12, no. 3 (June 1929): 187–96.

71.   Ralph Gundlach, "The Dependence of Tonal Attributes Upon Phase," *The American Journal of Psychology* 42, no. 4 (October 1930): 505–43.

72.   He published the results of these studies, the first of which analyzed the characteristics of selected American Indian songs that he learned through recordings and transcriptions. In a later study, he used examples from Western art music. (Forty very brief selections were played for 112 observers who characterized each excerpt's emotional content.) Ralph Gundlach, "A Quantitative Analysis of Indian Music," *The American Journal of Psychology* 44, no. 1 (January 1932): 133–45; and "Factors Determining the Characterization Of Musical Phrases," ibid. 47, no. 4 (October 1935): 624–43.

73.   "Round About" column, *Seattle Post-Intelligencer,* March 19, 1939.

74.   The Henmar Press catalog of Cage works erroneously lists *Imaginary Landscape No. 1* as performed at Cornish on December 9, 1939. It also lists a performance in 1940, but the work in question here is *Imaginary Landscape No. 2*, later rejected, as discussed below.

75.   A document in the Cornish scrapbooks projects a performance of *Marriage at the Eiffel Tower* on March 10, 1939. It is not clear whether there was a production of the work preceding the March 24/25 performances or whether the original performance date was delayed. (Considering the large amount of publicity for the March 24/25 event, I tend to favor the latter hypothesis.) The program was repeated on April 26.

76.   "Hilarious Curtain Opener" and "Ritournelle" were published in the *New Music Quarterly* in October 1945 during the single year in which Lou Harrison was editor. In a letter to Bird on January 9, 1939, Cowell described his plans for the pieces, including a 3 $\frac{3}{4}$ minute introductory piece, a "peppy" finale, and three "middle pieces." In another letter (April 2, 1939), he responded to one in which Bird apparently described the performance. Cowell apologized for the "unyielding meter" of his ritournelles, which apparently made them inappropriate for the choreography. (Letters in private collection.) In 1949 and 1950 Bird staged Cocteau's play again, this time at Reed College's summer festival of dance and theater, with a totally new score composed by Harrison, who was her composer-in-residence for both summers.

77.   Private communication from Bird's daughter, Heidi Smith, who heard the story repeatedly from her mother. See also William Fetterman, *John Cage's Theatre Pieces: Notations and Performances* (Amsterdam: Harwood, 1998), 8. The accident in class likely led to the home experiments Cage described in Stephen Montague, "John Cage at Seventy," *American Music* 3, no. 2 (Summer 1985): 209–10.

78.   Cage, "Composer's Confessions," 11.

79.   Weston entered Cornish in 1937; like Cunningham, he began as a theater student. There he met Dorothy Herrmann, whom he married shortly before returning to California in 1940. See *Cole Weston: Eighteen*

Photographs (Salt Lake City: Peregrine Smith, 1981), introduction by Charis Wilson; and *Cole Weston: Fifty Years* (Salt Lake City: Peregrine Smith Books, 1991), introduction.

80.   The concert took place on May 7, 1942 at the Holloway Playhouse in the Fairmont Hotel, San Francisco.

81.   Lou Harrison, personal communication.

82.   Many thanks to Laura Kuhn of the John Cage Trust for providing me with a copy of this score.

83.   Virginia Boren, "Cornish Dance Group Gives Refreshing Concert," *Seattle Times*, May 8, 1940.

84.   Copies of many of these letters may be found in the Cage Archive at Northwestern University. Patterson, "Appraising the Catchwords," also discusses Cage's contacts with Black Mountain College in 1942 on the same matter.

85.   Letter from Bonnie Bird to Mrs. W.W. Scruby, Nov. 2, 1939 (courtesy of Heidi Gundlach Smith).

86.   After attempting to support an independent dance school in Seattle for a year, she explored an alternative career in the medical sciences. She soon returned to dance, however, and collaborated with Harrison, among others, in later years. On Bird's career, see Karen Bell-Kanner, *Frontiers*. On her later collaborations with Lou Harrison, see Leta E. Miller and Fredric Lieberman, *Lou Harrison: Composing a World* (New York: Oxford University Press, 1998). Bird died on April 9, 1995.

87.   Letter, Cage to Harrison, University of California, Santa Cruz, Library, Special Collections (undated, but the envelope bears the postmark April 20, 1939). Quoted by permission of the John Cage Trust.

88.   For further details on Cage's work during this year, see Miller, "The Art of Noise."

89.   Calvin Tomkins, *The Bride and the Bachelors* (New York and London: Penguin Books, 1962), 88.

90.   Nancy Wilson Ross, foreword to Cornish, *Miss Aunt Nellie*, ix.

3. No Ear for Music: Timbre in the Early Percussion Music of John Cage

Christopher Shultis

For Tom Siwe

> I don't have an ear for music, and I don't hear music in my mind
> before I write it. And I never have. I can't remember a melody. A
> few have been drummed into me, like "My Country 'Tis of
> Thee," but there will come a point in even those songs that I'm
> not sure of how the next note goes. I just don't have any of those
> things that are connected with solfège and with memory and with
> what you might call, imagination . . . all those things which most
> musicians have, I don't have.[1]

Thus spake John Cage, with a literally Zarathustrian authority that
kept him and his work mostly free of serious criticism for an entire
lifetime. What follows is intentionally critical of Cage's point of view.
In the quote above, Cage was speaking from his own perspective in
the late 1980s. But as Norman O. Brown has written, "Cage in 1959
is not the same as Cage in 1974."[2] Nor is Cage in the late 1980s the
same as Cage in the 1930s and 1940s. It is that earlier Cage, specifically Cage the percussion composer, who is the subject of this essay.

Cage the composer was in many ways a formalist from the very
beginning. Like Schoenberg, his former teacher, he was looking for a
fundamental principle, a method of organization based upon music's
"nature." And while he appreciated Schoenberg's so-called twelve-
tone system, Cage the experimentalist, follower of Cowell, Varèse
and Russolo, was ultimately not able to attach himself to a method
that based its organizational principles on pitch. Cage himself
explained in 1948:

> In the field of structure, the field of the definition of parts and
> their relation to a whole, there has been only one new idea since
> Beethoven. And that new idea can be perceived in the work of
> Anton Webern and Erik Satie. With Beethoven the parts of a com-
> position were defined by means of harmony. With Satie and
> Webern they are defined by means of time lengths. The question
> of structure is so basic, and it is so important to be in agreement
> about it, that one must now ask: Was Beethoven right or are
> Webern and Satie right? I answer immediately and unequivocally,
> Beethoven was in error, and his influence, which has been as
> extensive as it is lamentable, has been deadening to the art of
> music.[3]

Those familiar with this quote often associate it with the lecture's
original context: a room full of German émigrés at Black Mountain
College. They were certainly outraged in 1948; Cage's remarks still
rankle today. This younger Cage paints a much more zealous portrait
than that of the elder statesman Cage who regarded music in a much
more egalitarian way. Responding to a question concerning whether
or not "more people will compose with the methods you've brought
forth," this elder Cage replied: "No, I think we're going in a multiplicity of directions. If I performed any function at all, it's one that
would have been performed in any case: to take us out of the notion
of the mainstream of music, and into a situation that could be likened
to a delta or field or ocean, that there are just countless possibilities."[4]
These countless possibilities would include Beethoven, one presumes,
but once again Cage's remark in this case was made in 1980. In 1948,
Cage saw Beethoven as opposing "the truth": "it took a Satie and a
Webern to rediscover this musical truth [that if] sound is characterized by its pitch, its loudness, its timbre, and its duration, and that
silence, which is the opposite and, therefore, the necessary partner of
sound, is characterized only by its duration, you will be drawn to the
conclusion that of the four characteristics of the material of music,
duration, that is, time length, is the most fundamental."[5] This statement's veracity is, of course, debatable. However, it well represents
the purpose behind Cage's own experiments in rhythm and his
method of structuring music through a temporal patterning called
"square root form."

Square root form has an equivalent "macro/microcosmic" structure which is determined prior to writing any given piece. It first
appears in Cage's *First Construction (in Metal)*, composed in Seattle in
1939. In this case, the square root is 16 x 16, which means that there
are 16 large sections made up of 16 measures each. Another charac-

teristic of square root form is the division of the piece into a form/phrase structure that mirrors the square root idea. In *First Construction*, this structure is symmetrical: 4, 3, 2, 3, 4. That is, the piece is divided into a formal structure that divides the 16 large sections into groups of four (i.e., four 16-measure sections), followed by three 16-measure sections, then two sections, three sections and finally four sections. This is the "macrocosmic" level of organization. Correspondingly, and on the "microcosmic" level, each individual 16-measure section is also divided into a phrase pattern of four measures, 3 measures, 2 measures, 3 measures, and 4 measures. The number 16 and its 4, 3, 2, 3, 4 division is thus the organizing principle behind the piece.

Example 3-1, a manuscript of this piece in Cage's hand, clearly illustrates the division of the phrases at the microcosmic level. The opening four-measure phrase features a solo for string piano (accompanied by thundersheets). The subsequent three-measure phrase then adds the sleigh bells, which become oxen bells in the published score. The next two-measure phrase employs orchestra bells, brake drums and turkish cymbals in half notes, while the three-bar phrase after that adds muted gongs to the piano of the first phrase and the sleigh bells of the second. The final four-measure phrase is almost a summation of the entire section, combining the musical ideas of the first and second phrases with those of the third.

Like *First Construction*, the instrumentation for *Second Construction* (Seattle, 1940) includes metal instruments (gongs, sleighbells and thundersheets); it also expands this arsenal by using glass wind chimes, maracas, tom-toms and a snare drum. *Second Construction* also uses a 16 x 16 square root form, but unlike its predecessor, its macrocosmic and microcosmic proportions are *not* identical. On the microcosmic level, each 16-measure section is divided into 4, 3, 4, 5 (this last section of 5 sometimes subdivided into 3 and 2). But at the macrocosmic level, the 16 large sections are apportioned as 4, 3, 5 [3, 2], 4.[6] There is a fermata that subdivides the 5 section of the macrostructure into 3/2, which is also how it works at the phrase level. Not surprisingly, and as Example 3-2 demonstrates, in the microstructure there are groupings of five in the third phrase, which is four measures long.

As this comparison of *First Construction* and *Second Construction* demonstrates, Cage's use of square root form was constantly changing. The organization method of *Second Construction* moves beyond that of its predecessor by manipulating the *linear* order of the form's segments. *Third Construction* (San Francisco, 1941) complicates the form even further by manipulating its vertical dimension. Unlike the previous two Constructions, *Third Construction*

Example 3-1.
John Cage, *First Construction (In Metal)*, manuscript.
Used by permission of the John Cage Trust.

Carl Fischer, Inc. New York.
No. 104 –12 lines.

Example 3-1 (cont.)

Example 3-2. John Cage, *Second Construction*, mm. 1–32.
Used by permission of the John Cage Trust.

Example 3-2 (cont.)

does not have a consistent phrase order; instead each part has its own phrase order. In his volume, *The Music of John Cage*, James Pritchett outlines this macro/microcosmic structure as follows:

> *Player 4*: 8 2 4 5 3 2
> *Player 1*: 2 8 2 4 5 3
> *Player 3*: 3 2 8 2 4 5
> *Player 2*: 5 3 2 8 2 4

As Pritchett puts it, Cage's structure in this case consists of "rotations of the same series." The musical result of this procedure, he notes, "avoids some of the blockiness and predictability of the textural changes found in the earlier Construction pieces, since phrase boundaries are rarely aligned among the four players."[7]

Square root form continued to be an important means of musical organization for Cage throughout the 1940s. Ultimately, this method would enable him to give equal weight to both sound and silence, since the structure was not "determined by the materials which were to occur in it; it was conceived, in fact, so that it could be as well expressed by the absence of these materials as by their presence."[8]

While rhythmic organization and the use of silence were perennial concerns to Cage, his focused interest in aspects of timbre was more intermittent and varied. Cage's participation as a performer of his own works was an important factor contributing to that interest. As Cage himself said in 1957: "Composing's one thing, performing's another, listening's a third. What can they have to do with one another?"[9] Cage the composer usually concentrated on structure when discussing his work. In the following pages, we will rely upon Cage the listening performer who interpreted his own music compositions. He took great care in both the selection of sounds and the interpretive context in which those sounds appear. Furthermore, those sounds and interpretive contexts are not only beautiful to hear, they are beautiful in the very traditional sense of the word that Cage seems to deny in the statement beginning this essay.

The origins of Cage's beautiful sounds were percussive. However, timbre was not his primary concern when he began writing for percussion instruments. The *Quartet* (1935), Cage's first composition for percussion, specifies no instruments at all,[10] and the *Trio* (1936) uses a decidedly minimal collection of percussion instruments chosen after the piece was written. In either case, the musical interest is almost entirely rhythmic in nature.

On the other hand, Cage had heard a good deal of percussion music that did have a strong timbral component. He heard Varèse's *Ionisation* at the Hollywood Bowl in 1933, and it is likely that he would have heard Henry Cowell's *Ostinato Pianissimo* for percussion

(1933) while taking courses on ethnic musics (which may have even included a course on percussion) with Cowell at the New School for Social Research.[11] And even though the *Quartet* did not specify instrumentation in the score, Cage and three others practiced the music using "whatever was at hand," tapping "tables, books, chairs," and then invaded the kitchen, using "pots and pans. Several visits to junk-yards and lumber-yards yielded more instruments: brake drums from automobiles, different lengths of pipes, steel rings, hardwood blocks. After experimenting for several weeks, the final scoring of the *Quartet* was finished. It included the instruments that had been found, supplemented by a pedal timpani and a Chinese Gong which lent to the whole a certain traditional aspect and sound."[12] As a result, one can see that Cage the composer's initially unspecified instrumentation was eventually determined by Cage the performer. One might also assume that the weeks of experimentation were for the purpose of choosing a sonically pleasing result.

Unfortunately, when performers interpret Cage's early music, in particular his percussion pieces, their method of sound source selection is often highly uncritical, choosing whatever instruments happen to be at hand without giving consideration to their sonic properties in relation to their historical past. In my opinion, this approach is painfully flawed, for it is only those instruments for which these percussion composers wrote that actually produce the sounds that these composers had heard—and therefore intended—as they wrote these pieces. That is, even if we take Cage at his word as "not hearing music" before he wrote it, at the very least this music was what he heard when he himself interpreted and performed his pieces. While what the composers themselves heard need not determine instrument choice, it does seem appropriate for interpreters to be aware of what those original instruments were, and what they sounded like, before ultimately choosing a percussion instrument. Brake drums, for example, such as those that Cage found in junk yards, were made of spun steel in the 1930s; when suspended, they rang like bells. The newer versions, which most percussion ensembles use today, sound entirely different, hardly ringing at all.[13] As such, using these original instruments (or substitutes that can duplicate their sound accurately) produce results that are frequently not only more historically accurate, but actually sound better.

As fascinating as the questions of form are in Cage's early percussion pieces, the issues related to timbral content are what attracted attention to these pieces when they were first performed. Timbre, along with rhythmic variety, continues to be what attracts us to them now. As the discussion of both *First Construction* and *Second Construction* has shown, the pieces are not complex from a formal standpoint; their sound world, however, even after multiple hearings, *is* complex.

The opening measures of *First Construction* are a case in point (see Example 3-1). Four of the six players shake suspended pieces of sheet metal that Cage calls "thundersheets," while the piano plays an ostinato-like combination of four notes (D, D♯, E, F) for seven measures in a rhythmic pattern that alternates between groupings of fours and threes, thereby mirroring the four-plus-three phrasing (the piano plays through the first two phrases) essential to Cage's pre-determined formal requirements (16 x 16 equals 4-3-2-3-4). The sleigh bells enter at the fifth measure using rhythmic groupings similar to those previously heard in the piano. Three of the four thundersheets drop out by the fifth measure, once again mirroring the formal structure (since there were four thundersheets playing during the first four-measure phrase); the only one left (but minus *three*—absence of sound thus creating as much of a formal presence as sound itself) then sustains for the required three measures of the second phrase. The two-measure phrase follows, consisting of half notes performed by the three who dropped out prior to the immediately preceeding three-measure phrase. Instruments used are the orchestra bells (player one), brake drums (player two), and Turkish cymbals (player three).

Completion of the internal phrasing requires a three-measure phrase followed by a four-measure phrase. The missing players who did not play half-notes now enter for the next three measures, playing either previously heard material (string piano, sleigh bells) or new material (muted gongs). It should be noted that all of the rhythmic material is related, coming from various groupings of twos, threes, and fours. The resultant texture is imitative (measure eleven between player six and players two and three, followed by player two then three in measure twelve), but not unusually so. When the half notes return in measure thirteen, the other three parts continue motivic exchanges rooted by the continuance of player two, whose phrase is seven measures long, with some variation in the parts of players three and six since their material is now in two-measure phrases.

Such structural considerations are not uninteresting; however, I would contend that they are not interesting enough in themselves to merit either the kind or level of attention this piece has received. Such consideration requires the inclusion of timbre into the mix.

The opening measures of *First Construction* are a prime example of Cage's timbral complexity (see Example 3-1). First, the very use of thundersheets—let alone four of them—yields a timbrally striking beginning to the piece. From their opening *sforzando*, the thundersheets, which are normally used to simulate thunder in theatrical productions, are given a prominence not commonly found in written music. This sound becomes the undergirding of the next sonic entrance—a"string piano," which is performed by an assistant placing and holding a metal rod on the strings while the pianist plays the notated keyboard part.[14] When properly actuated with the bar pressed down hard upon the strings, the sound is remarkable. The technique is quite close to the "bottleneck" technique found in certain schools of guitar playing (named after the pressing of a glass bottle on the guitar strings). However, when the metal is pressed on tightly drawn piano strings, the result is much more unsettling. Coming soon after the shock of the thundersheets, the piano equally problematizes the listening experience; the exotic quality of the sound achieved through the novel use of the instruments produces an unexpected result, even considering the fact that the listener is already prepared visually by the unusual "look" of the combined instruments' appearance on stage. By the time so-called "normal" percussion instruments (orchestra bells, turkish cymbals) arrive—albeit accompanied by the then less-than-normal brake drums—the aural scene has been set, and even these instruments have lost any traditional sense of musical place.

There is no question that factors other than just timbre make *First Construction (in Metal)* what David Nicholls has called Cage's "earliest masterpiece." Some of those factors, according to Nicholls, include "Cage's interest in using all available sounds and his search for new sounds, these partially combined with the employment of percussion instruments; the use of extramusical—often mathematical—systems to determine musical parameters (especially pitch); and the quest for a structure other than Western harmony/tonality with which to build form."[15] I would argue that there is a more hierarchical means by which to determine what qualifies *First Construction* as a "masterpiece." One can imagine hearing Cage's percussive sounds in another structure or using another form and still being interesting in themselves: sweeping a gong beater over piano strings, "metal rod on piano string" glissandos or Cage's now-famous invention, the water gong (in which one strikes a gong while inserting it into or retracting it from a tub of water, thereby producing a glissando effect). The history of early percussion ensemble music is filled with examples of pieces in which timbre is of such primary interest regardless of structure and form. On the other hand, it is hard to imagine the formal structure of *First Construction* being as interesting without the unusual timbres. Consequently one might argue that timbre is the essential parameter of the piece, surpassing form in its importance.

Second Construction (1940) clarifies this issue. In retrospect, at least, Cage himself didn't like this piece very much, commenting, "I think the *Second Construction* is a poor piece. I wasn't quite aware that it was poor when I wrote it; I thought it was interesting. But it has carry-overs from education and theory; it's really a fugue, but of a novel order. In this day and age, I think fugues are not interesting (because of the repetition of the subject)."[16] As usual, Cage discussed his concerns about the piece according to what were, in his mind, its formal problems. However, even if one concedes that interest in Cage's percussion pieces is due more to timbral rather than formal qualities, *Second Construction* is also the least timbrally varied of the three Constructions.

The timbres of this piece are less varied and less unusual due to the use of more commonly found percussion instruments as well as their more traditional deployment; the snare drum, for example, is found nowhere else in the early percussion pieces of John Cage other than the *Second Construction*. Although it is used in ways that would be regarded as untraditional in orchestral circles, the snare drum *is* still used in a way similar to that of drumset players, especially in a jazz-like context (e.g., the "swish" of the wire brush and the tap of the snare drum stick in combination). Certainly Cage's association with composer and jazz enthusiast William Russell was a strong influence in this regard. Other instruments—maracas, tom-toms, the tam-tam—are less traditional in the context of Western European music but are used in ways that do not necessarily emphasize what makes them unusual; that is, they are used in ways that do not emphasize their extra-European origins.

After repeated listenings, the overall timbral quality of *Second Construction* seems to lack the same novelty that the other two Constructions continue to have. This is partially due to the general lack of vertical rhythmic complexity that makes *Third Construction* a more multi-faceted piece than either of its predecessors. Furthermore, the lack of timbral variety occurs because of the particular combination of instruments and more importantly (at least in this context), the lack of timbral complexity *within* one particular sound source. This complexity is an essential characteristic that makes *First Construction* so interesting timbrally. Because it only uses metal instruments, and because it uses metal instruments of so many types that are played in so many ways, there is a diversity within a single sound source (metal) that is very complex.

Second Construction uses all three instrument groupings that are stereotypically characteristic of percussion: metal, wood, and skin. These include sleigh bells, temple gongs, muted gongs, tam-tam, thundersheet, and a water gong (metals); maracas and a rattle (wood); tom-toms and a snare drum (skin). It also uses glass (the windchimes). Its emphasis on soloistic lines and its use of fairly traditional accompaniment figures suggests the element of timbre as perhaps more important here than in either of the other two Constructions, an idea reinforced by the fact that the rhythmic structure of this piece is the least complex of the three. When the subsidiary lines take on more than an accompanimental role, they are primarily imitative and do not necessarily add much to the vertical complexity of the work, either timbrally or rhythmically.

Timbres are often heard individually, and even when they are combined they rarely contain more than two moving lines. In *Second Construction*, one either does or doesn't find the sounds interesting in themselves. Even though there are several instruments of several types, there is not enough timbral diversity either within those types or in the combining of those types to stimulate interest on its own terms. The beginning of the piece exemplifies this. It begins (see Example 3-2) with a four-measure sleigh bell solo, consisting of two- or three-note rhythmic groupings, followed by a stroke in the center of the tam-tam that sustains for three bars. The sleigh bells return for another four measures, this time in longer rhythmic groupings of fours and fives; they are followed once again by the tam-tam, this time with two strokes: the first is played in the center and held for three measures, and the second is played on the edge and held for two measures. The rhythmic figures (the twos and threes combine to produce five in this instance) thus mirror the macro-micro structure of 4, 3, 4, 5, which is, of course, also the phrase structure as described.

All four players enter in the second section, beginning at Rehearsal no. 1. The string piano, using a variation of the first phrase that contains both its beginning and its end, is accompanied by the snare drum which adds an imitative three-plus-two figure towards the end of the first four-measure phrase. The other two parts, a rattle and a thundersheet, are simply shaken at low dynamics. After the string piano completes its solo, which uses the first two phrase lengths of four and three, the sleigh bells take over for four measures, using a variation of its second phrase (fours and fives). It is accompanied by maracas rolling in half notes and a return of the thundersheet. The final five measures, split again into three plus two, contain the same tam-tam figure that ended the first section, which now accompanies the string piano playing the figure that opened the second section both altered and somewhat reversed (quarter notes, sometimes lengthened to dotted quarters, followed by the eighth-note figures of twos, threes, and fours).

The opening two sections, one soloistic and the other *tutti*, contain both the form and rhythmic structures as well as the instrumental diversity characteristic of Cage's early percussion pieces. However, if Cage's negative opinion of *Second Construction* has any validity, it is likely the result of its more conventional structural *and* timbral elements.

Third Construction departs from both the timbral and structural conventions of its immediate predecessor while at the same time diversifying further its instrumental resources. This piece contains Cage's most complex percussion orchestration as well as what was, at that time, his most complex formal design (Example 3-3). Completed in 1941, *Third Construction* received its premiere in May of that same year in a concert of works composed by either Cage or Lou Harrison. By that time, Cage had collected over one hundred percussion instruments; he had catalogued these in a detailed list which included one snare drum, two bass drums, five Chinese tom–toms, one Japanese Noh drum, and one tortoise shell, among others. According to B. Michael Williams, Cage's collection of instruments "would eventually number over three hundred."[17]

The John Cage Archives at Northwestern University also houses a notebook entitled "John Cage: Accounts in Connection with Percussion Instruments, Seattle 1939." This document includes a list of patrons, including author John Steinbeck, who responded to a request by Cage for funds to replace percussion instruments owned at the time by the German dancer Lora Deja, who had been on the faculty at the Cornish School in Seattle. Cage, who was on the faculty, had used them the year before in his first percussion concert at the Cornish School on December 9, 1938, but he had been informed that Deja had requested their return.

According to a letter written by Cage to Mr. and Mrs. John H. Ballinger, the instruments that could not be "borrowed, constructed, or invented" were "Chinese Gongs, cymbals, tomtoms and woodblocks . . ."[18] Indeed, as one peruses Cage's meticulous records, one discovers that the most expensive purchase is dated September 22: $81.43 was paid to the China Trading Company for five brass gongs, three brass cymbals, five tom-toms and three wood blocks. By 1939, Cage had come a long way from the "found" instruments of 1935. Furthermore, his powers of timbral discernment now encompassed the entire world of percussion, thanks in part to his associations with Cowell and Harrison, as well as to the availability of Lora Deja's instruments. None of Cage's three Constructions, most of which were written while at the Cornish School, could have been performed without these instruments. That is, they were written with these instruments and their respective timbres in mind.

In some cases Cage makes timbral distinctions by indicating specific differences in instrumental types. For example, while Cage in *Second Construction* asks for a "Wooden Indian Rattle," in *Third Construction*, his instrument choices are more specific. There are three rattles (not including the maracas that are used too often for all rattle types in performance): a Northwest Indian Rattle (wooden), an Indo-Chinese Rattle

Example 3-3. John Cage, *Third Construction*, mm. 1–24.
Used by permission of the John Cage Trust.

Example 3-3 (cont.)

2

(wooden, with many separate chambers), and a rattle made by placing tacks inside a tin can. The Northwest Indian rattle is probably the one used in *Second Construction*, since the piece was written in Seattle and the rattles found among the Native Americans in that area are wooden. Consequently, an instrumentation calling for other rattles might need to be explicit, and indeed, in these cases, Cage either describes the instrument that must be made (the tin can) or he describes the particularity of the material required to produce the characteristic sound of a pre-existent instrument (Indo-Chinese rattle). Obviously, the expectation here is not to duplicate the instruments. However, it seems clear that Cage's descriptions are meant to help the performer duplicate the specific timbre of those instruments.

Third Construction was written for Chinese Tom-Toms, but in the score it states "drums." Today, however, modern tom-toms have been affected timbrally by the appearance of plastic heads that yield a sound quality that was not available in the 1930s and 1940s. Are modern tom-toms, therefore, inappropriate or undesirable in performances of this work? This question is especially problematic because Cage requires the performers to distinguish between the sound produced at the center of the instrument and the sound produced on its edge. Chinese drums, which have animal-skin heads, produce very distinct timbres in those two spots. On the other hand, modern plastic heads have a "ring" that comes from a weakened fundamental and the predominance of upper partials. Furthermore, since drums do not have a strong fundamental in the first place, these overtones tend to produce a much less focused tone, and because of the plastic there is a much harsher attack. Skin heads produce a better fundamental pitch; however, because these heads come in a variety of thicknesses, it is equally important to consider not only the material but also its density. Chinese drums have a strong fundamental pitch and, at the same time, a good amount of resonance because the heads are not as thick as, for example, conga drum or bongo drum heads. Consequently one must also consider how much or how little skin heads resonate, in order to duplicate the sound Cage had in mind.

Cage's inclusion of instruments from variously distinct musical cultures, including the aforementioned examples from both Chinese and Native American musics, is not always respected by interpreters as a cue toward authenticity. The types of conch shell and cricket-callers used in *Third Construction* are of Polynesian origin (Figure 3-1). Making a substitute for the conch shell is not a legitimate possibility, and any potential substitute for cricket-callers (bamboo with the ends split into several small stick-like segments) would at least have to share similar material properties in order to produce their characteristic sound. In all likelihood, the result would reproduce the

Figure 3-1. Cricket-callers. Photo by Erica Jett.

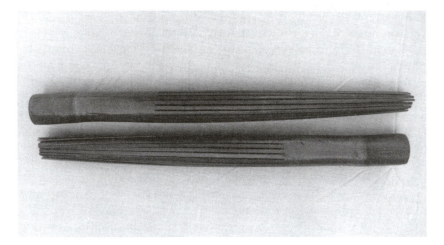

instrument rather than serve as a substitute. Today claves and maracas have become ubiquitous; it is easily forgotten that these were not commonly found in Western classical music of the early 1940s. In addition to these well-known instruments, Cage also used two other Latin American instruments that are much harder to find and have a sound that is very difficult to duplicate by synthetic means. These are the quijada and the teponaxtle [sic]. A vibraslap is often used in place of the difficult to find and preserve quijada which is typically the jawbone of a donkey. Knowing what a real quijada sounds like (in particular, how its resonance compares to that of the vibraslap) is essential.

Figure 3-2. Teponaztli. Photo by Erica Jett.

The teponaxtle (Figure 3-2) is named after one city of its origin, Tepoztlan, Mexico. It looks like a log drum and has two carved-out tongues that produce two distinct pitches which are often a minor third apart.[19] James Blades discusses the teponaxtle in his *Percussion Instruments and Their History*: "A slit drum of pre-Aztec origin is found in the Mexican teponaztli. The slit in this instance is in the shape of the letter H carved horizontally in the wood shell. The tongues are chiselled on the underside to different thicknesses (or the section between the longitudinal slits divided unequally) to produce two distinct tones."[20] A hand-made log drum is usually substituted in performance, but consideration is not always given to the distance between pitches, which I believe should be considered when duplicating this instrument.

Even "found" instruments pose similar problems, as in the case of tin cans, which are used extensively in *Third Construction*. First of all, tin cans in the 1930s and 1940s were made of a different combination of metals than they are today. However, the mere size of the cans themselves is a more serious problem, as they must be big enough to be aurally distinctive and, furthermore, they must be able to produce clearly distinct timbres between the center and the rim.

As previously discussed, this much larger array of instruments is complemented formally by a much more complex structure. Here is where form and content meet. While Cage the formalist preferred to discuss structure, the content of timbre is ultimately what best delineates the structure during this period. In *Third Construction*, the timbral complexity predominates, and on a sonic level it even determines the audibility of form. The score example (see Example 3-3) is the beginning of *Third Construction*. It is given as an example so that one can note the formal similarity between it and *Second Construction*, while at the same time noting how timbrally different the sonic result of each will be. It begins with a drum solo consisting of a five-measure phrase. The Northwest Indian rattle enters following two measures of rest (which constitute the first part of its structure) with an entrance that is sustained for eight measures, constituting the second part of its structure. Player two's drums are joined by those of player three in measure four, which includes the second (two measures) and third (eight measures) parts of player three's structure, which began with three measures of rest. The Northwest Indian rattle is joined by the tin can rattle in the ninth measure. The tin can rattle sustains for two measures (the second phrase for player four), preceded by eight measures of rest, which constitutes the first part of player four's structure.

The complexity increases as the entrances continue to overlap and as individual parts become more difficult. Player one's tin can entrance in measure thirteen has a four plus five phrase structure, beginning at the same time that player three is closing an eight-measure phrase. Player four's clave entrance in measure fifteen (a five-measure phrase) precedes the re-entry of player three on the drums (a four-measure phrase), while player one ends a five-measure phrase with a new dynamic level and a new rhythm (half-note triplets), just as player two is ending a two-measure phrase.

The result is "marvelous," as Cage himself might have characterized it. But while form and content, or structure and timbre, meet, it is essential to establish the hierarchical nature of the aural experience of the piece. Rhythm and structure can of their own accord determine formal characteristics, sometimes with the help of dynamics, as can be seen in measure twenty-one. However, when heard, there are no clearer divisions than those determined by timbral change.

These observations in their totality support the notion that Cage had, if not an "ear for music," at least a remarkable ear for timbre. Without detracting from the obvious importance of rhythm in his early percussion pieces, Cage's careful instrumentation greatly adds to one's musical enjoyment and renders these works immediately accessible, even to the traditionally inclined. Choosing the right instruments and playing them well does indeed produce a beautiful sound.

In 1965, Cage said the following:

> Logically I thought that anything that is small and intimate, and has some love in it, is beautiful. Therefore, I wrote a piece for prepared piano, which is very quiet. It is called *Amores*, and it is about my conviction that love is something that we can consider beautiful. But then shortly I discovered that I was being divorced and going through all the troubles associated with disrupted love life; so that even love has its aspects which are not beautiful. So what is beautiful? So what's art? So why do we write music? All these questions began to be of great importance to me, to such a great importance that I decided not to continue unless I could find suitable answers.[21]

The rest is history. But one should never forget that those questions, which confirmed Cage's place as one of this century's most influential artists, were asked after he wrote these early pieces. *Amores* was a transitional four-movement work that included both the percussion music that was soon to be part of Cage's past and the prepared piano that was both his present and, through the 1940s, his future. If the John Cage of the 1980s was accurate in saying that "what most musicians have, I don't have," his percussion pieces and the prepared piano works that followed prove that he had what only a few musicians ever acquire: a meticulous sense of musicality combined with a highly refined sensitivity toward that which characterizes a beautiful sound.[22] As his early percussion pieces testify, Cage *did* have an ear for timbre; furthermore, they show that he had an exceptional ear for music, regardless of what he himself had to say.

Notes

This essay was presented in abbreviated form at the Annual Meeting of the Sonneck Society for American Music, March 8, 1997, Seattle, Washington. I also presented it in somewhat longer form, thanks to an invitation by Professor Thomas DeLio, at the University of Maryland-College Park as part of their Lectures in the History and Theory of Music series, December 8, 1997. I'd like to thank David Nicholls, whose *American Experimental Music, 1890-1940* (Cambridge: Cambridge University Press, 1990) is an important influence on this essay for his encouragement after hearing my presentation in Seattle. I'd also like to thank David Patterson for his patience and support, without which this essay would likely never have been completed.

1. William Duckworth and Richard Fleming, eds., *John Cage at Seventy-Five* [*Bucknell Review* 32, no. 2], (Lewisburg, PA: Bucknell University Press, 1989), 16.

2. Norman O. Brown. "John Cage" in Duckworth and Fleming, eds., 104.

3. John Cage, "Defense of Satie" (1948), in *John Cage: An Anthology*, ed. Richard Kostelanetz, (New York: Da Capo Press, 1991), 81.

4. Tracy Caras and Cole Gagne, eds., *Soundpieces: Interviews with American Composers* (London: The Scarecrow Press, 1982), 81.

5. John Cage, "Defense of Satie," in *John Cage: An Anthology*, 81.

6. David Nicholls keeps both macro- and micro-structures in four parts: "Thus, in the *Second Construction*—which is again 16 x 16 bars long—the supposed micro and macrocosmic structural proportions are 4:3:4:5. However, the effective macro-structure is actually 4:3:3:6, with the 6 section being a rhythmic fugue." The distinction is minor but my preference for splitting the fourth part (5) into 3/2, allows for a connection between macro-and micro-structure by simply reversing the third and fourth parts of the macro-structure with 3/2 combining into 5: 4, 3, [3:2], 4. See Nicholls, *American Experimental Music* (Cambridge: Cambridge University Press, 1990), 209.

7. James Pritchett, *The Music of John Cage* (Cambridge: Cambridge University Press, 1993), 19–20.

8. John Cage. "Composition as Process" (1958), in *Silence: Lectures and Writings* (Middletown, CT: Wesleyan University Press, 1961), 19–20.

9. John Cage, "Experimental Music: Doctrine" (1955), in *Silence: Lectures and Writings*, 15.

10. Neither of these compositions' dates is known to be exact. Cage himself has said that perhaps the *Trio* was written first. See an interview with Cage by B. Michael Williams, "The Early Percussion Music of John Cage, 1935–1943" in *Percussive Notes* 31, no. 6 (August 1993): 60–67.

11. Nicholls, 184.

12.   John Cage. "A Composer's Confessions" (1948), in *John Cage Writer*, ed. Richard Kostelanetz (New York: Limelight Editions, 1993), 31–32.

13.   According to Leta Miller, pre–World War II brake drums, "are indeed much better than more recent ones because the automobile industry changed from spun steel to cast iron after the war; the latter is more malleable but less resonant because of the graphite flakes in the iron." (Private correspondence, April 5, 1998).

14.   Nicholls, 206. Nicholls attributes the invention of the "string piano" generally to Henry Cowell and Cage's use of a metal rod on the strings specifically to Cowell as well: "This technique was first used by Cowell in the third movement of *A Composition* (1925)."

15.   Ibid.

16.   Gagne and Caras, eds., 70–71.

17.   B. Michael Williams. "The Early Percussion Music of John Cage 1935–1943," (Ph.D. diss., Michigan State University, 1990), 11.

18.   Letter to Mr. and Mrs. John H. Ballinger, September 14, 1939, from John Cage Archive, Northwestern University Music Library, Evanston, IL.

19.   According to Robert Stevenson, "In museum exemplars studied to date, the tongues emit notes a major second to a fifth apart. Which intervals, however, did the instrument makers prefer? Seconds? Fifths? So far as the fourteen teponaztlis tabulated by Casteneda and Mendoza are concerned, minor thirds prove the favorites." See Stevenson, *Music in Aztec and Inca Territory* (Berkeley: University of California Press, 1968), 64.

20.   James Blades. *Percussion Instruments and Their History*, revised ed. (London: Faber and Faber, 1984), 47.

21.   Richard Kostelanetz, ed., *Conversing with Cage* (New York: Limelight Editions, 1987), 59.

22.   One listen to Cage himself performing the piano movements of *Amores* proves this point better than words could possibly describe. The recording is *Concert Percussion*, the Manhattan Percussion Ensemble, Paul Price, director, Mainstream Records, MS 5011. Another future reference in this regard will be the recordings, once thought to be lost, that Cage made with his percussion ensemble, which he formed while in Seattle in the late 1930s and early 1940s. Gordon Mumma has those recordings in his possession and they are in the process of being restored.

4. John Cage's *Imaginary Landscape No. 1*: Through the Looking Glass

Susan Key

> *The artist picks up the message of cultural and technological challenge decades before its transforming impact occurs.*
>
> —Marshall McLuhan[1]

> *It's not a physical landscape. It's a term reserved for the new technologies. It's a landscape in the future. It's as though you used technology to take you off the ground and go like Alice through the looking glass.*
>
> —John Cage[2]

Two aspects of John Cage's 1939 *Imaginary Landscape No. 1* are generally acknowledged to have broken new aesthetic ground: its incorporation of electronic instruments and its use of rhythmic structures. Yet perhaps the most radical aspect of the piece is one that is generally overlooked: the composer's directive that it be executed in a radio studio and "performed" through either a live or recorded broadcast.[3] By making this distinction between realization and performance, Cage moved well beyond issues of harmonic or temporal structure, reformulating the fundamental relationship between a musical creation and its environment. In so doing, he also anticipated his own deeper philosophical inquiries into the role of "silence" from the late 1930s through the early 1950s.

Cage was fortuitously placed to exploit the new medium of radio. In 1939, he was employed as accompanist to Bonnie Bird's dance classes at the Cornish School in Seattle. Only three years earlier, the School had acquired a fully-equipped radio studio, reported as "the most modern and complete of its type in the West;"[4] it celebrated this new acquisition with a nationwide "gala broadcast" on May 13, 1936, that included contemporary music and an experimental, improvised radio drama.[5] In 1937, the Cornish Radio School officially opened as the first of its kind in the U.S.; NBC executive Franklin Dunham headed the advisory board, and various NBC studio personnel were engaged as instructors in radio education, production, arranging, and program building.[6] *Imaginary Landscape No. 1* was broadcast from Cornish's radio studio for a dance program in an adjacent theater.[7]

However innovative his first radio composition, Cage's interest in the medium placed him firmly within the mainstream of American culture. During the 1930s, radio's aesthetic possibilities, its potential to reach vast audiences, and its wealth of institutional resources attracted composers from a broad stylistic spectrum.[8] With the financial support of network music departments, many of America's most prominent composers, including Aaron Copland, Roy Harris, and Howard Hanson, experimented with various aspects of timbre, style, and genre in works especially designed for broadcast. While these efforts produced a number of interesting individual pieces, the composers rarely strayed too far from conventional compositional techniques, and the cumulative impact on twentieth-century composition was slight.

In more avant-garde circles, Edgard Varèse shared Cage's desire to use the new technology to expand the field of musical sound. Varèse worked throughout the decade on a radio composition entitled *Espace;* though never finished, the composer's working accounts of the piece in progress and one extant study sketch reveal in some detail his vision of radio's new spatial and timbral potentialities. Like Cage, Varèse responded both to radio's new sonic resources and also its more profound reconfiguration of the twentieth-century aural landscape, in which sounds from disparate sources mingle indiscriminately in new environments.

Cage was hardly unique in exploring the potential of radio. Yet *Imaginary Landscape No. 1* represents a unique challenge not only to conventional musical idioms but even to the conception of music itself. An examination of this particular piece illuminates issues of Cage's artistic development as well as the singular nature of his contribution to twentieth-century culture. This essay, therefore, addresses *Imaginary Landscape No. 1* within the context of contemporary attitudes toward radio music, with particular emphasis on the respective approaches of Cage and Varèse, ultimately arguing for the importance of radio to Cage's evolving aesthetic.

In the 1920s, it was clear to America's composers, critics, and performers that radio's "transforming impact" on America's musical culture would be genuinely profound. They understood that broadcasting would affect the kinds of music to which Americans listened as well as the environments in which they would listen, and that there were evident social implications in this technology that allowed music to cross boundaries of class and race. The Midwestern farmer listening to Vivaldi and the New England Caucasian listening to southern, African-American blues were indications of a new cultural mobility that was analogous to the physical mobility introduced by the automobile, and throughout the 1920s and 1930s, the musical community discussed this new cultural phenomenon in a stream of commentaries in books and periodicals, at conferences, and, of course, over the airwaves themselves.

One strain of commentary regarding radio and music is especially relevant to the innovations that Cage would introduce in *Imaginary Landscape No. 1*: namely, the widespread and deeply-rooted assumption that this new broadcast medium and fine-art music were fundamentally compatible, or even alike. As a result, even radio's most extraordinary consequences, such as a large-scale symphony emanating from a little box in a rural kitchen miles away from performers and the concert hall posed no challenge to the parameters of musical sound, musical perception, or musical meaning. Rather, this twentieth-century invention was seamlessly absorbed into a view of music that long predated its presence as a fixture in American homes.

The basis of this view is that the essence of fine-art music lies in its non-material, abstract, transcendental qualities. By extension, the physical parameters of music are disconnected from its basic nature; even its most basic physical manifestation—sound—is subordinate to its existence on a more abstract plane. Nurtured by German romanticism, this attitude was promulgated most eloquently by authors such as transcendentalist and critic John Sullivan Dwight. Michael Broyles has traced the dissemination of Dwight's transcendental aesthetic in nineteenth-century America, and he has discussed the ways in which a central canon of absolute symphonic music became allied with universality, spirituality, and moral purity, fostered by Boston's upper classes in particular.[9] By the end of the century, dialogue in the United States about both the nature of classical music and its cultural role reflected a solid dependence on Dwight's transcendentalism.

Divorcing the value of music from its worldly associations or physical environment involved a curious effacement of the relationship between performance, social context, and sound itself. In Dwight's philosophy, a concert of live music took place in a space that, in theory, was soundless. The boundary between a musical composition and its physical environment was at once clear and irrelevant: it was clear because the concert setting, no matter how elaborate, existed only to frame the music performed; it was irrelevant because the music's essence was independent of its physical environment. The social aspect of the concert hall was equally non-essential to music. As Dwight expressed, "One gets the best part of music, the sincerest part, when he is alone."[10] The effacement of physical reality extended to sound itself, which was always threatening to get out of hand and claim an identity for itself. Again, in Dwight's words:

> It is not the chief ambition of these concerts to exhibit models, either in surpassing brilliancy or fineness, of mere instrumental execution. . . . We call upon the orchestra to open for us, and read out to us, sealed volumes within which we know that treasures of beauty and divinist wisdom wait to be revealed.[11]

For Dwight and his fellow transcendentalists, then, performers and sound existed almost as a lamentable necessity in the attainment of spiritual enlightenment.

For the twentieth-century inheritors of this philosophy, radio merely extended the effacement of music's physical context from a theoretical level to an actual one; if anything, it enhanced music's immanent qualities, allowing one to experience the essence of music without visual distractions. As sound—the inescapable physical presence of music—was construed as the mere vehicle to a higher spiritual essence, the technology of radio was likewise construed as a mundane means toward music's intangible essence, and the radio broadcast as an extension of music's highest value—a "natural" medium for its dissemination. Radio seemed to embody the notion that music existed in some ideal, celestial realm and that through a new technological miracle, this realm could be accessed by any person who made the effort to "tune in." The modern radio listener could live out Dwight's ideal of solitary musical experience, as the strains of distant orchestras wafted through the living room.

The invocation of transcendental imagery affected conceptions of radio itself. Rather than being characterized as a deliberately-constructed *invention*, the medium was often described as having been *discovered*; as a music educator intoned in 1930: "*Radio* has always been in the air, but our finite minds have only now discovered it."[12] Pitts Sanborn, music critic at the *New York World Telegram*, referred to radio as "this intangible thing that has been summoned as though by magic from the vasty deep of a great silence" and "an entity, a living, all-pervading force."[13] In addition, the tangible aspect of studio equipment, paradoxically, performed sightlessly and soundlessly as though nonexistent—as though it were a framing device equivalent to the concert hall. As late as 1963, Benjamin Britten claimed that "[the loudspeaker] is not a part of true musical experience," again reflecting the notion that there is some kind of ideal musical essence that is separate from its physical manifestations.[14] Therefore, though recognizing radio's implications for the *dissemination* of music, most of the musical community saw radio as having no deep implications for the true nature and experience of music.

This idealistic theory about radio and music often collided with the reality of radio broadcast, which competed for audience attention with distractions not present in a concert hall. As Daniel Gregory Mason observed in 1928, "how can any artistic experience have value, in which the audience is in a purely passive condition—in which it may turn off at any moment the performance . . . or, what is even worse, turn it on at any moment as a not quite successfully ignored background for conversation?"[15] Though Mason complained of audience passivity, in fact, it is precisely the opposite phenomenon that bothered him: the ability of listeners to take a kind of action not allowed within the confines of the concert hall. The mistake is revealing; had Mason allowed for the possibility of an active audience, he might also have had to allow for the possibility that the environment in some way affected the essence of the music or opened the boundaries of musical sound to question. A passive audience allowed classical music—and thus a transcendental conception of its essence—to remain intact.

Critics and educators were not the only ones who accepted the transcendental paradigm. Although American composers produced numerous works for radio, they generally accepted the old concert hall model without critical scrutiny. Their innovations were generally those of timbre, or of the use of accessible idioms in deference to the mass radio audience, rather than any more radical conception of radio or the listening experience. With the exception of Varèse, America's new radio composers posed no fundamental challenge to the notions of John Sullivan Dwight.[16]

While the dominant view of radio stressed compatibility with and continuity of nineteenth-century perspectives, a few who were working with new media prophesied that radio would have a far more profound impact not only on the modern aural experience, but on basic approaches to creativity itself. German psychologist and critic Rudolf Arnheim's 1936 treatise on radio represents the most thoroughly developed early theory of radio and sound. There is no evidence that Arnheim's writing had any direct influence on Cage. Even so, the critic's celebration of an inclusive world of sound and his observations about its effect on modern listeners are strikingly relevant to the creative leap the composer would make in *Imaginary Landscape No. 1*. For Arnheim, who began his career as a film critic, radio constructed an experience based on the aural rather than the visual, creating a new artistic unity between categories of sound that formerly inhabited separate realms:

> In wireless the sounds and voices of reality claimed relationship with the poetic word and the musical note; sounds born of earth and those born of the spirit found each other; and so music entered the material world, the world enveloped itself in music, and reality, newly created by thought in all its intensity, presented itself much more directly, objectively and concretely than on printed paper: what hitherto had only been thought or described now appeared materialised, as a corporeal actuality.[17]

Arnheim cautioned that "wireless must not take any part in enlarging the gap between music and natural unmusical sound,"[18] and in passages such as this, he stressed the new relationship between the "musical" and the "extra-musical," highlighting the role of radio in allowing natural sounds to interact with speech and music in an intense, concrete aural world.

Arnheim's discussion of the ways in which radio opened up the world of sound extended to the recognition of new patterns of perception that the twentieth-century listener might develop:

> The new aural education by wireless, which is so much talked about, does not consist only of training our ear to recognise sounds, so that it can learn to distinguish the hissing of a snake from that of steam, and the clanking of metal from the clatter of porcelain. Such a discrimination is doubtless desirable: it brings about, so to speak, the enrichment of the aural vocabulary by whose help the loudspeaker describes the world. But it is more important that we should get a feeling for the musical in natural sounds; that we should feel ourselves back in that primeval age where the word was still sound, the sound still word.[19]

Clearly, by creating a world through sound unmediated by visual input, radio had the ability to suggest images "more directly, objectively and concretely than on printed paper" and could allow the listener not only to hear more but to hear *differently*.

German filmmaker Oskar Fischinger was another contemporary whose experiments with sound and new media actually had a direct influence on Cage. In the early twenties, Fischinger began a restless search for film-making tools and techniques in order to advance his goal of creating "color music," that is, film in which the unfolding of visual images mirrored the "absolute" and abstract qualities of music. For Fischinger, the music in his films was to aid the audience in "understanding and accepting abstract visual images."[20] His films were accompanied by scores in many styles, which ranged from jazz and light concert music to Richard Strauss and Paul Hindemith.

Among his projected enterprises were filmed accompaniments to Leopold Stokowski's transcription of J.S. Bach's *Toccata and Fugue in D Minor* and Paul Dukas's *Sorcerer's Apprentice*—ideas that eventually bore fruit in Disney's 1941 animated classic *Fantasia*, although ultimately Fischinger was never associated with this project.[21]

One particular concept espoused by Fischinger directly affected Cage: the correlation between an object's sound and its spiritual essence. One day, Fischinger's wife dropped a key in another room, and he was fascinated by the fact that he could ascertain immediately the identity of the object. He went on to theorize that an object's characteristic sound was an emanation of its spirit, therefore documenting the unity of the outward, material world of science and the inner truth of spirituality.[22] In his own creative work, this notion led to experiments with drawing and filming objects directly onto the soundtrack portion of the film in order to achieve a unity of visual image and sound. To Cage it implied an expanded and idealized conception of musical sound to include objects that were not conventional musical instruments. As Cage often stated when recalling Fischinger's impact on his own music:

> [Fischinger] made a remark to me which dropped me into the world of noise. He said: "Everything in the world has a spirit, and this spirit becomes audible by its being set into vibration." He started me on a path of exploration of the world around me which has never stopped—of hitting and scratching and scraping and rubbing everything, with anything I can get my hands on.[23]

As Calvin Tomkins observes, Fischinger's idea expanding the potential boundaries of music ultimately facilitated Cage in his own quest to liberate music from the pitch-based compositional models with which he was becoming increasingly frustrated.[24]

Overall, then, the musical community hailed radio's advent primarily in terms of its effects on the dissemination of music across new social and geographical boundaries, and secondarily in terms of the desirability or undesirability of the new physical contexts in which music was consumed. The legacy of nineteenth-century transcendentalism obscured the importance of radio as a technology in favor of its role as an intangible, ineffable medium and consequently its potential as a creative tool. Within this cultural context, however, a few isolated individuals looked beyond these parameters, investigating the means by which radio's de-contextualized sounds raised both new aesthetic issues and creative possibilities.

When Cage himself turned to radio as a compositional device with *Imaginary Landscape No. 1*, he drew both from these new conceptual models as well as from the general aural landscape that had been reconfigured by this technology. As suggested at the beginning of this essay, in many ways this work's most fundamental departure from tradition centers around its specification that it must be realized in a radio studio, while the actual "performance" would occur through a live or "pre-recorded" broadcast. The first page of the score indicates the setup and procedure to be followed:

> This composition is written to be performed in a radio studio. 2 microphones are required. One microphone picks up the performance of players 1 and 2. The other, that of players 3 and 4. The relative dynamics are controlled by an assistant in the control room. The performance may then be broadcasted and/or recorded.[25]

These straightforward instructions constitute a direct challenge to the more popular perception of radio as an unseen, natural, even spiritual vehicle for musical dissemination. Radio is no longer an intangible medium for the transmission of pure musical substance; instead, Cage's simple words thrust the technology itself to the forefront of both the performance and listening experiences.[26]

Cage's insistence on broadcasting as essential to the work also has important ramifications for the relationship between music and its environment, responding to the way in which radio, and to a lesser extent recording, radically disrupt the boundaries of traditional musical composition. For example, within a traditional concert hall framework, performers can be perceived visually, and it is clear to both eye and ear when any given composition begins and ends. Even in those instances when performers are placed offstage or in the orchestra pit, their sounds are contained within the ostensibly soundless frame of the concert hall. An individual may enter or leave, but the stable existence of the hall ensures that this is only an issue of individual experience and does not affect the organic unity of the music itself.

On first consideration, it might seem that radio merely substitutes the distant broadcast studio for live performers, and that whatever context in which the broadcast is received substitutes for the frame of the concert hall. If this were so, the boundaries of the musical composition would be as stable as in a traditional concert hall, merely increasing the listener's freedom to enter and leave any performance in perfect anonymity, tuning in or out at will. Yet radio places the sounds of a musical composition into environments that are not soundless frames. They contain sounds, both natural and constructed, that are essential to their functions. Whereas in a concert hall the sound of a person changing position, for example, is incidental to its purpose, the opposite holds true in a kitchen. Thus the listener who hears a radio broadcast of a Beethoven quartet in a kitchen where someone is cooking confronts sounds that cannot merely be reabsorbed into a silent frame but assert themselves as autonomous, with equal claim as constitutive elements in the experience. In this kind of physical environment, the individual sounds of a broadcast composition assume a new relationship both to each other and to the listener. Since there is no frame marking the boundaries between a composition's sounds and those of its environment, and thus no definitive way to relate individual moments to a greater whole, each sound exists not as an organic part of a whole but as a discrete entity. This allows—even forces—the listener to focus on the actual physical presence of the sound, and, as Arnheim described, encourages a finer discrimination of sound. Furthermore, these circumstances contribute to a renewed perception of both "natural" and "unnatural" sound, since both typically inhabit a broadcast listening space. Rather than a one-way relationship in which the listener receives sound in the relatively stable and neutral environment of the concert hall, the listener must be engaged actively in sorting through the heterogenous assortment of sounds (the cooking noises versus the Beethoven quartet), thereby constructing an artistic experience.

As *Imaginary Landscape No. 1* was immediately broadcast to a theater, it could be argued that the piece was re-inscribed within a soundless frame. It would be in later pieces, beginning with *Imaginary Landscape No. 4*, that Cage would tease out all the implications of revising the relationship between sound and its environment through the use of radio.[27] Yet the specific requirement of broadcast performance and the intentional use of broadcast technology in *Imaginary Landscape No. 1* presented a radical aesthetic proposition nonetheless, and it is against this backdrop that Cage's individual innovations in timbre and rhythmic structure are best understood.

Certainly the most obvious aural aspect of *Imaginary Landscape No. 1* is its timbre, in which the "non-instruments" of the studio claim equal prominence with acoustic instruments. Cage's performance instructions indicate the importance he attached to timbre. Handwritten notes in the score give instructions for the turntable that include "earthy" and "sensational." By "sensational," he seems to mean less that he wants the sound to be "astonishing" than producing a distinctive sensual effect. In the fourth section, the notes include "drama intensified" and "apparent distance." The timbres in this piece derive from two variable-speed phono-turntables, frequency recordings, muted piano, and cymbal. Cage's use of frequency recordings—the test tones of the studio—as the generator of meaningful sound, is particularly significant. As Frances Dyson has observed, in using these recordings, Cage transforms the radio studio itself into an instrument, since the tones were considered part of the studio apparatus—in essence, part of the medium—consequently breaking down the dichotomy between object and process:

> Entering the radio studio, Cage leaves behind the everyday notion of objects and locales, positioning the aural within a continually shifting field where sound fluctuates between the acoustic and the electronic or radiophonic, the object and the quasi-object, the produced and the reproduced.[28]

In other words, Cage takes the formerly neutral medium and foregrounds its relationship to both its environment and its end result.

Cage's choice of frequency recordings has a corresponding impact on a listener's perception. No listener would immediately perceive this sound emanating from a speaker as falling within the boundaries of a musical piece; in fact, this particular sound traditionally defined a space that was not only explicitly non-musical but was not intended to be noticed by the listener at all. *Imaginary Landscape No. 1* forces the listener to disengage the actual sound from its conventional use and meaning, consciously apprehending it first as a discrete phenomenon and then as an aesthetic object, all the while becoming conscious of the instantaneous and normally unconscious process of assigning meaning to sound. In this way, the use of frequency recordings goes far beyond the mere expansion of the instrumental spectrum, simultaneously challenging the nature of radio and of musical sound itself.

Cage's interplay between the acoustic and electronic instruments in this work reinforces this aesthetic and perceptual reorientation. As stipulated in the performance instructions, the two groups are divided by microphone, (players one and two on electronic instruments on one microphone, players three and four on acoustic instruments on the other), establishing an initial opposition of the acoustic and the electronic in performance. These are merged, however, in the broadcast performance, and the displaced listener receives the sounds as a single stream. The piece begins with the electronic instruments, which predominate throughout the first section; however, both the electronic turntables and the acoustic piano ultimately use glissandi, establishing an equivocal relationship by reconciling opposed instruments through common gestures. This electronic opening suddenly gives way to a staccato pattern in the piano accompanied by the cymbal, a fully acoustic timbre in stark contrast to the opening section. By the end of the piece, however, this acoustic/electronic dichotomy dissipates, as all of the sound sources appear carefully layered with one another, finally fading into silence.

In addition to innovations in timbre, *Imaginary Landscape No. 1* features a sectional form based on time and rhythmic structures rather than on pitch structures. In Cage's own words:

> Four 15-measure sections divided into three equal parts alternate with three interludes and a coda. Each interlude is one measure longer than the preceding one. The first, one measure long, introduces three rhythmic elements which one by one are subtracted from the interludes to be added one by one to the middle parts of the second and third and to the final part of the fourth 15-measure section. The completion of this process reestablishes the original form of the interlude, which, by means of repetition (first of the whole and then of the second half only), is extended, concluding the piece.[29]

The rhythmic units for this work and their evolution are illustrated in Example 4-1.[30]

The dependence on time-based structures occurs at both the level of local rhythmic pattern, most obviously in the interlude, and of larger structural units, creating a fluid and somewhat ambiguous effect. The interlude's $\frac{6}{4}$ time signature is hard to classify, having no standard division into groups of two or three. Cage's opening triplets suggest 3 + 3, but the subsequent rest and ensuing rhythm patterns undermine any consistency of metric subdivision. The pitches of the interlude also reinforce the idea of freedom from patterning. The first two rhythmic triplet groups nonetheless have a pitch pattern suggesting 2 + 2 + 2, while the third group consists of a pitch repeated twice. Unlike these microcosmic rhythmic groupings, the overall sectional form is regular, although the coda interrupts this regularity. Cage himself describes the coda as a four-measure section, but those four measures are virtually identical to the last two measures of Section IV, thereby extending issues of local rhythmic ambiguity to the higher level of formal organization.

For Cage, the move from pitch-based to time-based structures was inextricably linked with the expansion of the sound world through the use of a wider spectrum of timbres. As he observed at a Seattle symposium organized by Bonnie Bird: "Percussion music is a contemporary transition from keyboard-influenced music to the all-sound music of the future . . . Methods of writing percussion music have as their goal the rhythmic structure of a composition."[31] Lou Harrison explained that Cage's rhythmic structure "makes possible a delicacy of structural balance and freedom of poetic thought quite impossible if one tries to employ older structural ideas in the use of new, especially percussive material."[32] Indeed, the construction and evolution of Cage's rhythmic materials exemplify the kind of freedom that Harrison identified.

Example 4-1. John Cage, *Imaginary Landscape No.1*,
rhythmic units.

Interlude 1

Section II.2

... (5 meas.)

Interlude 2

Section III.2

Interlude 3

Section IV.3

If Cage's innovative use of timbre reflects Arnheim's vision of the enriched world of sound made available by radio, the relationship of timbre to rhythm and form reflects an even more radical extension of its compositional implications. As noted above, the interlude of *Imaginary Landscape No. 1* is distinguished by the use of acoustic timbres, and subsequent interludes are also fully acoustic; therefore "identity" comes about not simply through the use of selected rhythmic patterns but through signature timbres that remain identifiable, even as they are broken apart and manipulated in the four 15-measure sections. As the local rhythmic patterns of the interlude are gradually broken apart and define the piece's larger form—the interlude is inserted within the middle of sections with its rhythmic elements in fragmentation—this contrast emphasizes the relationship of timbre and form. When the original acoustic material of the interlude, however, is re-established within Section IV, it is fully integrated with electronic timbres—a long-range effect perhaps best described as moving into an imaginary aural landscape in which familiar acoustic patterns are first disengaged from each other and eventually swallowed by fantastic and unfamiliar electronic sounds.

The element of time (both rhythmic patterning and formal structure) is also linked to timbre through imitation of timbral effects, as Example 4-1 demonstrates. The alternation of triplets and sixteenths in Section III.2, for example, creates the same effect as a turntable's mechanical slowing-down and speeding-up, embedding timbre within the rhythmic material. Since this effect was previously associated with the electronic instruments, the effect further reinforces the contradictory relationship between acoustic and electronic instruments. In larger structural units, the beginning of Section IV.3 states the one-measure interlude twice, but over a three-, rather than two-measure span. The cumulative effect not only undermines the form as it has been reiterated throughout the entire composition, but it recreates both the duple/triple ambiguity of the original pattern, and, in larger units, the effect (both timbral and rhythmic) of slowing down that had been created in the sixteenths and triplets. Finally, the overlapping of Section IV and the Coda simultaneously stretches that Section and contracts the Coda—again, echoing in structural terms the effect of mechanical slowing down and speeding up.

In all aspects of *Imaginary Landscape No. 1*, Cage's procedures might be summarized as "assemblage," in that he seems to have put together scraps of sound rather than develop a single idea organically. This approach underscores the way in which radio broadcasting can undermine a composition's organic unity by placing it in a less than neutral environment; it relates, more generally, to the developing twentieth-century aural experience, wherein the listener first assembles and must then sort through bits of disconnected sound—as the hypothetical listener to Beethoven at dinner time. At a deeper level, the idea of "displacement" typifies this work. The local rhythmic patterns are based on displacement of the beat; on the larger scale, rhythmic patterns are progressively disassembled and re-assembled, carrying displacement to the level of overall structure in the composition. Ultimately, these various levels of compositional displacement become an extension of the displacement between sound, object, and listener that radio entails.

From the smallest surface element to the fundamental structures, then, *Imaginary Landscape No. 1* marks a creative response to both tangible and intangible changes in the twentieth-century environment facilitated by radio. The piece also signals a pivotal point in Cage's development, for when his explorations incorporated the electronic devices of the radio studio, consequently enabling the musical elements to function in a different relationship, his philosophical conception of sound took an important step. Cage's later work with silence and chance operations in the 1950s is inconceivable without the awareness of sound as "a continually shifting field" in which the boundaries of art and environment are no longer clear—or, as Arnheim expressed, "the sounds and voices of reality [claim] relationship with the poetic word and the musical note."[33] Cage's chance compositions built on this initial experience in which the incongruous, almost arbitrary nature of sound with no visible means of production suddenly illuminates the world of all sound, embracing even that which is presumably separate from the act of composition. For Cage, the issue was no longer that of a "pure" musical essence that existed separate from its environment but rather a "continually shifting field" in which the boundaries of sound, its medium, and its environment were infinitely movable:

> Urgent, unique, uninformed about history and theory, beyond the imagination, central to a sphere without surface, its becoming is unimpeded, energetically broadcast. There is no escape from its action. It does not exist as one of a series of discrete steps, but as transmission in all directions from the field's center. It is inextricably synchronous with all other, sounds, non-sounds, which latter, received by other sets than the ear, operate in the same manner.[34]

Cage's incorporation of specific mass media terminology ("broadcast," "transmission," "received by other sets") is evidence of the influence of the technology on his conception of sound. But even without such literal clues, the perspective of sound as "a sphere without surface," describes a sonic world reconfigured by the effects of technology, or as perennially *becoming* rather than *constituting* a unidirectional, congruous and stable element. Of his work specifically for radio, Cage said, "It wasn't really a leap on my part; it was, rather, simply opening my ears to what was in the air."[35]

While Cage was tinkering within the radio studio at Cornish during the late 1930s, Edgard Varèse labored over *Espace*, a radio work of major proportions on which he ultimately spent more than a decade's worth of effort. And while both composers explored the potential of the new medium and drew inspiration from artistic innovations in other media, their underlying aesthetic orientations were radically different. Varèse, on the one hand, conceived of a grand piece exploiting radio's potential to unify humanity; Cage approached the medium out of his interest in abstracted, individual sounds. Or, in terms that Marshall McLuhan popularized three decades later, Varèse sought to expand his message through the dimensions of its medium (radio) by composing a piece unconstrained by outmoded technical limitations. Cage's work unified medium and message at a more concrete level, making a sound-object of the medium itself.

Like Cage, Varèse turned to radio for both its concrete new timbres and for its more theoretical aesthetic promise. Further, he was similarly influenced by the work of Oskar Fischinger, whom he apparently met in the United States.[36] The filmmaker's philosophy of sound and spirit resonated with a phrase that Varèse himself frequently invoked: that of Hoëne Wronsky (1778–1853), who claimed that music was "the corporealization of the intelligence that is in sounds."[37] The composer's odyssey in search of materials by which to realize his artistic visions was propelled by these romantic concepts of the relationship between sound and spirit, as well as an interest in the expanded possibilities of twentieth-century media.

Espace, therefore, was one step in a larger quest, one in which Varèse spent years on a series of multi-media compositions with idealistic themes. As Olivia Mattis has described, *Espace* was to be:

> . . . the utopian work that haunted the composer for most of his "silent years." It was to be a space-age theatrical production, combining text, music, color, movement and projected lights or film. The composer was forever searching for the perfect text to express his conception, and so the project took a variety of names: *The-One-All-Alone, Sirius, Espace, Il n'y a plus de firmament* and *L'Astronome*.[38]

The composer's aesthetic conception of this work incorporated a political dimension, at least in the broadest sense of "politics" as the outward revelation of ideology. This is made evident in his description of the text and plan for *Espace*, published in 1941:

Chorus is to be used to the full extent of its possibilities: singing laughing, humming, yelling, chanting, mumbling, hammered declaration, etc. Theme: TODAY. The world awake! Humanity on the march. Nothing can stop it . . .

Rhythms change: quick, slow, staccato, dragging, racing, smoothe. [sic] The final crescendo giving the impression that confidently, inexorably the going will never stop . . . projecting itself into space . . .

Voices in the sky, as though magic, invisible hands were turning on and off the knobs of fantastic radios, filling all space, criss-crossing, overlapping, penetrating each other, splitting up, super-imposing, repulsing each other, colliding, crashing. Phrases, slogans, utterances, chants, proclamations. China, Russia, Spain, the Fascist states and the opposing Democracies all breaking their paralizing crusts.

What should be avoided: tone of propaganda as well as any journalistic speculating on timely events and doctrines. I want the epic impact of today stripped of its mannerisms and snobbisms . . .

Also some phrases out of folk-lore, for the sake of their human, near-the-earth quality. I want to encompass everything that is human, from the most primitive to the farthest reaches of science.[39]

If Varèse's manifesto gives little sense of his technical approach, it does make clear that modern technology was to transcend the old boundaries of art and pre-existent ideology, combining the unconscious eloquence of ritual with the hyper-conscious eloquence of abstract art.

Although *Espace* took different forms over the period during which Varèse labored over it, radio was a consistent essential to Varèse's conception. The work would be broadcast from points around the globe:

Varèse had imagined a performance of the work being broadcast simultaneously in and from all the capitals of the world. The choirs, each singing in its own language, would have made their entries with mathematical precision. The work would have been divided up into seconds, with the greatest exactitude, so that the chorus in Paris—or Madrid, or Moscow, or Peking, or Mexico City, or New York—would have come onto the air at exactly the right moment. All men could have listened simultaneously to this song of brotherhood and liberation.[40]

Radio, therefore, was fundamental both from the technical perspective of the work's performance and from its symbolic role as a unifying force among disparate peoples. Even so, the composer disparaged the idea of devising compositional techniques specifically for an existing medium, including the microphone, feeling rather that composers should write whatever they heard, contending, "it is up to the engineers to transmit what you want."[41]

Perhaps it is fitting that the score for a radio work should have vanished into thin air.[42] The only tangible result of over a decade's work on *Espace* was *Etude pour Espace*, a sketch performed in 1947 at the Greenwich House Music School in a concert sponsored by the New Music Society.[43] Clearly, the composer's conception had evolved significantly from the original plan. The unpublished score distills but one step in the process, yet the sixty-nine-measure piece for two pianos, chorus (with individual soloists) and a large percussion section is revealing. Elliott Carter, who attended the performance, recalled the piece as "a most stimulating score, suggesting a whole world of new possibilities not thought of at that time."[44]

In *Etude pour Espace*, the chorus sings no identifiable words but rather vocalized syllables. Fernard Ouellette comments:

> Perhaps for the first time in the history of music, Varèse dispensed with a coherent text having a meaning of its own and instead selected various phrases from different languages, none having any meaning in relation to the others, and perhaps not even in itself, since one would at least have to know all the languages to begin with.[45]

Virgil Thomson's review of the 1947 performance alluded to the text as "poems in English and Spanish, plus invented syllables."[46] It is difficult to know which is correct, for although there are isolated syllables that could be construed as being in English or Spanish (e.g., "out," "yet," "mind," "*sin*" [Spanish *without*], "*o chay*" [Spanish *eight*]), there is no way to determine if meaning is deliberate, implied or simply coincidental. The instructions to the vocalists include "mumbled, like in trance," "almost mumbled," "nasal—closed mouth," "hissing," and "hum."[47] Whatever the source of the vocal parts, it is clear that Varèse intended the words to reach the listener as incoherent fragments. Ouellette points out that the variety of sonorities in the chorus make it "a sort of percussion section."[48] This revised relationship between traditional musical sound and speech recalls Arnheim's contention that listeners should place themselves "back in that primeval age where the word was still sound, the sound still word."[49]

Varèse's radio-indebted conception of space operated on multiple levels. "Espace," or "space," refers in this case to the great geographical territory embraced within radio's potential: "Voices in the sky, as though magic, invisible hands were turning on and off the knobs of fantastic radios." The term also refers to Varèse's concept of the compositional potential of space. Rather than a fixed element—or dimension—that never forms part of a composition (even while limiting it), Varèse moved space to the forefront, emphasizing the element as equal to time and frequency (pitch). As he expressed in 1936:

> I became conscious of a third dimension in the music. I call this phenomenon "sound projection," or the feeling given us by certain blocks of sound. Probably I should call them beams of sound, since the feeling is akin to that aroused by beams of light sent forth by a powerful searchlight. For the ear—just as for the eye— it gives a sense of prolongation, a journey into space.[50]

Much later, Varèse voiced his notion in this way:

> I think of musical space as open rather than bounded, which is why I speak about projection in the sense that I want simply to project a sound, a musical thought, to initiate it, and then to let it take its own course. I do not want an *a priori* control of all its aspects.[51]

Space, then, is an element composed directly into the score. While Varèse did not embrace aleatory methods for *Espace*, his use of broadcasting from disparate sources into disparate environments clearly acknowledges the implications of a world in which new technology allowed for the realization of sounds that were beyond the dictates of the composer.

Example 4-2 illustrates the beginning of *Etude pour Espace*. In the opening measures, Varèse establishes a set of shifting relationships among three sonorities: piano, voices, and percussion.[52] In addition, he creates a framework in which the texture seems governed by the spatial rather than the temporal dimension; that is, the musical elements emerge as though appearing and reappearing on scattered planes rather than progressing through a linear development. Robert Morgan described this aspect of Varèse's manner of manipulating pitches:

> Each pitch appears to occupy more a position in musical space than a moment in musical time. . . . In Varèse the pitches appear not so much to "move" to other pitches as to be "displaced" by them: certain positions in the tonal gamut simply give way to others. The effect seems spatial rather than temporal.[53]

In comparison to the composer's unique manipulations of spatial texture, the melodic and harmonic procedures involved in this work seem far less innovative. Both the diminished chord in the opening

Example 4-2. Edgard Varèse, *Etude pour Espace*, mm. 1–3.

solo as well as the reiterated fourths, for example, borrow from musical techniques traditionally used in programmatic works to invoke a "primitive" and ritualistic mood. Indeed, Varèse's fluctuating use of various types of seconds, thirds, and sevenths keeps the piece anchored, if not in genuine tonality, at least in triadic sonorities. However, categorizing the piece primarily in melodic and harmonic terms misconstrues its nature, for rather than linear and vertical relationships that produce traditional textures that can be described as homophonic, polyphonic, etc. (horizontal and vertical processes within a fixed spatial grid), the relationships in *Etude pour Espace* allow even traditional tonal passages to exist in a new kind of spatial relationship.

Varèse left no specific commentary explaining the procedures used in *Etude pour Espace*. Certainly, however, the configuration of sounds into disparate points and planes complements the original plan of simultaneous broadcast from disparate geographical points. The performance conditions of the *Etude* obviously precluded literal reception of sounds from different points, but even within the resources available, the techniques discussed above built in a new kind of spatial dimension among the parts. As in *Imaginary Landscape No. 1*, the elements reflect the composer's conception of radio's potential; in particular, the innovations in vocal sonority and texture are tied to the radio-based conception of the text.

No version of *Espace* was ever performed again in Varèse's lifetime.[54] Instead, *Déserts* represents the ultimate result of the composer's dream. The importance of radio for *Déserts*, while not on the grand scale he had originally conceived for *Espace*, was still integral. The premiere was broadcast by two radio stations, each with half the signal; in order to achieve the intended effect, a listener had to tune into two different stations.[55]

Imaginary Landscape No. 1 and *Espace* represent the most original musical responses to radio in Depression-era America. Both Cage and Varèse broke from convention by approaching their works from the perspective of broadening definitions of musical sound, devising works that included "noise" and were structured on bases other than pitch. Yet both works were dependent on radio more profoundly than in the narrow sense of being broadcast, or even in the sense of being conceived idiomatically for this medium. Both emanated from the new sensory environment of radio—an environment that was also a result of phonograph, film, and the other technologies of modern life. Both works—and both composers—epitomize Marshall McLuhan's later declaration that: "The serious artist is the only person able to encounter technology with impunity, just because he is an expert aware of the changes in sense perception."[56] Even so, their respective sensitivities led these two composers in opposite directions in their work with radio.

Varèse operated within a paradigm that emphasized radio's potential for enhanced musical expression. In a 1962 lecture he contended: "Our new medium has brought to composers almost endless possibilities of expression, and opened up for them the whole mysterious world of sound,"[57] and for Varèse, this "whole mysterious world of sound" facilitated the grand re-integration of music with its environment. The choral "non-language" text of *Espace*, for example, was designed to be more expressive than language—not to deny the possibility of expression.

Ouellette touched on the relationship between Varèse and his environment when he declared that: "Varèse assumed our age as it is, and lived it in its totality. That is why his music is much more tragic than it is nostalgic . . . there is no analogy between a tragic vision and a nostalgic impulse."[58] The tragic vision requires the ability to extrapolate from the individual level to one larger-than-life; as Varèse declared, "the epic interests me."[59] Varèse's struggle to find both a medium and a message capable of expressing his epic vision makes him difficult to classify in terms of the modern dichotomy of "progressive" and "conservative" tendencies. In commenting on this aspect of Varèse's work, Mattis cites Joan Peyser's characterization of Varèse as "romantic" and concludes, "Varèse's conception of the 'human point of view' was the quest—indeed, his own personal quest—for the unknown, the unheard and the unseen."[60] His approach to radio, therefore, encompasses one of the central issues of twentieth-century art: how to sustain a coherent personal vision within a world that lacks coherence not only in its substance but in its media. The sense of a personal quest could indeed be classified as romantic, even though Varèse's attitude toward a new realm of sound separated him from romantic epigones, composers whom Varèse dismissed as "too timid to trust themselves to go forward without a guide."[61]

Both Varèse and Cage faced the same creative paradox, namely, that any artwork that made sense as a self-contained system was incompatible with the dislocations and abstractions of the twentieth-century aural environment, while any that reflected these dislocations was no longer an artwork—at least in the traditional sense. Cage, however, made the choice to collapse the boundary between environment and artwork, a choice that Varèse found untenable. If Varèse incorporated the tragic and the nostalgic within a personal vision, Cage dealt with the new environment simply by sidestepping any such personal aesthetic quests in order to return the listener's attention to sound itself. It is telling that although both composers were influenced by Fischinger, Varèse seized on the spiritual, expressive aspects of Fischinger's ideas, while Fischinger's legacy to Cage was more in terms of focusing attention on sound, on "hitting and scratching and scraping and rubbing" everything in his environment. The epic, transcendent vision of Varèse contrasts sharply with that of Cage, who operated within a paradigm in which the nature of the medium was also the nature of the composition: a creative tautology that negates any possibility of transcendence.

This creative tautology is clear in the way that Cage's score uses what we might term "sound effects," a concept that acquired a new meaning with radio. The use of specific imitative effects within a musical composition is well known (for example, the bird-noises of Renaissance madrigals or the storms in Vivaldi's concertos), and in this context, while a flute or violin solo may sound like a bird, it always retains its identity as musical language. The case of radio-style sound effects is somewhat different, as the displaced listener accepts the aural meaning not as what the sound "really" is (birdseed dropping on a board) but rather what its *effect* is (rain). This substitution separates the source of a sound from its understood meaning and allows transcendence into the imaginative realm of drama. Beginning with *Imaginary Landscape No. 1*, Cage explores sound effects in a tautological sense, in which the sound effect equals sound. The frequency recordings in this piece, for example, achieve their meaning not by leaving the fixed and unassuming realm that they had previously inhabited to assume a different, "musical" role but by ignoring the transparent distinctions between sound and music.

The above suggests that in Cage's approach, he does not seem to enlarge boundaries so much as deny them, and his understanding of the distinction between these two strategies demonstrates how far ahead of his time he was in his comprehension of radio's implications. Decades later, McLuhan discussed the attitude that contended that the medium created no fundamental break in the nature or perception of reality, an attitude he dubbed "somnambulism." In particular, he cited David Sarnoff's assertion that "the products of modern science are not in themselves good or bad; it is the way they are used that determines their value." McLuhan noted that Sarnoff "ignores the nature of the medium," and further responded: "It has never occurred to General Sarnoff that any technology could do anything but *add* itself on to what we already are."[62] Not surprisingly, Cage fell under the spell of McLuhan, saying in 1967 that "not a moment passes without my being influenced by him and grateful to him."[63]

Ultimately, both Cage and Varèse sought an enriched aural vocabulary. But Varèse sought the capture of a totality—"the epic impact of today," while Cage pursued the essence that McLuhan called "integral and decentralist."[64] For Varèse, the broadcast needed to be worldwide and in perfect synchronicity all over the globe in order to fulfill his goals. *Imaginary Landscape No. 1* was broadcast to the dance studio a few steps away—a geographical fact that had absolutely no bearing on the work's aesthetic conception: the broadcast had no purpose except to be itself. Cage underscored these aesthetic differences in his own comments on Varèse in 1958. While celebrating Varèse as the one who "fathered forth noise into twentieth-century music," Varèse's innovative techniques, such as those in *Espace*, ultimately operated within a personal vision that could be expressed in ideological terms. As Cage wrote, "the presence of [Varèse's] imagination is strong as handwriting in each of his works . . . in these respects Varèse is an artist of the past. Rather than dealing with sounds as sounds, he deals with them as Varèse."[65]

The history of *Espace* traces one artist's search for coherence and consonance between the ideology and technology of his day. In radio, Varèse found the potential for both a geographic and an ideological space that was "open rather than bounded." Perhaps he understood that any realization would have necessarily bounded the space, inevitably imposing fixed interpretations on a piece he wanted to leave open-ended. This is perhaps responsible for Varèse's gradual disillusionment with radio; by 1945 Varèse wrote to André Jolivet deploring commercials and Hollywood-style radio.[66] He expressed similar sentiments in 1948 in the journal *possibilities*, sneering that "music is reaching the level (let's hope it is the bottom—it seems hardly possible to sink lower) of radio, Hollywood and their audiences."[67] In the long run, radio's potential remained unfulfilled, and Varèse's vision was finally frustrated; Ouellette refers to it as "tragic."

Cage, in contrast, was gradually won over to the medium. After his years in Seattle, he sought to take advantage of the forward-looking programming available on network broadcasts. Upon moving to Chicago in 1941, he contacted Davidson Taylor of CBS and as a result was commissioned to provide music for a Columbia Workshop play. Cage recalled that he originally wanted Henry Miller to write the script, but that Miller turned down the opportunity, and that he next selected Kenneth Patchen. Their collaboration produced "The City Wears a Slouch Hat," scored for six instrumentalists.[68] The instruments and sound effects include a wide variety of traditional percussion instruments (bell, maracas, claves, etc.), special effects with traditional instruments (piano struck with a gong beater), and sound effects such as a thundersheet, an alarm, and a record of a baby crying.[69] Later Cage recalled his desire to "elevate the sound effect to the level of musical instruments."[70]

In subsequent years Cage continued exploring the possibilities of radio. In *Imaginary Landscape No. 4* for twelve radios, the dials were manipulated according to directions that Cage arrived at through chance operations, turning around the creative tautology of *Imaginary Landscape No. 1*; rather than using radio's electronic instruments to broadcast, the composition uses radio's broadcasts as its instruments. The most significant radio work of Cage's later years was for West German radio, beginning in 1979 with *Roaratorio*. And in contrast to Varèse's disillusionment, he even incorporated radio into his own daily environment, commenting, "I now frequently compose with the radio turned on, and my friends are no longer embarrassed when visiting them I interrupt their receptions."[71]

The results of Cage's denial of the boundary between environment and artwork inevitably resulted in compositions that reflected the displaced, fragmented nature of the twentieth-century aural landscape. This quality has led Charles Hamm to describe Cage as "thoroughly postmodern":

> Postmodern criticism has given us a lovely set of words to associate with the style of Cage's music: open, play, disjunctive, anarchy, chance, silence, process, participation, dispersal, anti-narrative, mutant, polymorphous—qualities present in Cage's music long before postmodern critics developed their vocabulary.[72]

It is noteworthy that this "postmodern" quality of Cage's music is directly related to the way broadcasting changed the twentieth-century musical experience. And while *Imaginary Landscape No. 1* may initially seem most interesting for its new approaches to sound and structure, in the larger view, these elements are surface reflections of a more significant reorientation of the relationship between sound and its environment.

Cage once remarked that:

> Having written radio music has enabled me to accept, not only the sounds I there encounter, but the television, radio, and Muzak ones, which nearly constantly and everywhere offer themselves. Formerly, for me, they were a source of irritation. Now, they are just as lively as ever, but I have changed. I am more and more realizing, that is to say, that I have ears and can hear. . . . Machines are here to stay, or for the time being. They can tend toward our stupefaction or our enlivement. To me, the choice seems obvious and, once taken, cries out for action.[73]

Cage's career played out this cry for action. From the structural innovations of the 1930s through the radical philosophies of the 1950s and after, his use of musical materials increasingly reflected an aesthetic posture whose roots are in *Imaginary Landscape No. 1*. As David

Nicholls observes, "it is debatable whether Cage's vision of 'the entire field of sound' and the 'all-sound music of the future' is realised in the work."[74] While we can agree with Nicholls that this work falls short of achieving Cage's all-encompassing vision, we can appreciate nonetheless the extraordinary aesthetic step taken in *Imaginary Landscape No. 1*—a gesture even more impressive in the context of contemporary "somnambulism" toward radio. By confronting technology directly, Cage absorbed its transforming impact; by engaging technology as both medium and message, he allowed an imaginative leap "through the looking-glass" into the future of aural experience.

Notes

1.   Marshall McLuhan, *Understanding Media: The Extensions of Man*, 2nd ed. (New York: Signet, 1964), 70.

2.   From an interview with Richard Kostelanetz in "A Conversation about Radio in Twelve Parts," in William Duckworth and Richard Fleming, eds., *John Cage at Seventy-Five* [*Bucknell Review* 32, no. 2], (Lewisburg, PA: Bucknell University Presses, 1989), 277.

3.   The score, including performance instructions, was published by Henmar Press in 1960.

4.   "Cornish School," *Musical Courier*, Feb. 8, 1936, 33.

5.   "Radio Highlights," *Musical Courier*, May 23, 1936, 31.

6.   "New Instructors for Cornish Radio School," *Musical America* (July 1936), 29. A short account of the founding of the radio school can be found in Nellie Cornish, *Miss Aunt Nellie: The Autobiography of Nellie C. Cornish* (Seattle: University of Washington Press, 1964), 245–9.

7.   From an interview with Richard Kostelanetz in *Conversing With Cage*, ed. Richard Kostelanetz (New York: Limelight Editions, 1988), 157.

8.   For a full discussion of these issues, see Susan Key, "'Sweet Melody Over Silent Wave': Depression-Era Radio and the American Composer," (Ph.D. diss., University of Maryland at College Park, 1995).

9.   Michael Broyles, *"Music of the Highest Class": Elitism and Populism in Antebellum Boston* (New Haven: Yale University Press, 1992), 7. The transcendental view of fine-art music also associated it with elite social status.

10.   John Sullivan Dwight, "Music a Means of Culture," *Atlantic* 26 (September 1870): 330.

11.   *Dwight's Journal of Music*, October 4, 1873, 103. Reprint ed. 33, no. 13 (New York: Arno Press, Inc., 1967).

12.   Frances Elliott Clark, "Education Through the Air," *Music Teachers National Association Proceedings* 1930 (Oberlin: Music Teachers National Association, 1931), 208.

13.   Pitts Sanborn, "Radio and Music Appreciation," *Yearbook of the Music Educators National Conference* (Chicago: Music Educators National Conference, 1936).

14.   From Benjamin Britten's remarks "On Winning the First Aspen Award," *Saturday Review,* Aug. 22 1964, 37–39, 51. Reprinted in Elliott Schwartz and Barney Childs, eds., *Contemporary Composers on Contemporary Music* (New York: Holt, Rinehart and Winston), 115–123.

15.   Daniel Gregory Mason, "The Depreciation of Music," in *The Dilemma of American Music and Other Essays* (New York: The Macmillan Company, 1928), 89.

16.   More interesting developments in music for radio were happening in Germany. See Nanny Drechsler, *Die Funktion der Musik im deutschen Rundfunk 1933–1945* (Pfaffenweiler: Centaurus-Verlagsgesellschaft, 1988); Joachim Stange, *Die Bedeutung der elektroakustischen Medien für die Musik im 20. Jahrhundert* (Pfaffenweiler: Centaurus-Verlagsgesellschaft, 1989). Also more interesting were developments in American popular music. I explore the issue of the relationship between radio and popular music in "A Simple Business Proposition: Early Radio and Popular Music," a paper delivered at the conference of the International Association for the Study of Popular Music, Los Angeles, CA, October 1998.

17.   Rudolf Arnheim, *Radio* (New York: Arno Press and The New York Times, 1971 [first published 1936]), 15. Trained as a psychologist, Arnheim left Germany in 1933; he spent six years in Rome and came to the U.S. in 1940, where he taught at Sarah Lawrence College, the New School for Social Research, Harvard University, and the University of Michigan. For an appraisal of his contributions to aesthetics and the psychology of art, see the *Journal of Aesthetic Education* 27, no. 4 (Winter 1993). The essays, all in honor of Arnheim, assess his impact on theories of perception, of artistic production, and of arts education.

18.   Arnheim, *Radio,* 32.

19.   Ibid., 35.

20.   William Moritz, "The Films of Oskar Fischinger," *Film Culture* 58–60 (1974): 50.

21.   Disney's film was based on Fischinger's concept and, to some extent, his animations. See Moritz for a detailed history.

22.   Anecdote included in Moritz, 51–2.

23.   In William Duckworth, "Anything I Say Will Be Misunderstood: An Interview with John Cage," in *John Cage at Seventy-Five,* 18–19.

24.   Calvin Tomkins, *The Bride and the Bachelors* (New York: The Viking Press, 1965), 86.

25.   As explained on the first page of the score. (New York: Henmar Press, 1960).

26.   Caroline Jones has addressed the importance of Cage's relationship to technology in "Finishing School: John Cage and the Abstract Expressionist Ego," *Critical Inquiry* 19 (Summer 1993): 628–665. Her analysis is mainly concerned with the prepared piano, which she calls his "first mature statement" in his search for the "technological sublime." Here I argue for a different perspective on Cage's use of technology: not as an obvious intrusion into an organic environment, but one that renders any such categories problematic.

27.   See Kostelanetz, "Radio and Audiotape," in *Conversing with Cage*, 157–71 and the same author, "John Cage as a *Hörspielmacher*," *Journal of Musicology* 8, no. 12 (Spring 1990): 291–99.

28.   Frances Dyson, "The Ear that would Hear Sounds in Themselves: John Cage 1935–1965," in Douglas Kahn and Gregory Whitehead, eds., *Wireless Imagination: Sound, Radio, and the Avant-Garde* (Cambridge, MA: The MIT Press, 1992), 373–407. Dyson also traces the philosophical journey that led to Cage's re-evaluation of silence and its relationship to non-intentionality, especially his experience in the anechoic chamber that made him conclude that there was no such thing as pure silence.

29.   In *John Cage: Writer*, ed. Richard Kostelanetz (New York: Limelight Editions, 1993), 7.

30.   Deborah Campana examines the rhythmically-based template in her dissertation, "Form and Process in the Music of John Cage" (Northwestern University, 1985). Campana concentrates on the piece as the first example of Cage's use of a rhythmic structure. David Nicholls discusses the way in which the various textures are combined and recombined. (See Nicholls, *American Experimental Music, 1890–1940* [Cambridge: Cambridge University Press, 1990], 204–6.) Neither addresses the issue of Cage's instructions that the piece be performed as a recording or broadcast.

31.   John Cage, "The Future of Music: Credo" (c. 1940), in *Silence: Lectures and Writings* (Middletown, CT: Wesleyan University Press, 1961), 5.

32.   Quoted in James Ringo, "Jokes, Portraits and Collages," *Bulletin of American Composers Alliance* 6, no. 1 (Autumn 1956): 22.

33.   Arnheim, 15.

34.   John Cage "Experimental Music" (1957), in *Silence*, 14.

35.   Cage, interview with Richard Kostelanetz in *Conversing with Cage*, 159.

36.   Moritz gives the date as "around 1940" ("The Films of Oskar Fischinger," 52), although Varèse's multi-media work during the 1930s suggests an earlier date.

37.   See the lectures "Music as an Art-Science" (University of Southern California, 1939) and "Spatial Music" (Sarah Lawrence College, 1959), reproduced in Schwartz and Childs, 199–201 and 204–207.

38.   Olivia Mattis, "Varèse's Multimedia Conception of *Déserts*," *Musical Quarterly* 76, no. 4 (Winter 1992): 570. The "silent years" of Varèse lasted from 1936 until the premiere of *Déserts* in 1954.

39.   Dorothy Norman, "Edgar Varèse: *Ionization-Espace*," *Twice A Year* 7 (Fall-Winter 1941): 259–60. Ellipses in the original.

40.   Fernand Ouellette, *Edgard Varèse*, trans. Derek Coltman (New York: Orion Press, 1968), 132.

41.   [Calla Hay], "River Sirens, Lion Roars: All Music to Varèse," *Santa Fe New Mexican*, Aug. 21, 1936, 2.

42.   Chou Wen-chung surmises that Varèse threw the sketches out, saying that they "were getting in his way" (Post-symposium discussion in Sherman Van Solkema, ed., *The New Worlds of Edgard Varèse: A Symposium* [New York: Institute for Studies in American Music, 1979], 89).

43.   Ouellette gives the date of performance as Feb. 23, 1947. The correct date is April 20, as given by Olivia Mattis and by Chou Wen-chung in "A Varèse Chronology" (*Perspectives on American Composers*, Benjamin Boretz and Edward Cone, eds., New York: W. W. Norton, 1971). There is a review of the concert in the *New York Herald Tribune* of Monday, April 21, 1947. Ouellette corrects the date in the second edition of his book, which only appeared in French (Paris: Christian Bourgois, 1989).

44.   Elliott Carter, "On Edgard Varèse," in *The New Worlds of Edgard Varèse: A Symposium*, 6–7.

45.   Ouellette, *Edgard Varèse*, 163.

46.   Virgil Thomson, "Music," *New York Herald Tribune*, April 21, 1947.

47.   According to Chou Wen-chung, there are three copies of the score, each with different emendations (*The New Worlds of Edgard Varèse*, 89). I am grateful to Olivia Mattis for providing me with a copy of one of them. All references to the score are from this copy.

48.   Ouellette, *Edgard Varèse*, 163.

49.   Arnheim, 35.

50.   "Varese Envisions 'Space' Symphonies," *New York Times*, Dec. 6, 1936, N7.

51.   Gunther Schuller, "Conversation With Varèse," in *Perspectives on American Composers*, 38–39. I am grateful to Olivia Mattis for pointing out that this idea acquired further meanings for Varèse, including, apparently, a more aleatory approach in his work in a 1957 jam session with eight jazz musicians. Mattis discussed this musical collaboration in "The Physical and the Abstract: Varèse and the New York School," paper delivered Nov. 2, 1995 at the American Musicological Society, Sixty-First Annual Meeting, New York City.

52.   Chou Wen-chung points out that the instrumentation represents the available resources for that particular concert rather than Varèse's choice and that this was "absolutely contrary to Varèse's normal way of choosing his instrumentation" (*The New Worlds of Edgard Varèse: A Symposium*, 90). This fact limits the usefulness of commentary about the individual qualities of the sonorities. Yet the way in which Varèse put them together is certainly relevant.

53.   *The New Worlds of Edgard Varèse: A Symposium*, 10.

54.   Chou Wen-chung briefly alludes to the decision not to perform or publish *Espace* in *The New Worlds of Edgard Varèse: A Symposium*, 89–90.

55.   Mattis, "Varèse's Multimedia Conception of *Déserts*," 562.

56.   McLuhan, *Understanding Media*, 33.

57.   From a lecture entitled "The Electronic Medium" (Yale University, 1962), reprinted in Schwartz and Childs, 207–208.

58.   Ouellette, *Edgard Varèse*, 190. One might argue, however, that in a world in which technology traps the past within the present—in which we ceaselessly revisit the past—that nostalgia is inescapable.

59.   Quoted in Mattis, "Varèse's Multimedia Conception of *Déserts*," 574.

60.   Mattis, "Varèse's Multimedia Conception of *Déserts*," 577.

61.   "edgard varèse & alexei haieff questioned by 8 composers," *possibilities* 1 (Winter 1947/8): 96.

62.   McLuhan, *Understanding Media*, 26–27.

63.   From a 1967 essay, "McLuhan's Influence," in *John Cage: An Anthology*, ed. Richard Kostelanetz (New York: Da Capo, 1991), 171.

64.   McLuhan, *Understanding Media*, 23.

65.   John Cage, "History of Experimental Music in the United States" (1958), in *Silence*, 69; also "Edgard Varèse" (1958), in *Silence*, 83–84.

66.   Edgard Varèse to André Jolivet, Jan. 20, 1945. Transcription from the collection of Olivia Mattis.

67.   "edgard varèse & alexei haieff questioned by 8 composers," 96.

68.   Cage recalled this sequence in Richard Kostelanetz, "Radio and Audiotape," *Conversing with Cage*, 158.

69.   The score to *The City Wears a Slouch Hat* is in the New York Public Library.

70.   Kostelanetz, "Radio and Audiotape," 158.

71.   John Cage, "Composition as Process" (1958), in *Silence*, 30.

72.   Charles Hamm, "Epilogue: John Cage Revisited" in *Putting Popular Music in its Place* (Cambridge: Cambridge University Press, 1995), 384.

73.   John Cage, "Letter to Paul Henry Lang" (1956), in *John Cage: An Anthology*, 118.

74.   David Nicholls, *American Experimental Music, 1890–1940* (Cambridge: Cambridge University Press, 1990), 204–6.

5. "A Therapeutic Value for City Dwellers":
The Development of John Cage's Early Avant-Garde Aesthetic Position

Branden W. Joseph

One day [John Cage recalled of himself and Mark Tobey] we were taking a walk together, from the Cornish School to the Japanese restaurant where we were going to dine together—which meant we crossed through most of the city. Well, we couldn't really walk. He would continually stop to notice something surprising everywhere—on the side of a shack or in an open space. That walk was a revelation for me. It was the first time someone else had given me a lesson in looking without prejudice, someone who didn't compare what he was seeing with something before, who was sensitive to the finest nuances of light. Tobey would stop on the sidewalks, sidewalks which we normally didn't notice when we were walking, and his gaze would immediately turn them into a work of art.[1]

While this is not one of Cage's most frequently recounted stories, it is typical of him for the manner in which actual events become, in the telling, parables of his artistic development. The setting is Seattle, where Cage relocated in the fall of 1938 to take a faculty position at the Cornish School.[2] This move marked an important turning point in Cage's career, coinciding as it did with the abandonment of his interest in serial composition in favor of the percussion music that linked him to the "experimental" wing of the avant-garde.[3] Throughout the following decade, in ways both explicit and subtle, Cage would investigate a host of earlier avant-garde ideas, adopting and adapting them for his own ends, in what amounts to an important chapter not only in his own development but also in the broader history of the European avant-garde's translation into the American context.

Within the avant-garde of the late 1930s, stories of an artist like Tobey hoping to modify an individual's perception of the contemporary urban environment were already familiar.[4] Tobey must have been a particularly good companion for Cage's walk through the city, as the modern metropolis was one of his most significant artistic stimuli. Inspired by New York's Broadway, which he first painted in 1935, Tobey developed an abstracted, calligraphic style of painting to evoke the city's energy and dynamism.[5] (Figure 5-1) This was not an environment that the young Cage had previously viewed with any sympathy. Writing to his former teacher, Adolph Weiss, a few months after returning from New York to California in 1935, he lamented:

> Somehow I am very sad that you are staying in New York. It is rarely that fine things come out of immense cities. Rather, it seems to me, reality is sucked in there and becomes unreal, meaningless.[6]

It took Tobey's example (and the much less imposing metropolitan environment of Seattle) to open Cage to an "unprejudiced" vision of such things as urban shacks, alleyways, and sidewalks. Yet however important Cage's revelation with Tobey, it must have served primarily as a reinforcement of the Futurist-inspired aesthetic that he was already pursuing.

In the decade following his move to Seattle, Cage's principal artistic concern was to accommodate the modern subject to his or her social and environmental conditions, conditions which included not only the city's physical surroundings, but also the increasing development of social atomization. The dissolution of community and the cultural traditions by which it was marked had been of concern to Cage since the early 1930s, and as he looked out across the musical landscape he saw two predominant reactions to it. The first consisted of a retreat into traditionalism, an embrace of neo-classicism which Cage rejected out of hand, denigrating those whom he would accuse of "spend[ing] their lives with the music of another time, which, putting it bluntly and chronologically, does not belong to them."[7] Cage also openly disapproved of composers who modernized their subject without consequently modifying its form, lending a superficially progressive or revolutionary air to their otherwise traditional work. As Cage wrote disdainfully, "When this better social order is achieved, their songs will have no more meaning than the 'Star-spangled Banner' has today."[8]

The second camp that Cage perceived consisted of modernists who sought to develop musical form but did so by such individualistic means as to reflect, or even exacerbate, the phenomenon of social fragmentation. In the article "Counterpoint" of 1934, the 22-year-old

Cage lamented "the relative absence of academic discipline and the presence of total freedom" in contemporary music.[9] "Modern Music," he argued, did not properly exist, being only a heterogeneous grouping of more or less distinct individual styles. After listing and briefly discussing some of them, Cage called for the creation of a new universal style appropriate for the age:

> I sincerely express the hope that all this conglomeration of individuals, names merely for most of us, will disappear; and that a period will approach by way of common belief, selflessness, and technical mastery that will be a period of Music and not of Musicians, just as during the four centuries of Gothic, there was Architecture and not Architects.[10]

The contemporary situation was thus a dichotomous one in which musical production accurately reflected the dissolution of social cohesion. While the first reaction, neo-classicism, provided tradition and community at the cost of modernity, the second achieved modernity only by sacrificing a common aesthetic structure. This situation forms the background against which Cage's early avant-garde program developed.

Although Cage found affinities between himself and Tobey, his early artistic orientation was more closely allied with the work of László Moholy-Nagy whom he had met while teaching at Mills College in the summer of 1938.[11] Moholy-Nagy was one of the early practitioners of the avant-garde strategy of perceptual estrangement, the depiction of new and unfamiliar perspectives of the world in order to counteract outworn perceptual modalities. Decades before Tobey achieved his mature style, Moholy-Nagy was already using photography to create such effects. A Moholy-Nagy image, such as that of a Paris street-side drain shot from above and close-up, fulfilled a similar function as Tobey's pedagogical walk with Cage (Figure 5-2). Yet, while both focused perception onto previously unseen aspects of the city, Moholy-Nagy's explicit desire to modernize the individual's perceptual capabilities was closer to Cage's early position.[12] It is likely to have been around the time of their meeting that Cage read Moholy-Nagy's *Von Material zu Architektur* (the English title of which, *The New Vision*, succinctly summarized Moholy-Nagy's artistic project) and found it, "very influential for [his] thinking."[13] Indeed, Cage began to pursue essentially the same goal as Moholy-Nagy, which was, as Sigfried Giedion summarized it:

Figure 5-1. Mark Tobey. *Broadway*, 1935. Tempera on masonite board. The Metropolitan Museum of Art, Arthur H. Hearn Fund, 1942. (42.170) © 2000 Artists Rights Society (ARS), New York/ Pro Litteris, Zurich.

Figure 5-2. László Moholy-Nagy. *Street Drain (Rinnstein)*, 1925. Gelatin-silver print. Courtesy George Eastman House. © 2000 Artists RIghts Society (ARS), New York/ VG Bild-Kunst, Bonn.

> to bridge the fatal rift between reality and sensibility which the
> nineteenth century had tolerated, and indeed encouraged . . . to
> give an emotive content to the new sense of reality born of mod-
> ern science and industry; and thereby restore the basic unity of all
> human experience.[14]

In order to achieve the goal of modernizing *auditory* perception, Cage
allied himself with music's Futurist camps. Although he looked to
many contemporary Futurist composers, Cage held a place of particular importance for the Italian Futurist, Luigi Russolo, author of the
manifesto "The Art of Noises" and originator of modern percussion
music in the West.[15] Soon after arriving in Seattle, Cage began to associate himself with Russolo explicitly, explaining, for example, that,
"Percussion music really is the art of noise and that's what it should
be called."[16] In "The Future of Music: Credo" (c. 1940), Cage would
make his affinity with Russolo clear. Russolo's phrases such as "We
must break out of this limited circle of sounds and conquer the infinite variety of noise-sounds"[17] are clearly echoed in the first line of
Cage's manifesto:

> I believe that the use of noise to make music will continue and
> increase until we reach a music produced through the aid of elec-
> trical instruments which will make available for musical purpos-
> es any and all sounds that can be heard.[18]

Furthermore, Russolo would have been important to Cage not
only for providing indications of a Futurist musical practice[19] but also
for describing the musical equivalent of perceptual estrangement. In
characterizing the state of modern composition, Russolo spun an
apocryphal tale of music's development into an autonomous, transcendental realm:

> Among primitive peoples, *sound* was attributed to the gods. It was
> considered sacred and reserved for priests, who used it to enrich
> their rites with mystery. Thus was born the idea of sound as some-
> thing in itself, as different from and independent of life. And from
> it resulted music, a fantastic world superimposed on the real one,
> an inviolable and sacred world.[20]

Unfortunately, Russolo argued, this old, "sacred" realm of music had
degenerated into irrelevancy, its sounds losing their exotic and awe-
inspiring character and becoming so familiar as to seem, for a Futurist
at least, deadeningly boring.[21] In contrast, the use of noise served two
interrelated functions: it negated the sacred space of music's circum-
scribed sound field, thereby freeing listeners from their habitual perceptual modalities, and it called attention to modern acoustical experiences. As Russolo explained:

> Every manifestation of life is accompanied by noise. Noise is thus familiar to our ear and has the power of immediately recalling life itself. Sound, estranged from life, always musical, something in itself, an occasional not a necessary element, has become for our ear what for the eye is a too familiar sight. Noise instead, arriving confused and irregular from the irregular confusion of life, is never revealed to us entirely and always holds innumerable surprises.[22]

Cage adopted Russolo's understanding of noise as a means of jolting the listener out of his or her habitual acceptance of traditional, outworn sounds. Reinforcing Russolo's position, he declared, "Wherever we are, what we hear is mostly noise. When we ignore it, it disturbs us. When we listen to it, we find it fascinating. The sound of a truck at fifty miles per hour. Static between the stations. Rain."[23]

It was not, however, in "The Future of Music: Credo," but in the earlier and less evidently Futurist lecture, "Listening to Music," attributed to his time in Seattle, that Cage provided a more detailed description of his view of traditional music. In explaining that a focus on musical rules hinders an actual experience of the sounds, Cage's words recall Russolo's foundational myth of music as ideology. Similarly decrying the autonomy or separation of music from an audience's everyday experience, Cage noted:

> in the presence of a musician, the high priest who alone reads the books, most people are afraid to admit any reaction to music, for fear it be the wrong one, or that they mistook the Development for the Recapitulation. This state existing between audience and musicians amounts to an ever-widening gulf and is largely due to the musicians making music obscure, that is: difficult to understand.[24]

Cage went on to explain that "knowledge" of traditional musical structures only made matters worse, for it "often becomes a prejudice. The prejudiced ear is listening not to the sounds, but to the relationships of the sounds, and, not hearing the expected relationships, closes itself."[25] Adherence to such traditional knowledge also impeded music from developing the most modern means available. As Cage contended in his "Credo," "Although the [Theremin] is capable of a wide variety of sound qualities, obtained by the turning of a dial, Thereministes act as censors, giving the public those sounds they think the public will like."[26] Thus, the predicament faced by Cage's listeners was analogous to that which he himself had faced before Tobey taught him to see the urban environment with an unprejudiced eye: outdated musical preconceptions likewise inhibited perception of the modern world. Not coincidentally, perhaps, Cage—like Russolo before him—used a visual metaphor to characterize his opposition to worn-out sounds: "Just as I would recommend not keeping on one's walls pictures which one no longer sees," he wrote, "so I would recommend not listening at all to music which one no longer hears."[27]

In "Listening to Music," Cage argued that because modern and non-western musics violated, ignored, or operated utterly outside of the traditional rules established in the West, they were capable of achieving an estranging effect.[28] Such music, he proposed, ultimately made sound (and noise) audible again by invoking a purportedly direct form of "hearing" against a more prejudiced form of "understanding."[29] This opposition between a mediated and a supposedly unmediated perception has a long history within the avant-garde. In "Listening to Music," however, Cage's distinction is made more precise in the way it describes two types of musical reception.

On the one hand, Cage characterized the receptive mode that the listener adopted before traditional music. In this case, the forms are more familiar (Cage's example is the sonata), and the compositional rules more easily recognized. Consequently, he notes ironically, this mode of listening gives rise to such "games" as "HERE COMES THE THEME or What on Earth is Happening Now?" "Most people will get completely mixed up," he declares, "unless they have learned the rules by heart."[30] Within this mode of listening, the listener maintains self-possession, choosing at will whether to absorb him or herself within the work or remain engrossed within his or her own thoughts. As Cage's comments make clear, when faced with traditional music it is "very easy" for the listener to "[think] about something else while the music is being played."[31] Modern music, on the other hand, denies the listener the illusion of subjective autonomy and plenitude. As Cage explained, "One reason that modern music is not liked by some people is that it is more difficult to wonder what sort of weather there will be tomorrow when Bartok is being played than it is when we are listening to a symphony which we have heard at least twenty-five times."[32]

Between the ideas voiced in "Listening to Music" and those developed in his compositional practice, Cage seems to be struggling to understand the same type of distinction that Walter Benjamin had theorized a few years earlier in "The Work of Art in the Age of Mechanical Reproduction."[33] In this essay, Benjamin argued that the avant-garde practices of collage and photomontage were like cinema in fundamentally disallowing traditional, contemplative modes of reception. Cage's remark regarding Bartok recalls Benjamin's remark about the effect of moving film, quoting Georges Duhamel: "I can no longer think what I want to think. My thoughts have been replaced by moving images."[34] According to Benjamin, what disrupted Duhamel's ability to achieve this "free-floating contemplation"[35] in which he could "abandon himself to his associations,"[36] was the film's use of discontinuous and startling shock effects that were related not only to avant-garde aesthetic practices but also to similar effects produced by modern, and particularly urban, existence. In the modern world, Benjamin observed, "Man's need to expose himself to shock effects is his adjustment to the dangers threatening him."[37] Whether in cinema or avant-garde art, modern montage techniques, he contended, "correspon[d] to profound changes in the apperceptive apparatus—changes that are experienced on an individual scale by the man in the street in big-city traffic, [and] on a historical scale by every present-day citizen."[38]

Like Benjamin, Cage saw avant-garde aesthetic production as integrally related to contemporary metropolitan conditions. In much the same way that collage and montage directly incorporated bits of everyday life such as newspaper clippings and ticket stubs, Cage's early percussion music appropriated noises from urban existence and technological production: struck percussion and machine-made sounds. The perceptual modality thereby fostered was more closely related to that developed to cope with the shocks of modern everyday life. Cage explained this very clearly in one of his early press releases:

> Cage describes his work as the organization of sound. The source of his music lies not in primitive percussion music, but in the contemporary city sounds which are so integral a part of life today. He believes that through organization these sounds lose their nerve-wracking character and become the materials for a highly dramatic and expressive art form.[39]

According to Benjamin, the individual's confrontation with such shocks brought about a "heightened presence of mind" which was necessary to counter their onslaught and thereby cushion their "nerve-wracking" impact. However, Benjamin did not see the resultant mental attitude as a fully conscious form of knowledge or analytic understanding.[40] Instead, he argued that the examination of reality brought about by such aesthetic production was "an absent-minded one,"[41] a reformulation of the individual's habits that was accomplished in a state of "distraction." To a certain extent, this distinction corresponded to Cage's contention in "Listening to Music" that one need not "understand" modern music, but rather must experience, or "hear," it. For Cage, however, the shocks of modern existence seem to have been almost entirely mastered through habit, and his analysis was devoid of that component of dispassionate critical expertise that

Benjamin saw arising with the decline of contemplation and the "aura" associated with the traditional artwork.[42]

For Cage, the notion of updating habitual perception so as to render it capable of countering perceptual shocks was described in terms of "therapy." As he explained in 1943 to a reporter from *Time* magazine, "People may leave my concerts thinking they have heard 'noise,' but will then hear unsuspected beauty in their everyday life. This music has a therapeutic value for city dwellers . . . "[43] More than Russolo, Tobey, or Moholy-Nagy, it was the poet William Carlos Williams who most directly provided Cage with a characterization of music's therapeutic function. On a concert program for the premiere of his *First Construction (in Metal)* of 1939, Cage included a quote by Williams:

> I felt that noise, the unrelated noise of life, such as this in the subway, had not been battened out as would have been the case with Beethoven still warm in the mind, but it had actually been mastered, subjugated. The composer has taken this hated thing, life, and rigged himself into power over it by his music. The offense had not been held, cooled, varnished over, but annihilated, and life itself made thereby triumphant. This is an important difference. By hearing such music, seemingly so much noise, when I actually came upon noise in reality, I found I had gone up over it.[44]

Cage had appropriated this passage from "George Antheil and the Canteline Critics," an article that appeared in 1928 in the avant-garde literary journal *transition*.[45] In it, Williams lambasted the critics' reaction to Antheil's U.S. concert premiere and defended in particular his performance of the *Ballet Mécanique*. Invoking a bit of editorial license, Cage excised Antheil's name from the original quotation, thereby rendering it applicable to his own work. By including it on the performance program of his most Futurist piece to date, Cage apparently sought to inoculate his audience against the kind of unsympathetic response that had greeted Antheil over a decade before.[46]

Cage's familiarity with *transition* was not limited to a single article. Rather, it seems that the magazine played a significant, although heretofore unacknowledged, role in the development Cage's artistic ideas. *transition* was one of the most important means of transmitting information about the early European avant-garde to America, and it undoubtedly influenced Cage's understanding of developments on that side of the Atlantic. Introduced to *transition* in Paris in 1930 or 1931,[47] around the same time that he began to pursue modern art and music, Cage later listed it among the works having "the greatest influence on his thought."[48] Subsequently familiarizing himself with the entire run of the journal, Cage specified a preference for the issues of "the twenties," before the publication shifted to American soil and became affiliated with the more staid modernism of the Museum of Modern Art.[49] At the time of Cage's introduction, *transition* had the reputation of being a thoroughly avant-garde magazine associated with an "extremist clique" of aesthetic revolutionaries,[50] a factor that would have attracted Cage as much as the magazine's association with two of his favorite authors, James Joyce and Gertrude Stein. In a sense, Cage became *transition*'s "ideal reader," heeding its call for a new generation of American avant-garde artists and subsequently taking up that call himself.[51] Upon returning from Europe, he immediately set about composing music to accompany writings by Stein and others published in *transition*.[52]

Although primarily remembered today for its association with Surrealism and Joyce, *transition* had its own aesthetic vision known (among variants) as Verticalism. Verticalism was promoted in nearly every issue by the magazine's lead editor and ideologue Eugene Jolas, and he and his other editors' writings were incipient avant-garde manifestos that called for disruptive assaults upon outworn linguistic and artistic rules. Programmatically stating their goals at the end of the first year of publication, Jolas and Elliot Paul, another of *transition*'s founding editors, declared that the journal's evolution, "was directed primarily by the idea that a conscious attitude of disintegration is necessary in order to combat the orthodox inertia characterizing modern art and letters."[53] This avant-gardist attitude, from which *transition* would not swerve until its final issues, reached a culmination with "The Revolution of the Word Proclamation" in which the editors and some of the magazine's fellow travelers declared war on grammatical and syntactic laws, advocating their destruction through an unfettered literary invention of linguistic forms. In each issue, Joyce, Stein, and the more radical practitioners of Dada sound poetry were put forward as examples of the individual's "right to use words of his own fashioning and to disregard existing grammatical and syntactical laws."[54]

At times, not only Cage's outlook, but also his rhetoric seemed to echo *transition*'s style. Claiming in the article "Goal: New Music, New Dance" (1939) that "Percussion music is revolution," he declared that, "a healthy lawlessness is warranted" to emancipate music from its submission to the outmoded "restrictions of nineteenth-century music."[55] Like the "revolution of the word," proposed by Verticalism, Cage's revolution of the noise-sound was to free the entire range of acoustical production from artificially imposed limitations. "The conscientious objectors to modern music will, of course, attempt everything in the way of counterrevolution," he wrote, ". . . But our common answer to every criticism must be to continue working and listening, making music with its materials, sound and rhythm, disregarding the cumbersome, top-heavy structure of musical prohibitions."[56]

Although primarily a literary magazine, *transition*'s call for aesthetic revolution extended to all the arts. In the editorial "Super-Occident," where Jolas most programmatically addressed the future role of music, a young Cage would have found a call for music's modernization, an attack upon its ideological function, and a statement of its relationship to perceptual modernization. "Music, too, is liberating itself from historicism," wrote Jolas:

> The search for new instruments, a minimizing of the use of the old melodic instruments, such as the voice and the violin, a search for new percussions and new intervals that will require a re-education of the human ear, and for a new scale, the development of rhythms that are both violent and unfamiliar, and a complete departure from the concept of music as a drug, a balm, a soothing syrup, or as a literary-programmatic composition, an attempt to give it its place as one of the vital forces of modern life corresponding to the forces of our time—this is the direction music is now taking.[57]

The composer *transition* most prominently featured as accomplishing this goal was George Antheil, who had been the subject of the Williams article quoted by Cage. Between 1927 and 1929, Antheil was the subject of seven articles, far more than any other composer.[58] He was invariably accorded high praise, and statements like, "The *Ballet Mécanique* is surely the most significant musical composition since the *Sacre du Printemps*,"[59] were the rule rather than the exception. Undoubtedly, Cage's early Futurism was as encouraged by Antheil as by Russolo, and at the end of the thirties he began to correspond with the American composer.[60] Comments that Antheil made in the article "Music Tomorrow" about the use of technology, the increased use of silence, and the structuring function of lengths of time all reappear in Cage's own writings.[61] Furthermore, when looking toward Futurism as a means of moving beyond serial composition, Cage would certainly not have failed to recall Antheil's criticism of Schoenberg as "not in the first rank," nor his flatly stated contention that, "Atonality . . . too . . . will have nothing to do with the music of the future."[62]

As vehement as it often was, *transition*'s will to destruction was always tempered by a strong utopian striving for the absolute. The "revolution of the word" was only the initial step in a process that would ultimately lead to the dialectical sublation of the rational and the creative sides of humanity into a new unity, one that in turn would provide the foundation for a new form of organic community. "The creative effort of this age goes towards totality," Jolas explained in the first lines of "Notes on Reality." "To achieve the new image of the world which we dimly perceive on the horizon we disintegrate the universe with all the means at our disposal and transform chaos into cosmos."[63]

transition's emphasis on the dialectical sublation of fragmentation—on both the aesthetic and social level—strongly resonates with Cage's own understanding of the interdependence of the therapeutic and aesthetic functions of music. As his 1942 press release stated, it was through the "organization of sound" that noises were simultaneously to "lose their nerve-wracking character" *and* to create "a highly dramatic and expressive art form." Like Williams, whose description of Antheil emphasized the dialectical reformation of noise into a new artistic unity, Cage saw composition as the formulation of an organic whole. As he declared in "Listening to Music":

> In the case of music, we often find that this organizing has made otherwise startling sounds seem natural. From the beginning to the end of a fine piece of music the sounds follow one another in a natural sequence. The whole problem (. . .) of listening to music is this: Hear the sounds as belonging together. Let the composer spend his days making them belong together.[64]

Despite Cage's embrace of modernity, music was to play a therapeutic or compensatory role, providing a hint or "image" of a utopian moment of reconciliation in the face of the apparent chaos of modern life. As he stated at the conclusion of "Listening to Music," "the natural flow of sounds which music is reassures us of order just as the sequence of the seasons and the regular alternation of night and day do."[65]

Although in "Listening to Music" Cage referred only obliquely to the use of noise (as "startling sounds"), his emphasis on forming an organic totality plays a no less important role in his understanding of percussion music. In order to achieve a therapeutic function, in order for the listener to sublate or "go up over" noise, the mimetic incorporation of city noises alone did not suffice. Rather, as Williams had made clear, these noises had to be "mastered and subjugated" dialectically into the work of art. This idea was further elaborated in "The Future of Music: Credo," where Cage made certain to state that, "We want to capture and control these sounds, to use them not as sound effects but as musical instruments."[66] Here again, Cage's phraseology recalled that of Russolo, who had written:

> And as I conceive it, *The Art of Noises* would certainly not limit itself to an impressionistic and fragmentary reproduction of the noises of life. Thus, the ear must hear these noises mastered,

servile, completely controlled, conquered and constrained to become elements of art.[67]

In collage and photomontage, as well as in poetry and performance, the most radical practitioners of Dadaism specifically opposed the artistic formation of organic wholes. Indeed, a vehement opposition to totality is one of Dada's most important postulates, whether it is understood as the radically anarchic negation of traditional aesthetic rules; as a more sophisticated form of montage in which the inorganically assembled materials force, on a second level of reception, a cognitive grasp of their underlying structure; or as a fragmenting of the apparently inalterable image of the world which thus opens up spaces of action. Yet, Cage seems to have been unresponsive to the most radical, anti-organic strains of European Dada. In both music and the visual arts, the Italian Futurists of whom he had knowledge advocated the reformation of non-traditional and initially shocking aesthetic materials onto a new form of expressive, organic whole. In addition to this totalizing thrust of Futurism, however, a consideration of *transition*'s role in presenting the European avant-garde helps to understand Cage's organicist impulse. For the view that *transition* provided of Dada was one that had been thoroughly assimilated into Jolas's more spiritual and organicist Verticalism.

Despite a close association with André Breton, Jolas had strong misgivings about Surrealism and, in part, because of *transition*'s incessant conflation with Surrealism by critics, his editorials voiced these reservations often. By contrast, he seems to have been entirely content to present his views as an extension of Dada.[68] While publishing the sound poetry of Kurt Schwitters, Hugo Ball, and Tristan Tzara as examples of the revolutionizing of the word, Jolas's sympathies tended toward those examples of Dada that displayed religious or spiritual impulses which more closely accorded with his own interest in Romantic mysticism.[69] Jolas's personal contacts with Hans Arp (with whom he was the closest), Richard Huelsenbeck, and Raoul Haussman all reinforced his impression that spirituality was an important component of Dada, and he saw to it that those aspects of the movement were frequently touted within the magazine.[70] As Hugo Ball wrote in "Fragments from a Dada Diary," "What we are celebrating is at once buffoonery and a requiem mass."[71]

Jolas and the editorship of *transition* never advocated a pure formalism—art for art's sake—or the mere exaltation of the irrational. Although Verticalism was to begin with the revolution of the word, its ultimate goal was a change in social existence, a task in which the artist was to play an integral role. As Jolas affirmed:

> If the liberation of man is the chief aim of action, the function of
> the creator is as essential as that of the politician or the econo-
> mist. The creator liberates with the instrument of the word, the
> plastic organization, the rhythmic composition. His revolution
> aims at a complete metamorphosis of the world.[72]

Cage shared Jolas's understanding of art's effectiveness, arguing in
"The Future of Music: Credo" that music not only provided a model
of reconciled society, but was itself be a means of enacting such reconciliation.[73] In *Double Music* (1941), written in collaboration with
Lou Harrison, Cage attempted to create a musical situation in which
two individuals—in this case, composers rather than performers—
could come together in anonymity, and he equated this method of collaboration with the anonymity associated with Medieval art.[74]

If music was to address Cage's concerns about social fragmentation, however, it was not enough that it be composed in such a manner as to form a whole. Rather, the process of accustoming the individual to the experience of modern sounds had to be founded on a
universal structural principle. Cage speculated that once one or more
such universal musical forms were "crystallized" and had been
absorbed into the common practice, "the means will exist for group
improvisations of unwritten but culturally important music."[75] This
program for developing a universal aesthetic echoed Moholy-Nagy's
artistic outlook and could also be found in the early issues of *transition*. As Jolas wrote in "Literature and the New Man":

> If we wish to find a standard for life and literature, we cannot, of
> course, escape the results of the personal and collective experi-
> ences. But creative expression envisages the combined forces of
> the human spirit. The writer proceeds from his own individuality
> to a connection with the humanity around him. He does not shirk
> the dark and sinister aspects of life. He presents life in its univer-
> sal relationships and is not afraid to destroy in order to create his
> vision.[76]

With such an insistence on the direct connection between music and
society (in which a composition acts both as a model of a social order
for listeners and as an experience of reconciled society for performers),
the question of exactly what structure music should assume takes on
the utmost importance. From the outset, Cage showed himself atten-
tive to the social and political implications of compositional form. He
implicitly linked neo-classical, harmonic composition to a hierarchical structure where "each material, in a group of unequal materials"
was assigned "its function with respect to the fundamental or most
important material in the group."[77] Although in "Counterpoint"
Cage had idealized the Gothic period as one of organic social unity, he

had no interest in returning to such a residually aristocratic form of social inequality. On the other hand, because it functioned without a fundamental tone Cage initially saw Schoenbergian serialism as figuring a more holistic and democratic ideal. "Schoenberg's method assigns to each material, in a group of equal materials, its function with respect to the group," Cage explained, ". . . Schoenberg's method is analogous to a society in which the emphasis is on the group and the integration of the individual in the group."[78] At the time, Cage accepted such integration unproblematically as a worthy aesthetic and ethical ideal. Years later, in discussing his initial enthusiasm for Schoenberg, he would recount:

> . . . those twelve tones were all equally important. . . . one of them was not more important than another. It gave a principle that one could relate over into one's life and accept, whereas the notion of neo-classicism one could not accept and put over into one's life.[79]

Although Cage initially interpreted Schoenberg's aesthetic in relation to his own desire for holistic social cohesion, reinforcing his preference for integration over that of individuality, this would soon undergo a significant transformation. In a 1942 article entitled "South Winds in Chicago," Cage analyzed Paul Hindemith's *Concerto for Violoncello and Orchestra*. In it he reiterated the idea that music acts as an analogue of social structure, although in the case of Hindemith it was not the musical tones but the instrumental parts that were seen as representative of individuals. "It is a concerto in which the soloist is not merely displaying virtuosity," Cage proposed, "but one in which the cello is an individual and the orchestra is the group and the musical relationships are human relationships."[80] As presented by Cage, Hindemith's concerto was a drama of the individual's plight within, and ultimate capitulation in the face of, mass society:

> This is particularly clear in the last movement in which the orchestra sets forth in martial character, the cello remaining distinct and apart, poetic and not marching, having, as it were, another point of view. The cello maintains the individual point of view with increasing intensity and up to the last possible moment. It is clear then that the choice is one between insanity and conformance. The latter course is followed and the cello becomes a subservient part of an overwhelming orchestra.[81]

The social condition that Cage outlines here is related to the same isolation of the individual from the community that he had commented on in 1934. In Hindemith, however, Cage did not find a utopian reformulation of a modern Gothic age, but a representation of the individual's authoritarian subsumption into the mass, describing Hindemith's musical figuration of society not in terms of "common belief" and "selflessness," but through allusions to militarism and forced conformity. Hearing the concerto in the context of America's entry into the war and the domestic conscription it entailed may have been a factor in prompting Cage into reevaluating his earlier call for social unity. Particularly in light of the Italian Futurists' embrace of Mussolini, Cage may have looked back at the implications of his abandonment of serialism in the late-thirties in favor of the noise music of Russolo—who had wished to hear his materials "mastered, servile, completely controlled, conquered and constrained"—as somewhat more ominous.[82] Whatever the exact cause, over the next few years Cage's understanding of the requirements of a utopian, organic community would change. While never abandoning the hope of social unification, Cage would begin more clearly to defend individual difference as a necessary component within it, a stance in which may be found the beginnings of his later anarchist ethos.

In the polemical "Defense of Satie," delivered in the summer of 1948 at Black Mountain College, Cage made his revised position clear. In this lecture, he opened once again by decrying the contemporary state of social fragmentation:

> On the one hand, we lament what we call the gulf between artist and society, between artist and artist, and we praise (. . .) the unanimity of opinion out of which arose a Gothic cathedral, an opera by Mozart, a Balinese combination of music and dance. . . . We admire from a lonely distance that art which is not private in character but is characteristic of a group of people and the fact that they were in agreement.[83]

While continuing to place a positive valuation on cultural agreement—even holding to the example of Gothic architecture—Cage now carefully articulated his opposition to mass conformity: "I would say that in life we would not be pleased if all of us dressed alike. . . . We feel imposed upon by G.I. clothing, Baltimore housing, and we would not like poetry in standard English or Esperanto. In the area of material, we need and are enlivened by differentiation."[84] A certain individuality, in fact, must be preserved, Cage further explained; this is why, "we admire an artist for his originality and independence of thought, and we are displeased when he is too obviously imitative of another artist's work."[85] Cage's problem was one of finding a universal aesthetic form that would allow the preservation of individual difference, "an art that is paradoxical in that it reflects both unanimity of thought and originality of thought."[86]

In the remainder of his lecture, Cage attempted to determine which aspects of aesthetic production should be agreed upon and which not, deciding ultimately that it was the structure of the composition that had to become universal, while form (by which Cage meant something more akin to expressive content) should remain free from uniformity; the nature of the materials and the methods of connecting them could be either conventional or individualistic. That having been decided, the question once again became that of the proper structure for music to take. Cage's answer was that compositions should be based on divisions of time ("rhythmic-" or time-structures)—a technique he had used since his *First Construction (in Metal)*, but which he now firmly and flatly declared to be correct—while all compositions based on traditional forms of harmonic structure were deemed to be wrong. Blaming Beethoven for instigating modern harmonic composition, and crediting Webern and Satie with the invention of compositional structures based on lengths of time, Cage asked:

> Was Beethoven right or are Webern and Satie right?

> I answer immediately and unequivocally, Beethoven was in error, and his influence, which has been as extensive as it is lamentable, has been deadening to the art of music.[87]

Cage famously justified this declaration by arguing that only a structure constructed on time lengths could accommodate the entire range of acoustic possibilities without discrimination, including not only sound and noise, but also silence, which at this point Cage still understood as the absence of sound.[88]

If, during this second phase of his early development, Cage continued to reject harmony as a legitimate basis for composition, it was no longer because he understood it to represent an inegalitarian social formation, nor simply because he had never had any natural inclination for it. Rather, his increasingly vehement opposition to harmony reflected a different understanding of its role. In part, this can be attributed to Cage's introduction to the writings of Indian art historian Ananda K. Coomaraswamy, writings that greatly reinforced his convictions about the crisis of Western culture.[89] For Coomaraswamy, the contemporary social crisis was caused by the rise of individuality that began in the Renaissance and severed the individual's ties not only to the remainder of society but also to reality's more universal and spiritual manifestations. Post-Renaissance Western art was an expression of the individual's alienation, an alienation which, Coomaraswamy contended, distinguished it from the healthier outlook characterizing Asian and Medieval Western perceptions of art.[90] Although Cage seems to have come to understand harmony as a metonym of Western culture in general, his opposition to it was not simply motivated by a loose definition of the latter's spiritual bankruptcy. Rather, as he explained in "The East in the West" (1946), his opposition was predicated on an understanding of harmony's connection to commercialism. "This element, harmony, is not medieval nor Oriental but baroque," Cage declared in allusion to Coomaraswamy's ideas, "Because of its ability to enlarge sound and thus to impress an audience, it has become in our time the tool of Western commercialism."[91]

Earlier in 1946, Cage voiced his opposition to commercialism clearly in a stinging critique of George Antheil. In a short piece written for *Modern Music*, he outlined the progressive cooption by commercial interests of one of his former avant-garde models. According to Cage, the first corrupting influence to which Antheil succumbed was that of "Stravinsky and the business of neo-classicism," soon after which he "was persuaded to write operas with the pre-Hitler German opera-loving audiences in mind."[92] More devastating than either Antheil's embrace of harmonic structure or his purported flirt with fascist aesthetics, however, was the "spell of Hollywood," under which he fell after returning to the United States. "He took some time," Cage noted wryly, "to recognize Hollywood's commercialism as a bad influence, incompatible with serious composition."[93] Reproaching Antheil for a "cheap gaudiness" of character no less than of composition, Cage concluded by connecting these commercial interests to both harmonic structure and the desire to impress the masses through kitsch and musical pandering:

> The part of Hollywood that stays with him still is his interest in writing for the "great public." This confirms his present choice of models: late Beethoven, Mahler, Bruckner, and, as he himself says, "even Sibelius." There is no longer any remembrance of the dream; instead he dedicates the *Fourth Symphony* to "Hedy Lamarr and all the living heroes of all countries," the *Fifth* to "the young dead of this war, the young dead of all countries." Something quite empty is being inflated with a vast amount of volatile profundity.[94]

Two years later, Cage was even less reticent about linking harmony to commercialism, holding that the "decadence"[95] into which Beethoven had thrust music was at one with the crisis brought on by capitalism. Toward the end of "A Composer's Confessions," he reiterated his conviction that harmony served only "as a device to make music impressive, loud and big, in order to enlarge audiences and increase box-office returns,"[96] and shortly thereafter he launched into a veritable tirade about the current state of music and composition:

> I don't sympathize with the idealization of masterpieces. I don't admire the use of harmony to enlarge and make music impressive. I think the history of the so-called perfecting of our musical instruments is a history of decline rather than of progress. Nor am I interested in large audiences or the preservation of my work for posterity. I think the inception of that fairly recent department of philosophy called aesthetics and its invention of the ideas of genius and self-expression and art appreciation are lamentable. I do not agree . . . that what . . . should inspire others to write music today is the rising crescendo of modern industrialism. I think this and the other ideas I have just been ranting about may be labeled . . . as being sheer materialistic nonsense, and tossed aside.[97]

Although his views were augmented by Coomaraswamy's conviction of the West's cultural decline and the role that the idea of expressive genius played within it, Cage was still passionately lamenting the same social fragmentation he had lamented since the early thirties. Yet that which Cage previously credited to individual stylistic divergence he now attributed to the pursuit of commercial success. It was, he declared, the composer's desire for "fame, money, self-expression and success," that had "[brought] about the state of music as it is today: extraordinarily disparate, almost to the point of a separation between each composer and every other one, and a large gap between each one of these and society."[98]

For Cage, music's implication within the modern social crisis was not confined to neo-classicism, the Hollywood culture industry, or the associated cult of expressive genius. Avant-garde musical production was equally compromised by commercialism, especially the Futurist strain to which he had earlier been dedicated. For Cage, the current state of social fragmentation seems to have been attributed to the loss of spiritual belief and the rise of consumer society: "That which formerly held us together and gave meaning to our occupations was our belief in God. When we transferred this belief first to heroes, then to things, we began to walk our separate paths."[99] Rather than being an oppositional or even conciliatory force, Futurist music—with its pursuit of ever new sounds, noises, and the technological means to produce them—merely traveled in the wake of these developments, confronting a decaying cultural superstructure with the aesthetic possibilities of a modern economic base. By 1948, the realization of a homology between Futurism and capitalist development led Cage to renounce his earlier Futurist project. "In view of these convictions," he confessed, "I am frankly embarrassed that most of my musical life has been spent in the search for new materials." Connecting the modernist exaltation of the new to the perpetual manufacture of consumer desire, Cage explained of this declaration:

> The significance of new materials is that they represent, I believe,
> the incessant desire in our culture to explore the unknown. Before
> we know it, the flame dies down, only to burst forth again at the
> thought of a new unknown. This desire has found expression in
> our culture in new materials, because our culture has its faith not
> in the peaceful center of the spirit but in an ever-hopeful projec-
> tion on to things of our own desire for completion.[100]

In part, Cage's idealization of Eastern and pre-Modern Western cultures was based on the conviction that they were free of the corrupting influence of commodification. The interrelation between Cage's
turn toward the East and his opposition to harmony and commercialism was most clearly articulated at the conclusion of "Defense of
Satie":

> It is interesting to note that harmonic structure in music arises as
> Western materialism arises, disintegrates at the time that materi-
> alism comes to be questioned, and that the solution of rhythmic
> structure, traditional to the Orient, is arrived at with us just at the
> time that we profoundly sense our need for that other tradition of
> the Orient: peace of mind, self-knowledge.[101]

Cage's use of the term "disinterestedness" to describe this peace of
mind further supports the supposition that his opposition to commercialism played an important role in shifting his thinking toward
Eastern philosophy. If in the Huang-Po *Doctrine of Universal Mind*
the idea of disinterestedness refers to a dispassionate stance toward
worldly existence,[102] in "A Composer's Confessions," where Cage
first mentions it, its use seems weighted toward a meaning of "not for
commercial gain":

> If one makes music, as the Orient would say, *disinterestedly*, that
> is, without concern for money or fame but simply for the love of
> making it, it is an integrating activity and one will find moments
> in his life that are complete and fulfilled.[103]

Even as Cage brought more of the Eastern nuances of disinterestedness into play, he maintained the connotation of anti-commercialism
as an important aspect of his use of the term. As he wrote, for example, in the "Lecture on Nothing," "Continuity today, when it is necessary, is a demonstration of disinterestedness. That is, it is a proof
that our delight lies in not possessing anything."[104]

There is a second half to the story that Cage told about his
enlightening walk with Mark Tobey. The setting is no longer Seattle
but New York, to which Cage had returned in 1942 after spending a
year teaching in Chicago at Moholy-Nagy's New Bauhaus. The story's
second part largely replicates the first, with the difference that it is no

Figure 5-3. Mark Tobey. *Crystallization*, 1944. Tempera on paper. Private Collection. © 2000 Artists Rights Society (ARS), New York/ Pro Litteris, Zurich. Photo: Geoffrey Clements.

longer Tobey the artist but Tobey's art that provides Cage with an appreciation of the urban environment. "[T]here was an exhibition at the Willard Gallery which included the first examples of white writing on the part of Mark Tobey," Cage recalled:

> [W]hen I left . . . I was standing at a corner on Madison Avenue waiting for a bus and I happened to look at the pavement, and I noticed that the experience of looking at the pavement was the same as the experience of looking at the Tobey. Exactly the same. The aesthetic enjoyment was just as high.[105]

Cage subsequently purchased one of the paintings in that show, a work entitled *Crystallization* (1944) for which he paid on an installment plan over the course of a year (Figure 5-3).

Yet this half of the story is somewhat deceptive. For if, by 1944, the year of Tobey's show, Cage could declare himself accommodated to the physical aspects of the modern urban environment, he could not make the same claim with regard to its saturation by commercialism. He lamented the commercial nature of life in New York, which he referred to as "the center and the marketplace."[106] And although he claimed to be able to perceive even the pavement in an aesthetic manner (thanks to Tobey), he nonetheless conceded the necessity of turning away from the city to find the spiritual tranquillity he so desired. As he acknowledged in 1948, it was only within the relative retreat of his apartment on the East River, "which turns its back to the city and looks to the water and the sky," that he was able to contemplate the spiritual side of musical composition.[107]

Along with the change in Cage's characterization of the city came a change in his understanding of the social illness that it caused—the illness for which music was to serve a therapeutic function. Previously described in terms of a vague nervous disorder associated with perceptual shock, he now explicitly introduced the term "neurosis" to describe this social malaise. Somewhat humorously, Cage stated in "Defense of Satie":

> We go so far as to give some credence to the opinion that a special kind of art arises from a special neurosis pattern of a particular artist. At this point we grow slightly pale and stagger out of our studios to knock at the door of some neighborhood psychoanalyst.[108]

Although Cage may be referring to his own experience with psychoanalysis or to a more general interest in psychoanalytic therapies within the New York art scene, in "A Composer's Confessions" he provided a much more specific diagnosis, explaining that the cause of this neurosis was occupational specialization and the division of labor:

> The occupations of many people today are not healthy but make those who practice them sick, for they develop one part of the individual to the detriment of the other part. The malaise which results is at first psychological, and one takes vacations from his job to remove it. Ultimately the sickness attacks the whole organism.[109]

This idea resonated strongly with Coomaraswamy's ideas about the separation of individuals from spiritual knowledge. However, in addition to the unquestionable importance of Coomaraswamy and other sources of Eastern thinking, Cage's ideas about the contemporary individual's neurosis—as well as the clinical vocabulary he used to describe it—seem to have derived from sources with which he was already familiar, namely *transition* and Moholy-Nagy.[110]

Cage stated that one of the things that most interested him in Moholy-Nagy's *The New Vision* was the discussion of the plight of the modern individual. As Cage recalled:

> Near the beginning of Moholy's book there is a circle which describes the individual, an individual human being, and shows that the individual is totally capable, that is to say, each person is able to do all the things that any human being can do. But through circumstances and so forth we often become specialists rather than whole people.[111] (Figure 5-4)

Moholy-Nagy made clear that these circumstances were those of contemporary capitalism, specifically the division of labor foisted on individuals for the purpose of maximizing profits. "Today neither education nor production springs from inner urges, nor from urges to make goods which satisfy one's self and society in a mutually complementary way," Moholy-Nagy explained:

> The educational system is the result of the economic structure. During the frenzied march of the industrial revolution, industrialists set up specialized schools in order to turn out needed specialists quickly. These schools in very few instances favored the development of men's power. They offered them no opportunity to penetrate to the essence of things, or to the individual himself.[112]

Moholy-Nagy, of course, did not advocate a retreat from this situation, but, urging that "the future needs the whole man,"[113] he proposed reforming education to achieve a more integrated and well-rounded training.

Moholy-Nagy's call for the "whole man" closely resembles *transition*'s promotion of the "new man." As Jolas explained in "Literature and the New Man":

> The new man should combine in himself the possibilities for universality. He will not be the homo faber, the homo sapiens, the metaphysical man, the dionysian man, the automatic man, the economic man. He will be all of them in one. . . . The industrial revolution needs an individual who will blend the intellectual and emotional side of his nature, who will harness science to eternal humanity, who will nullify the antinomy of nature and man.[114]

Figure 5-4. László Moholy-Nagy. Graph of "Sectors of human development" from *The New Vision.* © 2000 Artists Rights Society (ARS), New York/ VG Bild-Kunst, Bonn.

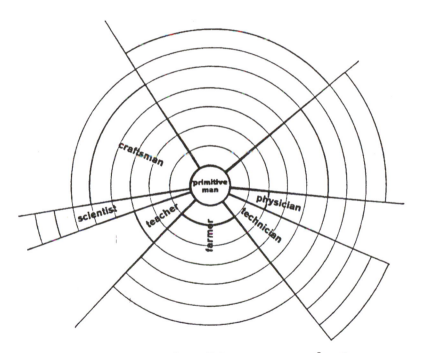

The primitive man combined in one person hunter, craftsman, builder, physician, etc.; today we concern ourselves only with one definite occupation, leaving unused all other faculties.

Although Jolas was as staunchly modernist as Moholy-Nagy, Cage would probably have found Jolas's description of the crisis of Western society and his interest in the spiritual impulses of humanity to have been more compatible with Coomaraswamy's ideas than Moholy-Nagy's were. The recognition of similar ideas within Jolas's uncompromisingly avant-garde program would have provided Cage with a means of overcoming Coomaraswamy's avowed anti-modernism and helped him justify integrating traditional Eastern thought into his still decidedly avant-garde position.[115]

Cage used the same clinical vocabulary as Jolas to describe the situation of contemporary social crisis. Jolas frequently made statements to the effect that the new man, "must needs be against the excessive, decadent individualism which produced the art of the neuroses."[116] Although he railed against such excessive individuality, Jolas resolutely held the view that a new, holistically unified individual was indispensable for achieving the thoroughly reformulated social totality of the future:

> The new man, represented by the creative spirit, will build his work on the consciousness of a purified individualism. It will be an individualism that is sufficiently deep to produce a compensation with groups, races, civilizations, economic systems, and even linguistic aggregations.[117]

Jolas's defense of the individual was categorical. Indeed, the most important principle of his Verticalism was that one had to fight unwaveringly against the contemporary forces of standardization. Throughout his life, Jolas staunchly opposed fascism, communism, and Western mass conformity, all of which he saw as threats to individual difference. He reiterated this opposition continually in *transition*, especially during the early period for which Cage expressed a preference.[118] As Jolas observed in the article "Notes":

> I know the tendency of this age is towards collectivism. . . . We consider the increasing tendency toward centralisation, both in the economic and political sphere, dangerous, unless curbed by a regional consciousness.
>
> . . . [T]he sense of universalism can only develop, when the sense of the indigenous remains as a catapulting force. That is why we regard the development of the collectivistic era in America with so many misgivings, having already observed during the brief period of its prologue how the regional particularities are being destroyed, how the mass consciousness becomes a paroxysm of parallel tendencies, how life in general becomes grey and monotonous.[119]

When Stuart Gilbert, another of *transition*'s editors, looked back over the journal's earliest phase, he characterized the defense of individual difference as its central and defining contribution. In "The Creator is not a Public Servant," Gilbert announced to his readers:

> Standardization is the creator's enemy, standardization of every kind: social, political, economic, linguistic. For standardization, a levelling out and a crumbling away, is the instrument of death, the antithesis of creation.[120]

Afterward, he concluded:

> The disease of our age, one of the many consequences of the war, no doubt, is the desire that every man should fall into line. *By the right . . . Dress!* Against such literary sergeant–majors, whether academical or demagogic, *transition* has waged a Three Years' War. Much ground has been won for the forces of individual creative effort and the occupied territory will be held.[121]

Within this "war," as Gilbert phrased it, one of the clearest communiqués of *transition*'s position was Jolas's editorial, "Super-Occident," the same article that had included his programmatic statement about the musical avant-garde. Here, Jolas summarized the current world situation as "deterministic and anti-individual," making abundantly clear that the emergence of mass movements on both the right and left posed equally troubling threats to individuality.[122] Describing this contemporary cultural leveling as the "metaphysical sordidness" of the age[123]—no less repellent than excessive individuality—Jolas went on to describe it explicitly:

> While concentration of wealth is getting more and more absolute, self-satisfaction, megalomania, cynicism run riot. Mad with mercantile-utilitarian vision, the power of the bankers has centralized everything so that all variations from their arbitrarily established norm are considered pathological cases. A wave of intolerance will sweep the country under the guise of democratic liberalism. The ruthless suppression of all protesting voices will be the result.[124]

Although the nihilistic element of *transition*'s agenda was in direct revolt against this form of cultural standardization, the ultimate end that Jolas was seeking through this agenda was still the utopian, social totality prefigured in Romanticism. This organicist vision differed from the actually encroaching mercantilist totalization of the world, however, because it would embrace difference rather than standardization. In reference to his idea of a "super-occident," Jolas wrote:

> The new Atlantic World . . . will be the prolongation of Europe and Asia combined. It will be made possible by the human adjustment to the mechanical civilization so that not only North-America, but also Latin-America, through mutual inter-penetration of eth-

nic and cultural and linguistic organisms can create a spirit which creates a totality.

But this totality cannot be achieved at the expense of differentiation.[125]

In this, Cage's position in "Defense of Satie" seems descended from the one that was advocated by Jolas and *transition* generally: a utopian social totality initially modeled in a universal aesthetic form, but which protected within its philosophy individual difference.

Before this revolutionary, utopian reconciliation of society could be achieved, however, the fragmentation of the modern individual had to be resolved. In a manner reminiscent of both Coomaraswamy and Moholy-Nagy, Jolas held that an increasing mechanization and industrialization had led to an unhealthy split within the subject, which, in Jolas's words, "made the clash between the rational and irrational a grave one."[126] For Jolas, the non-rational aspects of reality with which the individual had to be reunited lay in both the unconscious and the spiritual realms, and he drew frequently and explicitly upon the lessons of psychoanalysis. Although *transition* had evinced a sustained interest in Freudian psychology, as of late 1929 it began instead to champion the work of Carl Jung. In the editorial "Literature and the New Man," Jolas critiqued Freud (and the Surrealists who followed him) for being too focused on the individual's neurosis:

> Although we stand in reverence before the genius of the scientist who in *The I and the It* and more recently in *The Malaise in Civilization* has gone beyond his initial point of departure, we feel nevertheless that he does not entirely meet our conceptions of the creative spirit. By reducing everything to the dogma of a neurosis, he eliminates layers of the poetic genesis that are essential for esthetic understanding.[127]

In Jung's writings, Jolas found a contemporary understanding of the unconscious that related not only to the personal but also to the universal and "the collective life of humanity."[128] This more closely coincided with the spiritualist element of *transition*'s avant-garde position which likewise attempted to access universal totality. Jung's work also encouraged Jolas to seek the possibility of a therapeutic means by which to foster the individual's holistic integration. As Jolas hypothesized, the new man, who would unite in himself all aspects of human personality, "will become conscious to a very high degree, because he will finally, through [Jungian] analysis, come to know himself."[129]

It is probably then not coincidental that after "eighteen months of studying oriental and medieval Christian philosophy and mysticism," Cage "began to read Jung on the integration of the personality."[130] In a form compatible with Cage's interest in South Asian philosophy, Jung expressed the necessity of overcoming the limitations of the self, the individual ego, and the isolated neurosis in order to achieve artistic creation. With reference to Jung, Cage explained in "A Composer's Confessions":

> [A] composer may be neurotic, as indeed being a member of contemporary society he probably is, but it is not on account of his neurosis that he composes, but rather in spite of it. Neuroses act to stop and block. To be able to compose signifies the overcoming of these obstacles.[131]

Whatever Jung he read at the time, Cage would already have been acquainted with these ideas from "Psychology and Poetry," the article that Jolas translated for *transition* and for which his "Literature and the New Man" served as an introduction. In it Jung explained:

> [T]he essence of the work of art does not consist in the fact that it is charged with personal peculiarities—in fact the more this is the case, the less the question of art enters in—but that it rises far above the personal and speaks out of the heart and mind and for the heart and mind of humanity. The personal is a limitation, yes, even a vice of art.[132]

Like Jolas, Cage saw artistic expression as a way to fulfill the same function as Jungian psychoanalysis. As he pointed out in "Defense of Satie," "Music then is a problem parallel to that of the integration of the personality: which in terms of modern psychology is the co-being of the conscious and the unconscious mind, Law and Freedom, in a random world situation."[133] Or as he explained earlier in "A Composer's Confessions":

> Music does this by providing a moment when, awareness of time and space being lost, the multiplicity of elements which make up an individual become integrated and he is one.[134]

In statements such as these, we encounter a position reminiscent of that espoused by Cage a decade earlier in "Listening to Music," a position that emphasizes the moment of individual reconciliation within an encompassing musical experience. Cage still sought to fulfill a therapeutic function within society; however, by this time, the goal was no longer that of overcoming of the shock of modern acoustical stimuli, but of allowing the individual to experience a moment of unity that transcends a psychic fragmentation brought on by modern economic specialization. As he wrote in reference to performances of Webern and Ives:

> We were simply transported. I think the answer to this riddle [of the music's effect] is simply that when the music was composed

the composers were at one with themselves. The performers became disinterested to the point that they became unselfconscious, and a few listeners in those brief moments of listening forgot themselves, enraptured, and so gained themselves.[135]

Jolas's understanding of art's effectiveness—it's role in promoting or actually producing social and subjective change—led him to critique Freud for emphasizing individual fragmentation and neurosis over an integrative form of healing. Cage's likening of Schoenberg to Freud would seem to be a product of a similar line of thinking. Initially linking the two in "The East in the West," Cage wrote that "Schoenberg analyzes and fragmentizes his music, so that he seems with Freud to be a founding father of today's cult of the neurosis."[136] Later, Cage made an additional reference to the same idea in "A Composer's Confessions," citing "the cerebral, even psychoanalytical, and non-sensuous aspect of much twelve-tone music."[137]

Cage's rather oblique criticism of Schoenberg's music for not transcending the level of individual neuroses found its social and aesthetic parallel in his critique of the Viennese master's treatment of musical structure. If, in "The Future of Music: Credo," Cage contended that new compositional forms would likely bear "a definite relation to Schoenberg's twelve-tone system," by 1942 he would begin to critique Schoenberg's serialism for failing to provide music with a new structural basis.[138] Four years later, Cage would begin to argue that Schoenberg evaded or simply negated harmony rather than having founded a new compositional system. "[Schoenberg's] erstwhile avoidance of harmony is neither Eastern nor Western," he wrote in "The East in the West." "It suggests the Orient, since the East does not practice harmony; but, at the same time, since avoidance is an admission of presence, it suggests the Occident."[139]

Although never so bold or straightforward as he would be with regard to Beethoven, Antheil, or Hindemith, the evolution of Cage's thinking brought about a more critical re-evaluation of Schoenberg. By 1948, he fully discounted the possibility of Schoenberg providing a new form of musical structure. Upon making a strict distinction between structure and method in "Defense of Satie," Cage categorized serialism as a mere "method," a means of getting from one place to another within a structure:

> Tonality essential to the artificial harmonic structure of Beethoven disintegrated within fifty to seventy-five years, to bring into being the concept of atonality. This, by its denial of the meaning of harmony, required a new structural means or, let us say, the true structural means. Schoenberg provided no structural means, only a method—the twelve-tone system—the nonstructural char-

> acter of which forces its composer and his followers continually to
> make negative steps: He has always to avoid those combinations
> of sound that would refer too banally to harmony and tonality.[140]

Schoenberg's atonality represented, then, not the rejection or over-throw of harmony, but related only to the "disintegration"[141] or per-haps (considering Cage's allusions to Beethoven) even the "deca-dence" of harmony as a structure that once held sway. [142]

Within Cage's thinking, harmonic disintegration corresponded to the social fragmentation that had arisen with commercialism. Like Freudian psychology, Schoenbergian serialism revealed or reproduced, but did not transcend or remedy, the contemporary crisis of society and the individual. According to Cage, Schoenberg, devoid of a new means of structuring music, necessarily had to rely (albeit negatively) on earlier, outdated ones; as Cage later made clear, "Schoenberg made structures neoclassically."[143] Indeed, in merely representing society's plight under commercialization and the division of labor, Schoenberg, as Cage would come to characterize him, was "simply Beethoven brought up to date."[144] With this evaluation in mind, Cage's earlier observation that Schoenberg's work represented the integration of individuals within a group potentially takes on a different characteri-zation. A compositional model in which a fragmented and atomized musical material was held together by an outdated, neo-classical structure corresponded on a social level to the false sublation of the individual within the group—not the individual's eradication within the martial and conformist mass signaled by Hindemith's orchestra but his or her solitary integration into the "lonely crowd" of Western capitalism.[145]

As Cage first outlined in his critique of Antheil, harmony and commercialism were interrelated, in part, by their common interest in making things big, loud, and impressive. At the time of the Second World War, during which Cage's antipathy toward commercialism developed, he came to the opinion that "there seemed to me to be no truth, no good, in anything big in society," and cited the conglomer-ates "Life, Time and Coca-Cola" as negative examples.[146] "Half intel-lectually and half sentimentally," Cage was led to decide on account of this conviction "to use only quiet sounds."[147] Here, however, he was caught in a reactive stance, merely avoiding the impressiveness of harmony and commercialism. In this respect, the critique he leveled against Schoenberg applied to himself as well, for Cage too was mere-ly—if only more thoroughly—avoiding harmony, providing its simple negation, rather than overcoming or subverting it. In "A Composer's Confessions" of 1948, he seems to have recognized the problematic status of this situation:

My feeling was that beauty yet remains in intimate situations; that it is quite hopeless to think and act impressively in public terms. This attitude is escapist, but I believe that it is wise rather than foolish to escape from a bad situation.[148]

Upon this realization, Cage began to feel it necessary to reconsider the sounds of conventional, harmonic instruments. In "A Composer's Confessions," in which he famously announced his intention to compose a silent piece and a work scored exclusively for radios (realized respectively as 4'33" and Imaginary Landscape No. 4), he also stated his desire to work with a conventional orchestra. As he explained, "Writing for orchestra is, from my point of view, highly experimental and the sound of a flute, of the violins, of a harp, of a trombone, suggest to me the most attractive adventures."[149] This return to conventional instrumentation was not a retreat from his earlier, avant-garde program. Rather, it represented the fulfillment of his goal of formulating an aesthetic structure that could encompass the entirety of available sounds and would lead Cage to a series of significant aesthetic breakthroughs, first in the String Quartet in Four Parts (1949–50) and then in the Concerto for Prepared Piano and Chamber Orchestra (1950–51).

In the Concerto for Prepared Piano and Chamber Orchestra Cage succeeded in producing an example of the aesthetic and social program he had outlined in "Defense of Satie." Like Hindemith's Concerto for Violoncello and Orchestra, Cage's concerto was to act as an analogy of human relationships. In it, the piano plays the role of the individual while the orchestra functions as the group, as it did in the Hindemith work. The integration of Cage's soloist into the orchestral group, however, is figured differently. In Hindemith's concerto, the soloist was described as capitulating to the expressive needs of a uniform, militarist mass, a relinquishing of individuality (and the risk of neurosis) in favor of "conformance." In Cage's concerto, by contrast, the integration of individual and group takes on a different valence. Throughout, the orchestra evinces a disinterested movement from sonority to sonority as determined in an impersonal manner by Cage's use of compositional charts. The piano's progressive move from a subjectively written part to one similarly determined by a series of impersonal moves on the charts (including, in the third movement, Cage's first employment of the I-Ching) represents a release from individual concerns in favor of Eastern forms of disinterestedness. In the final movement of the work, the piano, now having overcome its expressive individualism, is able to come together with the orchestra in such a manner that its presence is never entirely subsumed. Thus, to James Pritchett's characterization of Cage's concerto as representing the resolution of the "law" of compositional structure and the "freedom" of musical content can be added its figuration of the utopian reconciliation of individual and society.[150] With the important role played by the *I-Ching* and the idea of disinterestedness, the work presents Cage's turn toward the East, not merely as a means of escaping the West, but as a means of attaining the new "Gothic" artform for which he had always longed.

Situated at the culmination of Cage's early aesthetic, the *Concerto for Prepared Piano* also marks the beginning of his work's next phase. Cage's integration of chance procedures into the process of composition would immediately be extended in the *Music of Changes* (1951) where even the work's structure would be submitted to the same form of chance determinations as the sequencing of sounds had been in the *Concerto*. Eventually, this would lead Cage to pursue the dissolution of the musical structure that he had sought for over a decade and to focus more explicitly on the independence of individual parts from any overarching organization. The social and political aspects of his thinking would nonetheless remain essential, as the holistic or organicist foundations of his earlier compositional thought were overturned and a pathway opened toward a more explicitly anarchist outlook that he began to espouse openly in 1960.

Notes

1. John Cage, in John Cage and Daniel Charles, *For the Birds* (New York: Marion Boyars, 1981), 158.

2. Cage moved to Seattle in September of 1938. Robert Stevenson, "John Cage on His 70th Birthday: West Coast Background," *Inter-American Music Review* 5, no. 1 (Fall 1982): 10. Both Calvin Tomkins and Michael Hicks erroneously state that Cage moved to Seattle in September of 1937. Calvin Tomkins, *The Bride and the Bachelors* (New York: Penguin, 1968), 89; and Michael Hicks, "John Cage's Studies with Schoenberg," *American Music* 8, no. 2 (Summer 1990): 130.

3. James Pritchett, *The Music of John Cage* (Cambridge: Cambridge University Press, 1993), 9–11. Richard Kostelanetz refers to this as the "chaotic" tradition of contemporary music. Kostelanetz, *John Cage (ex)plain(ed)* (New York: Simon and Schuster Macmillan, Schirmer Books, 1996), 8. On Cage's relationship to the musical avant-garde, see also David Nicholls, *American Experimental Music, 1890–1940* (Cambridge: Cambridge University Press, 1990).

4. See George J. Leonard's somewhat reductive comments on Cage's relationship to the early, historical period of the avant-garde. George J. Leonard, *Into the Light of Things: The Art of the Commonplace from Wordsworth to John Cage* (Chicago: University of Chicago Press, 1994), esp. 136–146.

5.   Eliza E. Rathbone, *Mark Tobey: City Paintings* (Washington, D.C.: National Gallery of Art, 1984).

6.   John Cage, letter to Adolph Weiss (late April, 1935), repr. in William Bernard George, "Adolph Weiss" (Ph.D. diss., University of Iowa, 1971), 310. On the date of this letter, see Hicks. Hicks has established that Cage traveled to New York to work with Cowell and Weiss in 1934 and returned to Los Angeles with Cowell only in December of that year to begin studying with Schoenberg in the spring of 1935. His studies with Schoenberg would last into the following year. (Hicks, 127–130). Nicholls also reports the same dates for Cage's studies with Cowell, Weiss, and Schoenberg. (Nicholls, 182). Calvin Tomkins, Ellsworth Snyder, and, more recently, Thomas S. Hines, however, all erroneously report Cage as having been in New York in the spring of 1933, and having begun studies with Schoenberg the following year. (Tomkins, 84; Ellsworth J. Snyder, "Chronological Table of John Cage's Life," in *John Cage: An Anthology*, ed. Richard Kostelanetz [New York: Da Capo, 1991], 36; and Thomas S. Hines, "'Then Not Yet "Cage"': The Los Angeles Years, 1912–1938," in *John Cage: Composed in America*, ed. Marjorie Perloff and Charles Junkerman [Chicago: University of Chicago Press, 1994], 91–92).

7.   John Cage, "Defense of Satie," (1948) in *John Cage: An Anthology*, 78.

8.   John Cage, "Credo," handwritten manuscript, 1940, John Cage Archive, Music Library, Northwestern University, Evanston, Ill. Repr. in Barry Michael Williams, "The Early Percussion Music of John Cage, 1935–1943" (Ph.D. diss., Michigan State University, 1990), 229.

9.   John Cage, "Counterpoint," (1934) in *Writings about John Cage*, ed. Richard Kostelanetz (Ann Arbor: University of Michigan Press, 1993), 16.

10.   Ibid., 17.

11.   That Cage met Moholy-Nagy at Mills College in the summer of 1938 is recounted by Tomkins, 89.

12.   By the time Cage met Tobey and Moholy-Nagy, he was not entirely unaware of the strategy of perceptual estrangement. Indeed, in the early thirties, when Cage practiced as a painter as well as a musician, he adopted a certain form of perceptual estrangement himself. As he recalled about his early paintings: "What it was was that I would look at a landscape and instead of seeing it straight, I would see it as though it were spherical. As though it were reflected in the headlight of an automobile. . . . I would look at houses and make them in this curious roundness." Paul Cummings, "Interview with John Cage," transcript of tape-recorded interview, May 2, 1974, Archives of American Art, Washington, D.C., 4. What had such an effect on Cage, then, walking with Tobey, seems to have been less Tobey's artistic procedure than the particularity of the urban setting in which it was practiced.

13.   John Cage and Hans G. Helms, *John Cage Talking to Hans G. Helms on Music and Politics*, S-Press Tapes, cassette tape. Excerpts printed in Hans G. Helms, "John Cage," in *Musik-Konzepte: Sonderband John Cage* I, ed. Heinz-Klaus Metzger and Rainer Riehn (Munich: text + kritik, 1990), 18–40 and as John Cage, "Reflections of a Progressive Composer on a Damaged Society," *October* 82 (Fall 1997), 78–93. Cage recalled having read *The New Vision* in the early thirties. However, it seems equally likely that he actually

read the book in the later thirties, probably after having met Moholy-Nagy in person. Cage also notes the importance of *The New Vision* and "various books about the Bauhaus" in John Cage and Joan Retallack, *Musicage: Cage Muses on Words Art Music* (Hanover, N.H.: Wesleyan University Press, 1996), 87.

14.   Sigfried Giedion, "Moholy-Nagy," (1935) in *Moholy-Nagy*, ed. Richard Kostelanetz (New York: Praeger, 1970), 199.

15.   In 1960-61, Cage listed Russolo's "The Art of Noise" as one of the books with the greatest influence on his thinking. John Cage, "List No. 2," in *John Cage: An Anthology*, 138. On Russolo's role as the initiation of the radical avant-garde aesthetic in music, see Cage's comments in Kostelanetz, *John Cage (Ex)plain(ed)*, 63; and in "A Composer's Confessions," (1948) in *John Cage: Writer*, ed. Richard Kostelanetz (New York: Limelight Editions, 1993), 32. Barry Michael Williams quotes a letter written from Cage to the music critic Peter Yates around 1941, in which Cage relates his "Imaginary Landscape No. 1" to Russolo's work. Untitled document in notebook, *John Cage Professor Maestro Percussionist Composer* vol. I, John Cage Archive. Repr. in B. Williams, 203. B. Williams takes Cage's statement "I did not have the background . . . for my work in this field," to mean that "his knowledge of Russolo's work was retrospective." However, from the letter quoted, it appears that Cage is discussing his work prior to 1938, and neither his work nor his thinking of that year or later.

16.   Program, "Percussion Concert," Cornish School Theater, Seattle, December 9, 1938 in notebook *John Cage Professor Maestro Percussionist Composer* vol. 1, John Cage Archive. Cited in B. Williams, 11. See also, Theresa Stevens, "Talent Trails: A Column of Chatty Gossip About Your Seattle Neighbors Who Write and Paint," *Seattle Star*, February 14, 1939, cited in Stevenson, 13.

17.   Luigi Russolo, *The Art of Noises*, trans. Barclay Brown (New York: Pendragon Press, 1986), 25.

18.   John Cage, "The Future of Music: Credo," (c. 1940) in *Silence: Lectures and Writings* (Middletown, CT: Wesleyan University Press, 1961), 3–4. On the date of this writing, see Leta Miller's essay in this collection, 54, 56.

19.   Although Cage's *Imaginary Landscape No. 1* (1939) employed a combination of variable-speed turntables and frequency recordings to create dynamic, sliding glissandi in a manner reminiscent of Russolo's descriptions in "The Art of Noises," Cage's actual knowledge of Russolo's music would have been extremely limited at that time. Cage applied the term "percussion" widely, using it to refer to any music incorporating noise (see "A Composer's Confessions," 32), and he felt that the music of the future had to be "free from the concept of a fundamental tone." Cage, "The Future of Music: Credo," 5. Russolo, on the other hand, was interested primarily in expanding, rather than doing away with, the notion of harmony, arguing that within all noises could be isolated a fundamental tone. See, for example, Russolo, 39. Russolo's famous "noise instruments"—even those with names such as "bursters" and "cracklers"—were not percussive, but involved rotary mechanisms that through variations in speed could, according to him, cover the entirety of a tonal range, creating a microtonal or enharmonic continuum that did away

with the separation in steps in the diatonic scale. For the names and a discussion of Russolo's instruments, see Barclay Brown, "The Noise Instruments of Luigi Russolo," *Perspectives of New Music* 20 (1981–1982): 31–48. Brown also points out that Russolo's actual music "has a clearly harmonic intent." Ibid., 36. (It should be noted that for the purposes of his art of noises Russolo redefines the "fundamental" as the loudest of the complex sounds produced by a noise instrument, not necessarily the actual harmonically fundamental tone.)

20.   Russolo, 23. Emphasis in original.
21.   "Everyone will recognize that each sound carries with it a tangle of sensations, already well-known and exhausted, which predispose the listener to boredom, in spite of the efforts of all musical innovators." Russolo, 25.
22.   Russolo, 27.
23.   Cage, "The Future of Music: Credo," 3.
24.   John Cage, "Listening to Music," (1937/38) in *John Cage: Writer*, 17.
25.   Ibid., 18.
26.   Cage, "The Future of Music: Credo," 4.
27.   Cage, "Listening to Music," 18.
28.   Ibid., 17.
29.   Ibid. For a discussion of the avant-garde strategy of peruptual estrangement and its Romantic pitfalls, see Simon Watney, "Making Strange: the Shattered Mirror," in *Thinking Photography*, ed. Victor Burgin (London: Macmillan, 1982), 154–176.
30.   Ibid., 16.
31.   Ibid., 18.
32.   Ibid.
33.   Walter Benjamin, "The Work of Art in the Age of Mechanical Reproduction," trans. Harry Zohn, in *Illuminations* (New York: Schocken Books, 1969), 217–251.
34.   Ibid., 238.
35.   Ibid., 226.
36.   Ibid., 238.
37.   Ibid., 250.
38.   Ibid.
39.   Statement attributed to John Cage in "John Cage Percussion Group Press Release" in 1942 file, John Cage Archive.
40.   Benjamin, 238.
41.   Ibid., 241.
42.   Benjamin's discussion of the dissolution of the "aura" can be found in "The Work of Art" essay. It is not at all certain that Cage fully shared the avant-garde project of destroying the aura of the work of art. Certainly, he sought through his Futurist music "the liquidation of the traditional value of the cultural heritage" mentioned by Benjamin. (Benjamin, 221). However, Cage's consistent relation of music and musical reception to spiritual impulses and experiences reveals an interest in retaining certain dimensions of art's traditionally cultic orientation. This may reflect Cage's adherence at the time to an outlook akin to that of Carlos Chavez, whose book *Toward a New Music: Music and Electricity* (New York: Norton, 1937) Cage found impor-

tant. (Cage, "List No. 2," 138). In it, Chavez draws conclusions about the role of technology and the technological reproduction of music that are diametrically opposed to those of Benjamin. For Chavez, the use of the mechanical reproduction and electronic transmission of music allow for an increased authenticity of performance and a better approximation of the intentions of the individual, and still hierarchically privileged, composer.

43.　"Percussionist," *Time*, Feb. 22, 1943, 70. Cited in David Wayne Patterson, "Appraising the Catchwords, c.1942–1959: John Cage's Asian-Derived Rhetoric and the Historical Reference of Black Mountain College" (Ph.D. diss., Columbia University, 1996), 108–109, and David Revill, *The Roaring Silence: John Cage: a Life* (New York: Arcade Publishing, 1992), 64.

44.　Revill quotes this passage as from a "note for the premiere of Cage's *First Construction* in 1939." Revill, 65.

45.　William Carlos Williams, "George Antheil and the Cantilene Critics: a Note on the First Performance of Antheil's Music in New York City; April 10-1927," *transition* 13 (Summer 1928): 240. Revill makes no reference to this quotation's original source, perhaps having been led to believe by Cage's program that Williams had provided the quote specifically for his performance.

46.　See also Cage's paraphrase of W.C. Williams in Program, "Cage Percussion Players," Reed College, Portland, Oregon, Feb. 14, 1940 in notebook *John Cage Professor Maestro Percussionist Composer* vol. I, John Cage Archive. Cited in B. Williams, 14–15; and William Fetterman, *John Cage's Theatre Pieces: Notations and Performances* (Amsterdam: Harwood Academic Publishers, 1996), 3.

47.　Hines, 81, and Cage and Retallack, 86.

48.　Cage, "List No. 2," 138. See also Cage's comment in *Conversing with Cage*, ed. Richard Kostelanetz (New York: Limelight Editions, 1994), 133.

49.　Cage, "List No. 2," 138. The first period of *transition* actually comes to a close in June, 1930 with the publication of nos. 19–20 and the suspension of publication at that time. It is almost certain that Cage is referring to the division made upon this break. On the difference in the periods of *transition*, see Dougald McMillan, *transition: The History of a Literary Era, 1927–1938* (New York: George Braziller, 1976), 70–71. A copy of *transition* 26 (1937) for which Duchamp did the cover, was located in Cage's library at the time of his death. That Cage had no other copies is not surprising since, as Patterson reports, Cage sold off his book collection for money during the 1950s. (Patterson, 134.)

50.　McMillan, 3–5.

51.　For *transition's* call for an American avant-garde, see, for example, The Editors, "Introduction," *transition* 1 (April, 1927): 135–138; Jean George Auriol, "The Occident," *transition* 2 (May 1927): 153–159; and Eugene Jolas and Elliot Paul, "A Review," *transition* 12 (March 1928): 139–147.

52.　John Cage, in *Conversing with Cage*, 57.

53.　Jolas and Elliot Paul, "A Review," 139.

54.　*transition* 16/17 (June 1929): 13.

55.　John Cage, "Goal: New Music, New Dance," (1939) in *Silence*, 87.

56.　Ibid. Cf., for example, Jolas: "But before this development is possible, a continuous subversive action will have to take place. Sympathy for any

creative action that tends to destroy the present system should be encouraged.
. . . Combating the sociological and esthetic defenders of this anachronistic
regime must be the fundamental aim." Eugene Jolas, "Super-Occident," *transition* 15 (February 1929): 13

57.   Jolas, "Super-Occident," 14.

58.   Elliot Paul, "Zukunftsmusik," *transition* 1 (April 1927): 147-150;
George Antheil, "Music Tomorrow," *transition* 10 (January 1928): 123–126;
Syd S. Salt, "Antheil and America," *transition* 12 (March 1928): 176–177; A.
Lincoln Gillespie Jr., "Antheil and Stravinsky," *transition* 13 (Summer 1928):
142–144; William Carlos Williams, "George Antheil and the Cantilene
Critics, op. cit.; George Antheil, reply to "Why Do Americans Live in
Europe?," *transition* 14 (Fall 1928): 101–102; and William Carlos Williams,
"The Somnambulists," *transition* 18 (November 1929): 147–151.

59.   Paul, "Zukunftsmusik," 148

60.   The first line of Cage's "Future of Music: Credo," which recalls
Russolo, echoes just as clearly Antheil's pronouncements in "Music
Tomorrow," published in *transition* 10 of January, 1928. On Cage's corre-
spondence with Antheil, see Revill, 64.

61.   See Antheil, "Music Tomorrow," 124. The relationship between
Antheil and Cage's early avant-garde musical aesthetic has repeatedly been
noted, although to my knowledge never fully explored. See Virgil Thompson,
"Expressive Percussion," (1945) in *John Cage: An Anthology*, 72; Henry
Cowell, "Current Chronicle," in ibid., 97–98; Paul Griffiths, *Cage* (London:
Oxford University Press, 1981), 11; Revill, 50; Nicholls, 208; and Pritchett, 12.

62.   Antheil, "Music Tomorrow," 124. Ellipses in original. Antheil's
statement would have received support in the same issue from Elliot Paul
who, in an article entitled, "The Schoenberg Legend," soundly thrashed
Cage's former teacher: "His recent series of concerts in Paris should, it seems
to me, remove any lingering suspicions that he is a *modern* composer." Paul,
"The Schoenberg Legend," *transition* 10 (January 1928): 142.

63.   Eugene Jolas, "Notes on Reality," *transition* 18 (November 1929): 15.

64.   Cage, "Listening to Music," 18.

65.   Ibid., 19.

66.   Cage, "The Future of Music: Credo," 3.

67.   Russolo, 86–87.

68.   McMillan, 102.

69.   On Jolas's interest in Romanticism, see McMillan, 32–34.

70.   McMillan, 102–103. Letters reveal Haussman and Jolas in agreement
on their interpretation of Dada, including a revolution in language, an avoid-
ance of political parties, and a certain level of mysticism or religious impulse.
See Andreas Kramer and Richard Sheppard, "Raoul Hausmann's
Correspondence with Eugene Jolas," *German Life and Letters* 48, no. 1
(January 1995): 39–55.

71.   Hugo Ball, "Fragments from a Dada Diary," *transition* 25 (Fall 1936): 73.

72.   Eugene Jolas, "Vertigral Workshop: Race and Language," *transition*
24 (January 1936): 111. This idea was as clearly articulated in *transition*'s
early issues. See, for example, "The Innocuous Enemy," Jolas's polemical

response to critiques launched by Wyndham Lewis, in *transition* 16–17 (June 1929): 208.

73. Cage, "The Future of Music: Credo" 5–6. Cage wrote in "Lecture on Something," "art is a sort of experimental station in which one tries out living." John Cage, "Lecture on Something," (1951) in *Silence*, 139.

74. Jean-Jacques Nattiez, et al., eds., *The Boulez-Cage Correspondence* (Cambridge: Cambridge University Press, 1993), 29.

75. Cage, "The Future of Music: Credo," 5.

76. Eugene Jolas, "Literature and the New Man," *transition* 19-20 (June 1930): 19.

77. Cage, "The Future of Music: Credo," 5.

78. Ibid.

79. Alan Gillmor, "Interview with John Cage," *Contact* 14 (Autumn 1976); quoted in Revill, 40.

80. Cage, "South Winds in Chicago," (1942) in *John Cage: An Anthology*, 68.

81. Ibid.

82. Perhaps on account of Marinetti's more visible embrace of fascism, Cage attempted to distance Russolo from him at the beginning of "The Dreams and Dedications of George Antheil," (1946) in *John Cage: An Anthology*, 73.

83. Cage, "Defense of Satie," (1948) in *John Cage: An Anthology*, 78.

84. Ibid., 79.

85. Ibid., 78.

86. Ibid.

87. Ibid., 81.

88. Ibid.

89. The most complete analysis of the presence of Indian art historian Ananda Coomaraswamy in Cage's thought is Patterson, chapter 2: "The Picture that is not in the Colors: Cage, Coomaraswamy and the Impact of India," 58–124. Patterson notes that Cage was most likely introduced to Coomaraswamy's writings by Joseph Campbell at some point soon after 1942 when Cage and his wife Xenia came to stay with Campbell and the dancer Jean Erdman to whom he was married. Patterson, 66.

90. Patterson, 74–75

91. Cage, "The East in the West," (1946) in *John Cage: Writer*, 25.

92. Cage, "The Dreams and Dedications of George Antheil," 74.

93. Ibid.

94. Ibid.

95. Cage, "Defense of Satie," 81.

96. Cage, "A Composer's Confessions," 40.

97. Ibid., 42–43.

98. Ibid., 44.

99. Ibid.

100. Ibid., 43.

101. Cage, "Defense of Satie," 84.

102. Patterson, 156–157.

103. Cage, "A Composer's Confessions," 42. Emphasis in original.

104.   John Cage, "Lecture on Nothing," (1950) in *Silence*, 111. More direct are Cage's comments in "Satie Controversy": "Satie, however, was disinterested....Forced, nervous laughter takes place when someone is trying to impress somebody for the purposes of getting somewhere. Satie, free of such interest, entitled his first pieces commissioned by a publisher *Three Flabby Preludes for a Dog*. It being fairly clear who is referred to by the word 'dog,' giving that title was evidently a social act militant in nature...." John Cage, "Satie Controversy," (1950) in *John Cage: An Anthology*, 89.

105.   *Conversing with Cage*, 174–175.

106.   Cage, "A Composer's Confessions," 38.

107.   Ibid., 41. Cage would later attribute a further transformaton in his appreciation of the city to the work of Robert Rauschenberg. See John Cage, "Letter to Paul Henry Lang," (1956) in *John Cage: An Anthology*, 118.

108.   Cage, "Defense of Satie," 78.

109.   Cage, "A Composer's Confessions," 41.

110.   Such a return to earlier sources is entirely characteristic of Cage's working method. Cage can be seen to have studied with increasingly thoroughness both his Eastern and Western sources, oftentimes over a period of several years, in pursuit of his own musical and artistic ends.

111.   Cage and Helms; and Helms, "John Cage," 21. Also in John Cage, "Reflections of a Progressive Composer on a Damaged Society," 78-79.

112.   Lázló Moholy-Nagy, *The New Vision*, trans. Daphne M. Hoffman, 4th rev. ed. (New York: George Wittenborn, Inc., 1947), 15.

113.   Ibid.

114.   Jolas, "Literature and the New Man," 17.

115.   On Cage's rejection of Coomaraswamy's anti-modernism, see Patterson, 108–111.

116.   Jolas, "Literature and the New Man," 17.

117.   Ibid.

118.   McMillan, 30–31, 44–46. Jolas's stance against the dehumanization caused by the forces of mechanization was developed even before he began *transition* and was maintained even in the face of the increasing pressures of communism and fascism. Hugh Fox, "Eugene Jolas and *transition*: the Mantic Power of the Word," *West Coast Review* 7, no. 1 (1972): 3; and McMillan, 183.

119.   Jolas, "Notes," *transition* 14 (Fall 1928): 181–182.

120.   Stuart Gilbert, "The Creator is not a Public Servant," *transition* 19-20 (June 1930): 148.

121.   Ibid., 149. Ellipses in original.

122.   Jolas, "Super-Occident," 12.

123.   Ibid., 13.

124.   Ibid.

125.   Jolas, "The Machine and 'Mystic America'," *transition* 19–20 (June 1930): 383.

126.   Jolas, "Super-Occident," 12.

127.   Jolas, "Literature and the New Man," 15. Cf. Cage's comment, "Surrealism . . . relates to therapy, whereas Dada relates to religion." Gillmor, "Interview with John Cage," 21.

128.   Jolas, "Literature and the New Man," 15.

129.   Ibid., 17.

130.   Cage, "A Composer's Confessions," 41.

131.   Ibid., 41–42.

132.   Jung, "Psychology and Poetry," *transition* 19–20 (June 1930): 40–41.

133.   Cage, "Defense of Satie," 84.

134.   Cage, "A Composer's Confessions," 41.

135.   Ibid., 42.

136.   Cage, "The East in the West," 25.

137.   Cage, "A Composer's Confessions," 34.

138.   Cage, "For More New Sounds," in *John Cage: An Anthology*, 66.

139.   Cage, "The East in the West," 22.

140.   Cage, "Defense of Satie," 82.

141.   Cage, "Forerunners of Modern Music," (1949) in *Silence*, 63.

142.   Cage, "Defense of Satie," 81.

143.   Cage, "Mosaic," (1965) in *A Year from Monday* (Middletown, CT: Wesleyan University Press, 1967), 45.

144.   See letter from Peter Yates to John Cage, June 9, 1960: "Now as to Schoenberg. Puttting aside your objection that S[choenberg] is simply Beethoven brought up to date, which is quite true . . . " Located in the John Cage Archive, Northwestern University, Music Library, Evanston, Ill.

145.   To a certain extent, this position coincides with Theodor Adorno's later assessment of Schoenberg's move from free atonalism to the twelve-tone technique. See Theodor W. Adorno, "Vers une musique informelle," (1961) trans. Rodney Livingstone, in *Quasi una fantasia* (London: Verso, 1994), 269-322.

146.   Cage, "Lecture on Nothing," in *Silence*, 117. Cf. Cage, "A Composer's Confessions," 39.

147.   Cage, "Lecture on Nothing," 117.

148.   Cage, "A Composer's Confessions," 40.

149.   Ibid., 44.

150.   Pritchett, 60–70.

have fairly frequent opportunities to interface with the Asian arts through any number of channels, including Harrison (who moved to New York himself in 1942), Jean Erdman, Joseph Campbell, artist Isamu Noguchi, or sculptor Richard Lippold, the last of whom shared both his own interest in the subject and his collection of recordings of non-western music with Cage on many occasions.[4]

Critical speculation regarding Cage's artistic debt to Asia first blossomed not on the west coast but in New York during the early 1940s, where commentators drew similes between the percussion ensemble works and the musical styles of Southeast Asia, and that of Bali in particular.[5] In hindsight, the value of these comparisons was decidedly limited, not only due to a relative unfamiliarity with the repertory and techniques of Asian music but to the very novelty of Cage's compositions themselves.[6] Today, scholars seem in implicit agreement that there is actually very little in Cage's works that reflects a genuine interest in Asian music *per se*, and there is no indication that he ever pursued the modes of experimentation typical among those composers whose interest in Asian music was more overt, such as Cowell, Harrison, Colin McPhee and Harry Partch. He did not exert any creative energies exploring non-western tuning systems, for instance, and predominantly his attempts to integrate authentically "Asian" instruments into western compositions were confined to the small handful of instruments included among the vast battery of devices found in the percussion works. Yet following the percussion ensemble compositions, the subsequent works for prepared piano only perpetuated critical suspicions of cross-cultural stylistic influence well through the 1940s and into the 50s, the instrument's timbral diversity and delicacy often interpreted as evidence of "orientalism."[7]

Cage never spent much time challenging those who drew connections between his works and Asian music, perhaps because these analogies afforded some degree of access into, or at least tolerance toward, his music. Nonetheless, he never personally credited the formal structures, timbres, or compositional techniques of Asian music as directive to his own development.[8] While his own musical statements from the 1930s, 40s and 50s do include occasional references to Asian music, these passages never identify particulars from this tradition as source materials for his own work. Instead, Cage's allusions to Asian music served as independent affirmation of his own thought; yet even in these cases, Asian music was only one of several musical styles that he cited for reinforcement. Early statements on modern rhythmic developments suggested analogues to "hot jazz" and "boogie-woogie"[9] (notions no doubt developed in part through his association with William Russell),[10] and both jazz and Asian music were important in their practice of allowing for "group improvisations of unwritten but culturally important music."[11] The square-root method of rhythmic organization that characterized Cage's works from the late 1930s through the early 50s was "a structural idea not distant in concept from Hindu tala (except that tala has no beginning or ending, and is based on pulsation rather than phraseology), the work of Anton Webern and Erik Satie and hot jazz."[12] Similarly, the prepared piano's timbral properties found a wide range of correlates in Navajo singing, particular string instrument traditions ("examples of this cross the world and the ages from Ancient China to the music of Anton Webern," Cage explained), the hot jazz piano, Henry Cowell's compositions, and the practice of the Bach Society in which thumbtacks pushed into the hammers of a piano created a pseudo-harpsichord.[13]

While claims of any causal relation between Asian music and Cage's compositions are highly contentious, both his interest in and appropriation of terms and concepts from Asian philosophy and aesthetics, on the other hand, are indisputable. However, the identification and specific dating of his earliest exposure to these subjects is problematic. Both Cage and Harrison have recalled the instance in 1936 in which Harrison first showed the *I Ching* to Cage in San Francisco, although developmentally, Cage was hardly at the point where it was of much interest.[14] Cage also made frequent reference to his attendance at a lecture entitled "Zen Buddhism and Dada" given by Nancy Wilson Ross at the Cornish School in Seattle, though this, too, seems an isolated instance of no obvious consequence.[15] Throughout the late 1930s, Cage's own musical rhetoric was consistently western in its expression,[16] and even during the war years his prose bore little overt sign of Asian influence. In 1944, for example, his mentality reflects that of the still-to-be-converted Westerner when he states, "personality is a flimsy thing on which to build an art. (This does not mean that it should not enter into an art, for, indeed, that is what is meant by the word *style*.)"[17]

Yet the war years are most likely those in which Cage first actively enhanced his own knowledge of Asian philosophy and aesthetics, and while seldom articulated in Cage scholarship to date, his initial frame of reference was not East Asian but South Asian. Among even the briefest biographical sketches of Cage, none omits mention of his reading of Ananda Coomaraswamy's 1934 publication entitled *The Transformation of Nature in Art*, a set of essays that derives a general theory of art from the examination of not only Indian and Chinese treatises, but through the writings of the fourteenth-century German mystic Meister Eckhart as well.[18] Cage discovered Coomaraswamy through Joseph Campbell, who had worked with Indologist Heinrich

Zimmer at Columbia University and was himself steeped in Indian artistic and aesthetic studies during the early 1940s, overseeing the completion of several of Zimmer's unfinished volumes. In addition to *The Transformation of Nature in Art*, Cage also cited *The Gospel of Sri Ramakrishna*,[19] a volume recording the life and lessons of an Indian mystic of the late nineteenth and early twentieth centuries, as influential to his life in the 1940s, although in the long run, this work most likely had a more meaningful impact upon his personal life than it did upon his artistic development.[20] Unlike his studies of Coomaraswamy, Cage's reading of *The Gospel of Sri Ramakrishna* can be dated conclusively within a period spanning the winter of 1946–47 through the spring of 1948, a period to which Cage referred in April of 1948, telling a Vassar audience of his recent completion of "eighteen months of studying oriental and medieval Christian philosophy and mysticism."[21]

In the case of either Coomaraswamy or Sri Ramakrishna, Cage's focused interest in Indian aesthetics and philosophy precedes his oft-cited studies of East Asian philosophy by several years, and specific principles derived from the above–mentioned texts can be traced into his own compositional agenda, revealing the impending stylistic shift toward indeterminacy in its earliest stages. In addition, several of Cage's compositions from this period bear some relation to India, whether through the programmatic use of distinctive Indian themes or through Cage's descriptions of his compositional procedures, which employ terms and concepts derived from his study of Indian aesthetics. Yet to date, no detailed explanation of Cage's affinities with and expression of these Indian texts and concepts has been offered.

Focusing especially upon *The Transformation of Nature in Art* and making use of additional texts by Coomaraswamy as auxiliary sources, the present essay initially offers a brief overview of Coomaraswamy's life and work. This is followed by a summation of "The East in the West," Cage's first article to reflect his interest in Indian philosophy. The greater portion of this essay then delves into the more specific affinities and incongruities of this relationship. With frequent reference to Cage's own remarks, Coomaraswamy's aesthetic is presented on two levels: 1) the identification of three assumptions essential to his aesthetic; and 2) the explication of particular corollaries to this aesthetic based on the interrelation of these assumptions, including the artistic value of *anonymity* and the requisite and related mental states of *self-naughting* and *dementation*. With these concepts explained, Cage's most frequent citation from Coomaraswamy's work is re-examined and interpreted: "Art is the imitation of nature in her manner of operation." Cage's borrowings from Coomaraswamy were hardly wholesale, and a study of their differences gives added definition to their respective contours. Following those pages devoted to aesthetic affinities, then, the subsequent section of this study reviews some of the most essential points of divergence between Cage and Coomaraswamy, and in particular, those centering around notions of *communication, tradition, originality* and *modernity.*

The accomplishments of Ananda Kentish Coomaraswamy (1877–1947) are legion, as were his professions: he began in the sciences as a botanist, geologist, petrologist and mineralogist, contributing articles in all of these fields, heading Ceylon's Mineralogical Survey and discovering the mineral thorianite. His sympathies with the emerging Indian nationalist movement soon gained expression, both explicitly, through his participation in groups such as the Ceylon Social Reform Society (which he also helped found), and implicitly, through his developing scholarly interests in ancient Indian culture and art. From scientist, then, Coomaraswamy evolved into art historian and aesthetician, and he made his greatest achievements in these fields. To this day, he is credited with almost single-handedly awakening both Indian and western peoples to India's cultural, artistic and literary heritage, and his writings remain one of the central foundations of contemporary Indian art scholarship.[22] Because of the spiritually-oriented aesthetic within which he set his artistic observations, many professionals in the field treat him as a philosopher, metaphysician and theologian as well. Coomaraswamy spent the last thirty years of his life in the United States.[23] In 1917 he joined the staff of the Boston Museum of Fine Arts, where he served as Keeper of Indian and Muhammedan Art; in 1933 he was appointed Research Fellow in Indian, Persian and Muslim Art. During this American period alone, Coomaraswamy published approximately one hundred twenty books and monographs, three hundred articles, some fifty scholarly book reviews, and left behind innumerable technical notes and letters.[24]

Within the highly complex system of Coomaraswamy's aesthetic, it is possible to extract fundamental assumptions that are operative throughout his scholarship, noting in turn some of Cage's remarks that at the very least suggest a sympathetic viewpoint, and in some cases may even indicate more direct borrowings on Cage's part from Indian systems of thought. Indian art scholar M. Sivaramkrishna distinguishes three such assumptions as essential to Coomaraswamy's aesthetic as it relates to the creative process:

1. that of a Unified Being, an Ultimate Reality, the evidence of whose existence is largely a matter of transcendental, undifferentiated experience;

2. that this power is present in all persons in an immanent form;

3. that one has to realize this immanent being in the totality of modes of knowledge and experience available: in this regard, art is the most significant mode.[25]

The nature of this Unified Being or Ultimate Reality lies beyond the scope of mere language or logic, and in line with most strains of Eastern philosophy, Coomaraswamy contends that while this Reality can be experienced, it cannot be explained, taught or even comprehended.[26] In those passages in his writings dealing specifically with this concept, Coomaraswamy repeatedly emphasizes Ultimate Reality as the time-transcendent origin of all ideas, perspectives, actions, and resultant products, as opposed to that more mundane level of reality in which one can speak of time, experience the specifics of a given culture or era and engage in the human processes of creation. Indistinguishable "even by a first assumption of unity," this Ultimate Reality "subsumes in its infinity the whole of what can be implied or represented by the notions of the infinite and the finite . . . "[27] At times, Coomaraswamy expresses this concept in more deistic terms:

> . . . from God's point of view ideas are all known at once in perfection and in one form; from our temporal point of view ideas are free and variably becoming, or as we now say evolving. From any point of view, ideas or forms (*nama*) are "living," not merely existing like standards fixed and deposited for safe-keeping—ideas not merely of static shapes, but ideas of acts.[28]

According to the second and third assumptions of Coomaraswamy's aesthetic as outlined by Sivaramkrishna, both levels of reality—Ultimate and Mundane—co-exist in all individuals, and the reconciliation of this fundamental duality may be realized fully through right-minded action.[29] The artistic process, Coomaraswamy contended, facilitates this reconciliation most effectively, since invariably any artistic action is illuminating, raising simultaneously one's awareness of "the basic reality which is one [Ultimate Reality] and the reality which is presented to the senses which becomes a world of multiplicity [Mundane Reality]."[30] In the course of this reconciliation, the artist will be faced with unanswerable questions and unsolvable paradoxes; yet these, Coomaraswamy explained, are not to be taken as discouraging, but should be appreciated as affirming manifestations of the all-encompassing, culture-transcendent issues that comprise the Perennial Philosophy of Mankind, or *philosophia perennis*, as Coomaraswamy identified it.[31]

While art is the "most significant mode" of reconciliation between Ultimate and Mundane Realities in Coomaraswamy's aesthetic scheme, it must be clarified that when he refers to "art," he typically invokes the term not in its contemporary Western sense but in a far more inclusive and antiquated sense, potentially embracing any and all actions that yield a resultant product. To Coomaraswamy, every action executed is linked inherently to an "aesthetic process, a succession of problem, solution and execution . . . whether [an individual] makes a house, or studies mathematics, or performs an office, or does good works."[32] Moreover, as creative endeavors pursued through this process, all such actions—whether of religion, philosophy, cooking, planting, teaching, sculpting, etc.—have the potential to draw one closer toward Ultimate Reality, and in so doing, must be considered "artistic." In Coomaraswamy's aesthetic, then, and in contradistinction to the typical Western view, "the artist is not a special kind of man, but every man is a special kind of artist," and one's particular "art" is simply determined by individual nature. In the course of substantiating this equation of life and art, Coomaraswamy draws from a vast system of cross-cultural citations:

> Indian literature provides us with numerous lists of the eighteen or more professional arts (*silpa*) and the sixty-four avocational arts (*kala*); and these embrace every kind of skilled activity, from music, painting, and weaving to horsemanship, cookery, and the practice of magic, without distinction of rank, all being equally of angelic origin.[33]

> "Demiurge" and "technician" are the ordinary Greek words for "artist" (*artifex*), and under these headings Plato includes not only poets, painters and musicians, but also archers, weavers, embroiderers, potters, carpenters, sculptors, farmers, doctors, hunters and above all those whose art is government, only making a distinction between creation (*demiourgia*) and mere labour (*cheirourgia*), art (*techne*) and artless industry (*atechnos tribe*).[34]

In taking this stance, Coomaraswamy purposefully challenged what he considered the unnatural, constricted, post-Renaissance perception of "art" (a perception he also held largely responsible for contemporary "decadence"), and recast the term instead within the far more expansive context of daily living. In the cultures of Asia and medieval Europe, he explained, art had been indistinct from life, and indeed, in eastern cultures, this was still the case: "Life itself—the different ways in which the difficult problems of human association have been solved—represents the ultimate and chief of the arts of Asia."[35] In contrast, Coomaraswamy contended that the modern (i.e., post-Renaissance) Western definition of art had alienated mankind against this experience of life as art, an unnatural segregation which had replaced universal humanity with a "spiritual caste system."[36] "All alike have lost," he lamented, "in that art being now a luxury, no longer the normal type of activity, all men are compelled to live in squalor and disorder and have become so inured to this that they are unaware of it."[37] The introduction of the museum to nineteenth-century European culture only compounded this rift, Coomaraswamy contended, for though this institution was intended to facilitate the preservation of art, it had in reality imprisoned it by extracting objects from their cultural environment, thereby stripping them of their innate purpose.

Lacking any conclusive documentation, it is still reasonable to speculate that Cage was reading Coomaraswamy's *The Transformation of Nature in Art* within months of his arrival in New York in the fall of 1942. His first extant reference to Coomaraswamy, however, does not appear until 1946 in an article entitled "The East in the West," in which he remarks, "There is, I believe, a similarity also between Western medieval music and Oriental. In other fields than music, Dr. Ananda K. Coomaraswamy has discussed such a relation."[38] However modest the citation, "The East in the West" signals the new role of Asia in Cage's creative thought and anticipates what would become his extensive use of Asian concepts and terms in his own aesthetic rhetoric. This article enumerates those contemporary western composers whose compositional techniques or attitudes "are similar to or characteristic of Oriental classical music, specifically, that of Hindustan." Before doing so, however, Cage instantly dismisses two types of cross-cultural appropriation from his discussion: 1) that too faithful to the Asian original to represent any genuine western innovation (a category into which Cage places McPhee); and 2) that which constitutes mere exoticism (e.g., Mozart's *Rondo alla Turca*). The following two-thirds of the essay then bring together a unique assortment of western composers in whose works Cage finds structural equivalents in Hindu music. Following a series of uncharacteristically obtuse (and perhaps far-fetched) comparisons between Schoenberg's twelve-tone system and the concept of raga, Cage makes more readily comprehensible remarks on the rhythmic techniques of Alan Hovhaness, the percussive sounds of Edgard Varèse, and the microtonality of Alois Hába. His deepest sympathies, however, appear to lie with those composers reserved for the final third of the essay, which deals with the psychological and spiritual elements of Hindu music. And while Cage never once mentions his own works, this passage may be taken as his first statement on the relation of eastern aesthetics to his own art. Cage groups Satie, Virgil Thomson, Carl

Ruggles, Lou Harrison and Messiaen as peers in this category, for aesthetically, all of these figures seek "to imbue their music with the ineffable," their compositions attempting "to express lofty sentiments in the most direct manner possible, rather than to evoke in any way the 'classical' tradition of music" (although the western-derived harmonic elements of Messiaen's music, Cage qualifies, "accounts for its occasional bad taste").

As the following pages will demonstrate, Cage's subsequent writings reveal affinities with Coomaraswamy far more intricate than the passing reference above may indicate. Yet in appropriating terms and concepts from this source, his borrowings did not constitute so much a faithful transcription of an aesthetic as they did a carefully constructed intellectual subversion. This is not to lend an insidious tone to the subject but more objectively refers to a particular type of appropriation whereby the basic elements and unifying structure of an idea are maintained, though the intended effect is first undercut and then reversed (i.e., subverted) by a motivation contrary to the idea's original purpose. This process is especially evident when Cage adopts Coomaraswamy's rhetoric to advance the cause of contemporary music. Of course, the notion of "subversion" could well apply to an even larger portion of Cage's activity during the 1940s, particularly in regard to the prepared piano, whose extraneous objects decisively thwarted the aesthetic function of the premiere instrument of the nineteenth century. In previewing any discussion of Cage's relation to Coomaraswamy, then, one might suggest that Cage used Coomaraswamy's aesthetic much as he used the standard piano—taking delight in the historical weight it derived from its tradition, then alienating it utterly from this original context, manipulating its internal arguments to sound to his taste, yet remaining sensitive enough not to damage its structure.

Like Coomaraswamy, Cage deemed contemporary museum culture a needless barrier between life and art, unequivocally equating the effect of the museum with ". . . refrigeration (which is a way of slowing down its liveliness) (that is to say museums and academies are ways of preserving);" consequently, he contended, "we temporarily separate things from life (from changing) . . . "[39] Yet Cage's aesthetic affinities with Coomaraswamy are demonstrable on far more fundamental levels. While he almost never invoked terms such as "Ultimate Reality" directly in his own writings,[40] for instance, his sympathies toward the notion seem to be expressed, albeit obliquely, in the occasional passing remark in various published articles or in some conceptual parenthesis in the course of a lecture. Coomaraswamy's statement that "the truth as a whole is an eternal, ever accessible, infinity, incapable as such of any improvement or

advancement,"[41] for example, is echoed in one of the many momentary themes in Cage's 1950 "Lecture on Something," when he notes:

> It all goes together and doesn't require that we try to improve it or
> feel our inferiority or superiority to it. Progress is out of the ques-
> tion. But inactivity is not what happens. There is always activity
> but it is free from compulsion, done from disinterest.[42]

Cage's adoption of Coomaraswamy's attitudes toward art as life and of
all persons as "artists," on the other hand, is nothing short of categorical, and the reader familiar with Cage can acknowledge readily the
status of these concepts as mainstays in his aesthetic for the rest of his
life; "Art's obscured the difference between art and life. Now let life
obscure the difference between life and art."[43] In speaking of this
reunion of art and life, Cage's tone was consistently hopeful. "The
heights that now are reached by single individuals at special moments
may soon be densely populated," he once predicted,[44] occasionally
summing up this position with the simple acronym, "H.C.E." ("Here
Comes Everybody").[45] In his earliest expressions of this idea, though,
the very language he chooses is clearly derived from Coomaraswamy;
in a 1950 rebuttal of criticisms leveled against Satie, his rhetorical pla-
giarism is flagrant:

> *Art is a way of life.* [Cage's italics] It is for all the world like tak-
> ing a bus, picking flowers, making love, sweeping the floor, get-
> ting bitten by a monkey, reading a book, etc., ad infinitum. . . . Art
> when it is art as Satie lived it and made it is not separate from life
> (nor is dishwashing when it is done in this spirit).[46]

Armed with the essential themes and terms of Coomaraswamy's aesthetic—the challenge to limited Western conceptions of "art," the
technique of juxtaposing examples of works of "art" with works of life
(and the ultimate equation of the two), and so forth—Cage often mod-
ified these materials to make specific claims for contemporary music
as to its function and value not only in life but as life. His contentions
are made clear in the 1958 essay, "Composition as Process," in which
he takes aim at the very same western conception of "art" to which
Coomaraswamy objects so strenuously:

> When we separate music from life what we get is art (a com-
> pendium of masterpieces). With contemporary music, when it is
> actually contemporary, we have no time to make that separation
> (which protects us from living), and so contemporary music is not
> so much art as it is life and any one making it no sooner finishes
> one of it than he begins making another just as people keep on
> washing dishes, brushing their teeth, getting sleepy, and so on.
> Very frequently no one knows that contemporary music is or
> could be art. He simply thinks it is irritating. Irritating one way or

another, that is to say keeping us from ossifying. For any one of us contemporary music is or could be a way of living.[47]

As Sivaramkrishna identifies them, the three fundamental assumptions of Coomaraswamy's artistic philosophy outline a progression of phenomena that culminates in a work or creation; that is, from Ultimate Reality, to Artistic Activity, to Resultant Product. The following chart summarizes the basic characteristics of each:

ULTIMATE REALITY	to	ARTISTIC ACTIVITY	to	RESULTANT PRODUCT
Great State of Undifferentiation, in which all "things" and "ideas" exist in perfection		Problem-Solution-Execution		Temporal/transient manifestation of Ultimate Reality
Eternal (i.e.,timeless; beyond temporal measure)		Man as Vehicle of Creation		Culture-specific
The non-created source of all creations		Culturally determined		Comprehended through the code of tradition

At the next conceptual level, Coomaraswamy's aesthetic derives several immediate corollaries based on the interaction of these phenomena. For example, the implications of an ever-present Ultimate Reality in which "ideas are all known at once in perfection" cast a new light on the nature and value of the Artistic Act, ultimately generating an inescapable thesis; since all things have already been fully perfected in this Ultimate state, it is therefore a non sequitur, if not simply nonsense, to speak of anything "new" in the profound sense of the term. All human activities and extant artifacts throughout all time and within all cultures are merely evidence of the endless cycle of "rediscoveries" of the same essential, immutable Reality that serves as the basis of all things. In the larger scheme of his scholarly output, Coomaraswamy attempts to prove this Reality through an elaborate system of multi-cultural cross-references, emphasizing similarities rather than temporal or cultural differences. Such differences, after all, are negligible, representing only the infinitely varied manifestations this Reality can assume. Not surprisingly, and as previous citations have already suggested, Coomaraswamy's scholarship makes few distinctions between sources, citing examples from European antiquity to support observations on Indian art, or those from medieval Christian mysticism to reaffirm the basic tenets of Buddhism.[48]

In assuming this timeless Reality as his focus, Coomaraswamy held a wholly indifferent attitude toward western historical disciplines, the motivations of which—biography, attribution of authorship, stylistic dating, etc.—he found merely symptomatic of a groundless culture that could not perceive the past "as the map of life and a means to the attainment of higher and less limited planes of consciousness."[49] Typically emphasizing the transient phenomena of any period rather than the underlying themes which unified a period with all others, the western historical approach was "harmless in itself, yet no better than the satisfaction of a curiosity."[50] Coomaraswamy explicitly countered the western agenda with his own multi-cultural, multi-temporal model whenever possible, arguing that "the wise man is therefore not interested in the history of aspects, but only in the validity of a given statement as a means conducive to the realization of invulnerable happiness."[51]

Coomaraswamy's appreciation of created products as transient manifestations of an Ultimate Reality rather than as culture- or artist-specific products is wholly eastern in fashion, and his subsequent observations on the nature and value of both the "artist" and the "artistic activity" stand in most obvious contrast to the typical western view. Extolling the artistic activity and denying outright any purpose to the study of the person of the artist, Coomaraswamy's "artist" is both anonymous and impersonal (i.e., forsaking self-expression) in his actions. Indian art scholar Betty Heimann illustrates this attitude succinctly, noting that in the making of a pot, for example:

> . . . Only the pot-making itself is of true importance. The potter, the artist, figures in this process of pot-making as a necessary, but accidental, agent. The potter, the clay, the material, and also the donkey which carries the clay to the site are all equally considered as subsidiary causes for the accomplishment of this purpose, the pot. As such it is no accident that in Indian visual art the name of the artist who has executed the work is hardly ever handed down to us. . . . This, in a way, deprives the artist of the personal honour of his achievement and of his individual appraisal. On the other hand, it values even the average Indian artist's work as a contribution to a supra-personal cosmic achievement.[52]

In these terms, it is clear why Coomaraswamy might consider the biographic facts of the artist meager contingencies in comparison to the totality of the artistic act itself.[53] Yet his aesthetic devalues the figure of the artist even further, for since Ultimate Reality is the source from which an artist receives ideas, he explains, the artist may lay no claim of ownership to that idea, a point of view which " . . . we all naturally endorse when we say that an idea has come to us, or that we have hit upon it, eureka, never that we have made it."[54] Among other sources, Coomaraswamy finds aesthetic confirmation in the Buddhist text, *Dhammapada*, which states, "to wish that it may be known 'I was the author' is the thought of a man not yet adult."[55] He also cites frequently the anonymity of ancient Indian art as a prime example of these principles in operation, contending that artists of this period were devoted to their calling, not to revealing their physical identity. (In sentiment, this perspective is quite similar to earlier western conceptions that depict the artist as one who labors, yet does not self-idolize the worker, intuiting that all artistic efforts are mere puppetry controlled by the hand of God.) Coomaraswamy's "artist," therefore, is not the doer, but only the instrument of the doing, a vessel through which Ultimate Reality might emerge as a resultant product. This artist does not express ideas derived from the Self, but receives them from a greater Reality, translating eternal truths into the temporal realm: "In action the workman is nothing but a tool," Coomaraswamy concludes, "and should use himself accordingly . . . "[56]

As a consequence, the interpretation of any resultant product as an accumulation of the artist's individual emotions would be mistaken, as would be its veneration as profound "Creation." Instead, Coomaraswamy explained, the resultant product is to be appreciated as the *translation* of an idea from one state of reality to another and valued as a contribution to its temporal and physical environment. As no claim of ownership may be made on the part of the artist, this product is inherently public property, enjoying a "pure objective existence as a part of life."[57]

Cage would express it even more compactly: "We are getting rid of ownership, substituting use,"[58] and his perception of the artist, at least by the late 1940s, was much in accord with that of Coomaraswamy. Coomaraswamy's remarks on artistic anonymity are clearly the textual source of Cage's early rhetoric on the same topic, though Cage modifies the argument to legitimize his own distaste for western harmony:

> I now saw harmony, for which I had never had any natural feeling, as a device to make music impressive, loud and big, in order to enlarge audiences and increase box-office returns. It had been avoided by the Orient, and our earlier Christian society, since they were interested in music not as an aid in the acquisition of money and fame but rather as a handmaiden to pleasure and religion.[59]

Like Coomaraswamy, Cage used the aesthetic ramifications of anonymity for aggressive purposes, challenging typical nineteenth-century characterizations of the "artist." The coronation of the Romantic artist as ultimate "creator," or the essential source of origin of an idea or action, Cage claimed, was an historical instance of aesthetic misdirection through which the culture had come to dire consequences. The common tendency to interpret a work as an expression of the artist's innermost psyche, for example, had not only skewed the understanding of the basic processes of creation, but had led to the ungainly inflation of the figure of the artist, culminating in the perverse practice of extolling the actor over the artistic actions themselves. Moreover, such misplaced idolatry gave impetus for a system of judgment which created an artistic hierarchy of sorts—a system Cage found unnecessary, if not simply delusional. Like Coomaraswamy's artist, Cage's artist is a conduit, and directly pitting this "artist" against the conventional western model, Cage prescribes that artistic endeavors (and their subsequent evaluations) not be caught up in issues of self-expression, but rather in their achievement of even a fleeting experience of the greater Reality from which such a work is derived:

> For instance: someone said, "Art should come from within; then it is profound." But it seems to me Art goes within, and I don't see the need for "should" or "then" or "it" or "profound." When Art comes from within, which is what it was for so long doing, it became a thing which seemed to elevate the man who made it above those who observed it or heard it and the artist was considered a genius or given a rating: First, Second, No Good, until finally riding in a bus or subway: so proudly he signs his work like a manufacturer. But since everything's changing, art's now going in and it is of the utmost importance not to make a thing but rather to make nothing.[60]

Like Coomaraswamy, Cage came to value the dynamic artistic process over any resultant product derived therefrom, and he explicitly understands this activity as inclusive of far more elements than the artist alone. In 1949, for example, he mirrors Coomaraswamy in his interpretation of any artistic action as a reconciling force, stating, "Activity involving in a single process the many, turning them, even though some seem to be opposites, towards oneness, contributes to a good way of life."[61] For the next twenty years, Cage's conception of art as activity would go unaltered; though again, following on the heels of his study of various social philosophers, he expressed the dynamics of this activity in human rather than cosmic terms:

> Art instead of being an object made by one person is a process set in motion by a group of people. Art's socialized. It isn't someone

saying something, but people doing things, giving everyone (including those involved) the opportunity to have experiences they would not otherwise have had.[62]

This "group of people" to whom Cage refers is not to be misunderstood in the western sense as consisting merely of composer, performer, and perhaps, impresario, but embraces a far more complex scheme of interrelations, much like that outlined in Heimann's potmaking analogy. Few passages in Cage's writings elaborate on this notion specifically; however, tucked within the somewhat daunting layout of the 1965 "Diary: How To Improve the World (You Will Only Make Matters Worse)," one particular epigram discloses this attitude precisely: "He wanted me to agree that the piano tuner and the piano maker have nothing to do with it (the composition). The younger ones had said: Whoever makes the stretcher isn't separate from the painting. (It doesn't stop there either.)"[63]

While "anonymity" refers to the proper status of the artist, Coomaraswamy invokes the term *impersonality* to refer to the proper manner in which such a figure is to execute tasks artistically. In this context self-expression, equated with "aesthetic exhibitionism," or "the substitution of the player for the play," is interpreted as an artistic vice, and Coomaraswamy continually warns of its degenerate nature. At the very least, the appearance of the artist's person in any work is intrusive; at worst, it is a glaring indication of defective workmanship. In several instances throughout his writings, Coomaraswamy explains the necessity of artistic impersonality through the example of Indian dramatic art and dance:

> As to the Indian drama, the theme is exhibited by means of gestures, speech, costume, and natural adaptation of the actor for the part; and of these four, the first three are highly conventional in any case, while with regard to the fourth not only is the appearance of the actor formally modified by make-up or even a mask, but Indian treatises constantly emphasize that the actor should not be carried away by the emotions he represents, but should rather be the ever-conscious master of the puppet show performed by his own body on stage. The exhibition of his own emotions would not be art.[64]

In the artistic process, therefore, even a momentary intrusion of the Self could jeopardize the integrity of the entire action. But this is not an exclusively eastern concept, Coomaraswamy insists. The interpretation of self-expression as an unnatural and destructive force exists even at the heart of Judeo-Christian cultures; it was, after all, an egomania which "occasioned the fall of Lucifer . . . thinking, 'Who is like me in Heaven or Earth?' . . . desiring to deify himself."[65] The true artist, then, is not deceived by those actions that aspire toward a freedom *of* Self, but rather is devoted whole-heartedly to those actions which will result in a freedom *from* Self.

Just as anonymity and impersonality imply self-denial, the specific process that readies the artist to receive and translate an image or idea from the conceptual motherlode of Ultimate Reality into mundane existence is also expressed through notions of negation. *Self-naughting* is the term Coomaraswamy uses to describe this process, and the most immediate proof of this condition as a prerequisite to any advanced spiritual state, he argued, is found in its universal institutionalization in the monastic societies of diverse religious systems:

> All initiations and, likewise, Buddhist ordination, which as in monasticism elsewhere is a kind of initiation, involve at the outset a self-denial . . . just as rivers lose their former name and lineage when they reach the sea . . . so men of the four castes . . . discard their former names . . . it is thus that the "exile" sets to work to "de-form himself of himself," as Eckhart expresses it . . . or, in other words, to "transform" himself.[66]

Self-naughting can be achieved, though, only when one no longer hesitates to structure thought in a conscious, rational manner, but simply acts, without even the momentary reflection it takes to distinguish the doer from the doing. Like any genuine experience of Ultimate Reality, Coomaraswamy asserts, this state of "right-mindedness," or as he more often identifies it, of *dementation*,[67] is beyond verbal description, " . . . a comprehension which is either a matter of experience, or no matter."[68] Through dementation, artists first awaken to the infinite number of "latent potentialities" in their work, intuitively comprehending and reconciling the function of their mundane actions with their higher, innate relationship with and participation in Ultimate Reality. As a consequence, conscious desire no longer acts as a locomotive force in the creative process, not because the artist is "apathetic," but because in this Reality in which all desires are already possessed in perfection, the notion of pursuit is simply inapplicable. Using the Hindu-Buddhist model of the *Arhat*,[69] Coomaraswamy explains, "if he is not curious about empirical truths . . . it is not because he does not know but because he does not think in terms of past or future, but is only now. If he is 'idle,' from our point of view who still have 'things to do,' it is because he is 'all in act' with an activity independent of time."[70] Ultimately, then, the goal of Coomaraswamy's artistic self-negation is not nihilistic but transcendent. Through dementation, self-naughting arises, a state which operates without the mediating process of conscious intellection. And in this state, "there is no longer a distinction of Knower from Known or of Knowledge and Being, but only a Knowledge as Being and a Being as Knowledge; when . . . 'Thought and Being are consubstantial.'"[71] The artist who achieves this condition, Coomaraswamy contends, enjoys the "constancy of the Supernal mind."

Apparently Cage concurred wholeheartedly with Coomaraswamy on all of these points, though again, in assuming such an aesthetic position, either on anonymity as a prerequisite to artistic integrity, or on the true place of the "artist" in the creative process, Cage framed his views as the antithesis to nineteenth-century European attitudes. In the 1952 "Juilliard Lecture," for example, he compares these two opposing attitudes, reinforcing his own position with references to the autonomy of sound, a central facet of his own aesthetic of indeterminacy. His aesthetic goal is again explicit—the reunification of life and art:

> The most that can be accomplished by no matter what musical idea is to show how intelligent the composer was who had it . . . the most that can be accomplished by the musical expression of feeling is to show how emotional the composer was who had it. If anyone wants to get a feeling of how emotional a composer proved himself to be, he has to confuse himself to the same final extent that the composer did and imagine that sounds are not sounds at all but are Beethoven and that men are not men but are sounds. Any child will tell us: this is simply not the case. To realize this, one has to put a stop to studying music. That is to say, one has to stop all the thinking that separates music from living.[72]

Cage's regard for artistic anonymity was far more, though, than a convenient means by which to engage in mock battles with the ghosts of composers past. Even his own musical heroes were subject to criticism should their works draw attention to the figure of the artist. At one point, even Varèse would be chided:

> What is unnecessary in Varèse (from a present point of view of necessity) are all his mannerisms, of which two stand out as signatures (the repeated note resembling a telegraphic transmission and the cadence of a tone held through a crescendo to maximum amplitude). These mannerisms do not establish sounds in their own right. They make it quite difficult to hear the sounds just as they are, for they draw attention to Varèse and his imagination.[73]

Though Cage never used the terms "self-naughting" or "dementation" in his writings or lectures, his comprehension of and aesthetic affinities with these concepts is entirely articulate. In the lecture-performance *45' For a Speaker* [1954], Cage's belief in the artistic necessity of the emancipation from Self is evident in one of the work's opening criticisms: "Composers are spoken of as having ears for music which generally means that nothing presented to their ears can be heard by them. Their ears are walled in with sounds of their own imagination."[74] A few pages later, Cage offers his corrective perspective, explaining, "what I think & what I feel can be my inspiration but it is then also my pair of blinders. To see one must go beyond the imagination and for that one must stand absolutely still as though in the center of a leap."[75] This same attitude is apparent in one of Cage's more general newspaper reviews of a European contemporary music festival from the late 1940s, surmising that composer Serge Nigg ". . . does not seem to have yet taken the walk around himself that Satie remarked was necessary before sitting down to compose."[76]

A handful of remarks from the late 1950s describe what Cage felt to be the mental state that facilitates artistic activity, a state so identical to Coomaraswamy's condition of "dementation" that one may well speculate on their genealogical kinship. One passage in "Composition as Process" reveals in fairly direct fashion the relation of Cage's thought to the classic Indian concept:

> One evening Morton Feldman said that when he composed he was dead; this recalls to me the statement of my father, an inventor, who says he does his best work when he is sound asleep. The two suggest the "deep sleep" of Indian mental practice. The ego no longer blocks action. A fluency obtains which is characteristic of nature. The seasons make the round of spring, summer, fall, and winter, interpreted in Indian thought as creation, preservation, destruction, and quiescence. Deep sleep is comparable to quiescence.[77]

Cage's most succinct description of dementation arose in the course of an informal conversation with Philip Guston in the late 1950s, telling the artist, "When you are working, everybody is in your studio—the past, your friends, the art world, and above all your own ideas—all are there. But as you continue painting, they start leaving, one by one, and you are left completely alone. Then, if you are lucky, even you leave."[78]

As the quoted excerpts above suggest, Cage was seldom direct in acknowledging Coomaraswamy's work, making it difficult at times to distinguish conclusively those coincidental instances of aesthetic parallelism from genuine appropriations. Over the years, his references to Coomaraswamy were both frequent and redundant of one another, citing the importance of *The Transformation of Nature in Art* to his aesthetic development. When asked for additional information on the subject, he merely contributed a reference to a single concept contained within this text: "Art is the imitation of Nature in her manner of operation."[79] Cage never went into detail as to his own interpretation of this statement; fortunately, Coomaraswamy clarified the meaning of each of the terms within this definition at various points in his own scholarship.

It is surprising to discover that the only direct quotation from Coomaraswamy found in Cage's aesthetic statements is, in actuality, not Coomaraswamy's at all, but a definition Coomaraswamy borrowed himself from the writings of St. Thomas Aquinas.[80] Both Aquinas and Coomaraswamy apply the term "Nature" in the broadest context, indicating the universal, natural order through which individual phenomena are created. Its implications are more cosmic than physical; it implies more immediately the cycle of the seasons than the characteristics of any individual artifact. To Aquinas, Coomaraswamy explains, "Nature" is synonymous with "'Mother Nature,' *Natura naturans, Creatrix, Universalis, Deus . . .* ":[81]

> Nature, for example in the statement "Art imitates nature in her manner of operation," does not refer to any visible part of our environment; and when Plato says "according to nature," he does not mean "as things behave," but as they should behave, not "sinning against nature." The traditional Nature is Mother Nature, that principle by which things are "natured," by which, for example, a horse is horsey and by which a man is human. Art is an imitation of the nature of things, not of their appearances.[82]

"'Imitation' (*mimesis*)," Coomaraswamy warns, is a word that can be "easily misunderstood."[83] Just as "art" required emancipation from its restrictive, contemporary western application, Coomaraswamy's interpretation of "imitation" broadens the base of this term considerably, and its meaning becomes clearer by perceiving the differences between art that is merely an imitation of nature and art that imitates nature *in her manner of operation*. The former, Coomaraswamy explains, constitutes the simple act of formal mimicry; it is only "a conception of art as something seeking its perfection in the nearest possible approaches to illusion."[84] An art that imitates nature in her manner of operation, however, reflects the process through which the artist invariably comes face to face "with the inner essence, with the spiritual essence of man."[85] Indeed, even this kind of imitation results in "the embodiment in matter of a preconceived form" (again, "preconceived" in that "the ideal pattern is pre-existent in the divine intellect"[86]), but by emphasizing art as the imitation of a dynamic, the resultant product becomes little more than a by-product of this more essential process.

Aquinas' definition, in other terms, describes an artistic act of creation that fashions itself after the same creative dynamic found in Nature. It is intelligent, yet it does not revert to the baser level of intellection; unmotivated by results and detached from "past" or "future," it acts only within the realm of the present. Coomaraswamy himself rewords Aquinas's statement on several occasions. Art is, for example, "an imitation of that perfect spontaneity—the identity of intuition and expression in those who are of the kingdom of heaven which is within us."[87] Making an allusion to Buddhist philosophy, he cites, "the first canon of Hsieh Ho, which asserts that the work of art must reveal 'the operation of the spirit (ch'i) in life-movement' . . . "[88] In more generic terms, Coomaraswamy asserts that by imitating Nature in her manner of operation, artists engage in the creative process much as God does, though admittedly with far fewer resources at their disposal:

> . . . the human artificer works like the Divine Artificer, with only this important distinction, that the human artificer has to make use of already existing materials, and to impose new forms on these materials, while the Divine Artificer provides his own material out of the infinitely "possible," which is not yet, and is therefore called "nothing," whence the expression *ex nihilo fit*.[89]

The aesthetic attitudes shared by Cage and Coomaraswamy demonstrate quite clearly why the two merit consideration in relation to one another. Still, it is imperative to acknowledge outright that they are hardly kindred spirits, aesthetically speaking. In fact, from certain standpoints, it is hard to imagine a philosophic attitude less sympathetic with Cage's than that of Coomaraswamy, and the study of these aesthetic divergences enhances an understanding of their relationship by mapping its boundaries and, more importantly, illuminating the specifics of Cage's appropriative subversions. The two figures seem compatible in their emphasis upon art as a creative process, for instance, and at first, Coomaraswamy's contention that "Works of art are reminders; in other words, supports of contemplation,"[90] appears wholly complementary to Cage's outlook. Yet their respective aesthetics include stark differences of opinion over the qualities a work of art must possess in order to function properly, a difference expressed through issues such as the relation between the object and its environment and the means by which an object interacts with an audience. Coomaraswamy qualifies that in order to inspire contemplation, and since the artist is "a rational being, it is taken for granted that every work has a theme or subject and a corresponding utility or meaning."[91] The "message" of any work of art, he contends, is three-fold, operating simultaneously on the levels of "denotation, connotation, and suggestion; statement, implication, and content; literal, allegorical, and anagogic."[92] A work of art, then, must consist of "a symbol or group of symbols having an ascertained rational significance and an even deeper content, not functioning only as means to recognition but as a means to communication and to vision."[93] It is, therefore, not only possible but expected that a work derive its value from its ability to communicate its theme:

> The fundamental judgment is of the degree of the artist's success in giving clear expression to the theme of his work. In order to answer the question, Has the thing been well said? it will evidently be necessary for us to know what it was that was to be said. It is for this reason that in every discussion of works of art we must begin with their subject matter.[94]

Underlying Coomaraswamy's system of aesthetic judgment, therefore, is a single, unflagging belief, which he restates time and again in the course of his scholarship: "the purpose of art is always one of effective communication."[95]

At the same time that Cage was absorbing *The Transformation of Nature in Art*, his own artistic experiences were impelling him toward very different conclusions. Cage had already begun to question the validity of art as communication during the war years, and by 1948 various remarks suggest that he had at least begun to resolve this issue. Conscious attempts at communication on the part of the artist, he theorized, were not at all responsible for the successful transmission of a work's "meaning," and could even be harmful to the work's integrity. Instead, the most important facet of any artistic experience was the mutual attainment of the proper, self-naughted mental state on the part of the creative artist, performer (if relevant) and audience member. Cage illustrated this idea through the example of a concert featuring the works of Ives and Webern that he attended with two friends, Lou Harrison and Mimi Wollner:

> I don't think it is a matter here of communication (we communicate quite adequately with words) or even of expressivity. Neither Lou nor Mimi in the case of Ives, nor I in the case of Webern, had the slightest concern with what the music was about. We were simply transported. I think the answer to this riddle is simply that when the music was composed the composers were at one with themselves. The performers became disinterested to the point that they became unselfconscious, and a few listeners in those brief moments of listening forgot themselves, enraptured, and so gained themselves. It is these moments of completeness that music can give, providing one can concentrate one's mind on it, that is, give one's self in return to the music, that are such deep pleasure, and that is why we love the art.[96]

By 1952, and under the compelling force of his Buddhist studies, Cage abandoned altogether any previously held beliefs in the expressive properties of art, phrasing his argument directly: "There is no com-

munication and nothing being said."[97] Later elaborations would
maintain his assertion that communication was the proper domain
and function of language, subsequently excusing the arts from this
responsibility. If the arts were to be appreciated, Cage insisted, they
were to be valued not for their "message" but for the sheer self-naughted nature of their execution and for the opportunity they provided to
an audience to experience the same, an attitude summarized in Cage's
program notes for a 1956 performance by the Cunningham Dance
Company:

> We are not, in these dances and music, saying something. We are
> simple-minded enough to think that if we were saying something
> we would use words. We are rather doing something. The mean-
> ing of what we do is determined by each one who sees and hears
> it. At a recent performance of ours at Cornell College in Iowa, a
> student turned to a teacher and said, "What does it mean?" The
> teacher's reply was, "Relax, there are no symbols here to confuse
> you. Enjoy yourself!" I may add there are no stories and no psy-
> chological problems. There is simply an activity of movement,
> sound, and light. The costumes are all simple in order that you
> may see the movement.[98]

The following year, Cage expressed this same sentiment more epi-
grammatically: "New music: new listening. Not an attempt to understand something that is being said, for, if something were being said,
the sounds would be given the shapes of words. Just an attention to
the activity of sounds."[99]

Not surprisingly, in valuing art for its communicative component,
Coomaraswamy also bestows primal importance on the idea of *tradition*. Any sensible artist would naturally value tradition, he asserted,
if for no other reason than as "a means to the conservation of energy;"[100] more significantly, though, as a time-honored system understood by all, tradition was the most effective means by which to communicate a work's theme. Artistic adherence to the pre-ordained rules
of a tradition, he explained, does not contradict the notion of a spon-
taneous, self-naughted creative process, but actually provides the necessary direction to this process, serving as:

> . . . the vehicle assumed by spontaneity . . . rather than as any kind
> of bondage . . . the artist does indeed become ever less and less
> conscious of rules . . . but at every stage the artist will delight in
> rules, as the master of language delights in grammar, though he
> may speak without constant reference to the treatises on syn-
> tax.[101]

While his aesthetic depreciated the notion of "originality" to a foolish
egoism, Coomaraswamy's insistence upon an artistic language rooted

in tradition amplified the negative implications of this term, transforming it from misnomer to pejorative. In India and China, for example, he points out that "it would be an insult to a thinker to praise the novelty or originality of his ideas, or his independence of authority," since "good form, in any and every sense of the word, consists in adherence to custom and precedent."[102] Moreover, he claimed, originality is scarcely a noteworthy factor in a work's reception, for although an audience may be diverse in its levels of artistic experience and knowledge, at no level of sophistication was originality of aesthetic consequence. Taking painting as his example, he explains:

> Everyone is interested in the subject-matter or application of the work, as a matter of course. More specifically, we find that learned men, pundits, are concerned about the correctness of the iconography; the pious are interested in the representation of holy themes as such; connoisseurs are moved by the expression of *bhava* [nature/sentiment] and *rasa* [the substance of aesthetic experience] and like to express their appreciation in the technical terminology of rhetoric; masters of the art, fellow artists, regard chiefly the drawing, and technical skill in general; ordinary laymen like the bright colors, or marvel at the artist's dexterity. Those who are in love are chiefly interested in portraiture reflecting all the charms of the original. Rarely do we meet with any mention of originality or novelty.[103]

From these and similar statements, one could well anticipate Coomaraswamy's particular distaste for the modernist movements of the twentieth century, and it is fair criticism to note that though espousing a *philosophia perennis* and the timeless, immutable principles which are supposedly engendered in the diverse artistic activities of all periods and cultures, he never sufficiently overcame his distaste for the post-Renaissance West to recognize or accept its art as a legitimate manifestation of this philosophy. The degree of this distaste is still debated. While some flatly brand Coomaraswamy a reactionary archaist, others judge him more moderately, noting only his curious estrangement from the modern world. Throughout his writings, this estrangement is tacitly implied through the almost total absence of contemporary citations; even within his elaborate network of cross-cultural references, documentation is based almost exclusively in antiquity, his examples seldom dating beyond the year 1400.

Western art of the twentieth century was especially irksome to Coomaraswamy, and his writings are intermittently spiked with seething invectives against the trends that had led to the "widespread confusion"[104] of this century. Primitivism, for example, was "superficial,"[105] "mere mannerism, and ridiculous,"[106] the spurious "caricature"[107] of genuine primitive models, and he cynically compared the "real" primitive artist with the contemporary "primitivist," noting, "[the] Neolithic formalist was not an interior decorator, but a metaphysical man who saw life whole and had to *live* by his wits."[108] Cubism, too, had misinterpreted the basic principle of artistic "imitation," and represented "not the technical and universal language of a science, but an imitation of the external appearances or style of the technical terms of sciences."[109]

But references to specific contemporary artistic movements such as those above are relatively rare in Coomaraswamy's scholarship, since he more often framed his objections to modern art through the general aesthetic issues relevant to the entire period. Having deemed artistic anonymity a moral imperative, for example, he openly loathed the "insistent self-expressionism"[110] of contemporary art, admonishing, "the way to liberty has nothing whatever in common with any wilful rebellion or calculated originality; least of all has it anything to do with functional self-expression."[111] Ultimately, the aesthetic implications of this contemporary self-expressionism foretold nothing less than cultural self-destruction:

> . . . in the last analysis the so-called "emancipation of the artist" is nothing but his final release from any obligation whatever to the God within him, and his opportunity to imitate himself or any other common clay at its worst; that all wilful self-expression is auto-erotic, narcissistic and Satanic, and the more its essentially paranoic quality develops, suicidal . . . [112]

Coomaraswamy conceded, however, that the western artist was not entirely to blame, citing the unnatural western practice of partitioning the arts into the categories of "fine" and "applied" as the origin of this aesthetic disaster. This division, he insisted, had led to the loss of true "art" in both fields; "applied" art had degenerated to the point of "artless manufacture in factories,"[113] and the "naive behaviorism" of modern fine art rendered it useless, "because it has no ends beyond itself, because it is too 'fine' to be 'applied,' and too 'significant' to mean anything."[114] Understandably, then, Coomaraswamy's attitude toward the contemporary notion of "art for art's sake" is utterly dismissive:

> The doctrine of art for art's sake is disposed of in a sentence quoted in the *Sahitya Darpana* V, I, Commentary: "All expressions, human or revealed, are directed to an end beyond themselves; or if not so determined are thereby comparable only to the utterances of a madman."[115]

Several of Cage's remarks from the 1940s and 1950s strongly suggest that he was well aware of the limits of his aesthetic alliance with Coomaraswamy, and though he never named him explicitly as an intellectual detractor, many of his statements from this period seem to respond directly to Coomaraswamy's objections to contemporary art. In contrast to Coomaraswamy's insistence upon the guiding role of tradition in the artistic process, for instance, Cage contended that it was pointless for contemporary artists to hold fast to the western tradition, since the tradition itself was both dysfunctional and in an advanced state of deterioration.

> . . . we are still at the point where most musicians are clinging to the complicated torn-up competitive remnants of tradition, and, furthermore, a tradition that was always a tradition of breaking with tradition, and furthermore, a tradition that in its ideas of counterpoint and harmony was out of step not only with its own but with all other traditions.[116]

Consequently, he argued, art needed to extract itself from its surroundings through non-conventional means (an attitude he shared with the Abstract Expressionists in general), where it might offer itself as a model of spiritual well-being. One of Cage's first references to this notion comes from 1943, when in the course of discussing what had been perceived as the "cacophony" of his percussion concerts, he explained that "people may leave my concerts thinking they have heard 'noise,' but will then hear unsuspected beauty in their everyday life. This music has a therapeutic value for city dwellers . . ."[117] Reviewing a Cage lecture five years later, a student newspaper recounted how he had "stressed the fact that in a 'right society, art is the handmaiden of tradition, but in our sick society, art is a guide to the integration of the personality.' For this purpose, he stated, music need not communicate, since one can get value in return for losing oneself in the material being heard."[118] In contrast to Coomaraswamy's disdain of contemporary artists as aesthetic infidels, these same persons were heroic figures in Cage's estimation, their very ability to create art in modern times proving that they had successfully secured themselves against various cultural ills that threatened mankind:

> . . . a composer may be neurotic, as indeed being a member of contemporary society he probably is, but it is not on account of his neurosis that he composes, but rather in spite of it. Neuroses act to stop and block. To be able to compose signifies the overcoming of these obstacles.[119]

Cage had established his own position on the purpose of art well before any of his Indian-based readings, and his perspective on this subject also differs markedly from that of Coomaraswamy. Even in his earliest days at the Cornish School in Seattle his fundamental conception of the purpose of music had little if anything to do the conveyance of meaning through the symbols of tradition—in fact, it had little to do with "meaning" at all. In 1937, he outlined the simple purpose of his own art concisely:

> Let us take a premise which seems apparent and elementary: music is made of sound. Every one with ears may hear it. The music is made to be heard. A piece of music is constructed, much as a chair or building is constructed. . . . The chair is useful for sitting, the home for dwelling, the music for hearing. From this point of view, the one which I am proposing, music need not be understood, but rather it must be heard.[120]

Some of Cage's later remarks from the 1950s deal specifically with the issue of "originality," and his position deflects Coomaraswamy's indictment of this term by qualifying that there are various *types* of originality, all but one of which, Cage claims, are false. It is not startling to discover that his examples of "false" originality come from the seventeenth and eighteenth centuries, implying as well those contemporary composers who continued to refer to these periods through their own compositions (not the least of which being those associated with the waning Neo-Classical movement):

> There are kinds of originality: several that are involved with success, beauty, and ideas (of order, of expression: i.e., Bach, Beethoven); a single that is not involved, neuter, so to say. All of the several involved kinds are generally existent and only bring one sooner or later to a disgust with art. Such original artists appear, as Antonin Artaud said, as pigs: concerned with self-advertisement. What is advertised? Finally, and at best, only something that is connected not with making history but with the past: Bach, Beethoven. If it's a new idea of order, it's Bach; if it's a heartfelt expression, it's Beethoven. That is not the single necessary originality that is not involved and that makes history.[121]

From a cultural standpoint, Cage explained, the only true brand of originality was utterly atomistic, depending upon unique individual efforts. "History," he remarked, "is the story of original actions,"[122] and tradition, which Coomaraswamy understood as a repetition of patterns necessary for the maintenance of culture and communication, only constituted redundancy and wasted labor in Cage's terms:

> That one sees that the human race is one person (all of its members parts of the same body, brothers—not in competition any more than hand is in competition with the eye) enables him to see that originality is necessary, for there is no need for eye to do what hand so well does. In this way, the past and the present are to be observed and each person makes what he alone must make, bringing for the whole of human society into existence a historical fact, and then, on and on, in continuum and discontinuum.[123]

In India, Coomaraswamy once explained, "it is constantly asserted that all art is intellectual, *citta-samjna*: the *Lankavatara Sutra*
expresses it thus: 'The real picture is not in the colour nor the surface
nor the saucer.'"[124] As stated in the opening passages of this chapter,
this attitude aptly expresses the position taken by the present study
on the issue of the detection of Indian stylistic borrowings in Cage's
actual musical works. Acknowledging these limitations, it is still possible to identify some "Indian" element in a variety of Cage's works
from the 1940s and early 1950s, although the nature and profundity of
these instances vary widely.

A handful of small projects in the 1940s, for example, specifically
explore the idea of anonymity. The first of these, *Double Music*
(1941), co-written with Lou Harrison for percussion quartet, was composed well before Cage's studies of Coomaraswamy, and is therefore
indicative of his pre-existent aesthetic sympathies with India rather
than demonstrative of any genuine Indian "influence." The story of
the work's creation is well-known. Each composer assigned to himself
two of the four parts to be composed, arriving through mutual agreement at the number of measures the work would contain. No other
specifications were prescribed, and the two, remaining purposefully
ignorant throughout the compositional process of the material being
created by the other, ultimately assembled the respective parts to
complete the piece. Cage found the possibilities this process afforded
intriguing, stating in 1948:

> . . . there is a deeply rewarding world of musical experience to be
> found in this way. The peculiarities of a single personality disap-
> pear almost entirely and there comes into perception through the
> music a natural friendliness, which has the aspect of a festival. I
> hereby suggest this method of composition as the solution of
> Russia's current musical problems. What could better describe a
> democratic view of life? . . . I am looking forward to working . . .
> with Lou Harrison and Merton Brown on finding a means where-
> by *Triple Music* can be written combining the techniques of their
> secundal chromatic counterpoint and my structural rhythm, and
> thereby providing a means with which three or four people can
> collaborate on a single piece of music. The pleasure here would be
> in friendliness and anonymity, and thus in music.[125]

Triple Music, though, was never realized. In a later article from 1951,
Cage made allusion to this same manner of creation involving the
fusion of parts independently conceived by multiple composers; the
resultant product, he asserted, "becomes a polyphony anonymous by
nature, but alive the way nature is."[126] Of lesser note, but still illus-
trative of the point, are the twenty *Party Pieces* (c. 1944–45), which

Cage co-wrote with Harrison, Virgil Thomson and Henry Cowell as a diversionary party game. As Harrison explains:

> Each composer present would write a measure, fold the paper at the bar line and, on the new fresh sheet, put only two notes to guide the next composer in his connection. The next composer would write a bar, fold at the bar line and leave two more black spots and so on. It seems to me that we would begin simultaneously and pass them along in rotation in a sort of surrealist assembly line.[127]

Beyond these instances, any direct or indirect relations between Cage's works and the principles drawn from his Indian source readings seems relatively superficial, consisting of little more than the programmatic themes found in some of his compositions:

> The *Sonatas and Interludes*, dedicated to the pianist, Maro Ajemian, were written when I began living at the East River, and first became seriously aware of Oriental philosophy. After reading the work of Ananda K. Coomaraswamy, I decided to attempt the expression in music of the "permanent emotions" of Indian tradition: the heroic, the erotic, the wondrous, the mirthful, sorrow, fear, anger, the odious, and their common tendency toward tranquility. These pieces were the first product of that effort. . . . [128]

As Cage acknowledges, the idea of the nine *rasas*, or permanent emotions, of Indian philosophy came directly from his study of Coomaraswamy. Yet while he may have explained the twenty *Sonatas and Interludes* as expressions of these *rasas*, the degree of literalness in his statement is indeterminable, and the work's history only compounds this uncertainty.[129] Originally, Cage wrote only four sonatas, which Maro Ajemian premiered in April of 1946. Entitled simply *Four Sonatas*, this collection constituted a "complete" set at the time, strongly implying that the expression of nine permanent emotions was not one of the original compositional goals. As those close to Ajemian recall, Cage's delight in her performance inspired him to expand the work over the next two years to include sixteen sonatas and four interludes.[130] Even if this final version ultimately assumed the nine permanent emotions as its overall theme, it is impossible to cross-match any one sonata to any one emotion, if in fact Cage's account is meant to be taken that literally at all. Consequently, the relation of these *rasas* to the *Sonatas and Interludes* seems doomed to be an eternally murky issue.

In contrast, the various parts of the *Sixteen Dances* (1950–51) are explicitly associated with individual *rasas*. But even in this case, such connections cannot be drawn between these *rasas* and any musical element of the work, for the nature of Cage's "transitional" chance compositional processes during 1950–51 all but precluded the possibility of extra-musical "depiction."[131] Instead, the *rasas* are manifested in the organizational plan of Cunningham's choreography, each dance expressing one particular *rasa*.[132] Using anywhere between one and four dancers and partitioned by interludes, these dances render the following structure:

I	Anger	(solo)
II	Interlude	(trio)
III	Humor	(solo)
IV	Interlude	(duet)
V	Sorrow	(solo)
VI	Interlude	(quartet)
VII	Heroic	(solo)
VIII	Interlude	(quartet)
IX	Odious	(solo)
X	Interlude	(duet)
XI	Wondrous	(solo)
XII	Interlude	(trio)
XIII	Fear	(solo)
XIV	Interlude	(quartet)
XV	Erotic	(duet)
XVI	Tranquillity	(quartet)

Cage's first orchestral score (and Cunningham's first ballet), *The Seasons* (1947), was "a further expression of still another Indian philosophical concept."[133] Cage's previously cited remark regarding the self-naughted, creative condition identified by Morton Feldman and its relation to the Indian notion of the seasons is one example of his explicit reference to this concept. Like the relation of the *rasas* to *Sixteen Dances*, however, any genuine relationship between the Indian concept of the seasons and the music Cage composed for the ballet is not demonstrable. While the dance is structured into sections which are identified with individual seasons, even Cunningham did not at first explain the work's theme through any connections with Indian concepts; the program notes that he and Cage wrote for the work's premiere, for instance, give no inkling of the role Indian thought may have played in the work's design or motivation, elaborating instead upon the structural organization of the music.[134] In the 1960s, however, Cage explicitly describes this work as "an attempt to express the traditional Indian view of the seasons as quiescence (winter), creation (spring), preservation (summer), and destruction (fall)."[135] Similarly, Cage related each of the four movements of the *String Quartet in Four Parts* (1949–50) to particular seasons. Yet again, his description lacks any explicit connection to his Indian readings, describing the work's theme as:

> ... that of the seasons, but the first two movements are also concerned with place. Thus in the first movement the subject is Summer in France while that of the second is Fall in America. The third and fourth are also concerned with musical subjects, Winter being expressed as a canon, Spring as a quodlibet.[136]

One final work includes the marked presence of Indian subjects, its narrative structured within the kind of multi-cultural system of cross-references that characterizes the scholarship of both Coomaraswamy and Joseph Campbell. In the 1948 lecture, "A Composer's Confessions," Cage announced plans for "several operas," the libretti of which would be written by Campbell.[137] Richard Lippold was apparently involved in the plans as well, for in a letter of that same year from Lippold to the administration of Black Mountain College, he made a similar reference to these projects.[138] The extant materials for the first of these "several operas," *Perseus and Andromeda*, comprise some nineteen pages of notes and libretto sketches in Campbell's hand, now among the materials in his estate.[139] While based on the Greek myth, this three-act work derived much of its dramatic imagery from Hinduism, such as the *kundalini* image of the dragon and the *uroboros* (the figure of a serpent in a perfect circle, head meeting tail, signifying harmony and renewal). The libretto sketches also include quotations from Psalms 72:6–9; 73:17; 73:19; and 74:14. Other portions, Campbell noted, were to be based on "religious mystical poems," such as those of John Donne and Gerard Manley Hopkins.

Campbell's tentative titles for some of the opera's scenes—"Music of the Infinite Void," "Music of the Island of Jewels," "Sky Ballet," "Andromeda sings the great solo of her life"—are tantalizing fodder for idle speculations on the sounds Cage may have been considering at the time. Unfortunately, not a note was ever composed, and Campbell's wife, Jean Erdman, explains that all such plans were dropped after Cage's final transition toward chance operations. While the *Concerto for Prepared Piano and Chamber Orchestra* and the *Sixteen Dances* may represent the beginnings of a new period in Cage's creative life, this uncomposed opera symbolizes the close of the previous period.

Cage's exposure to South Asian aesthetics through the writings of Coomaraswamy does not express itself in the actual materials of his musical compositions. Indeed, in this case, the picture is not in the colors. Yet this exposure remains essential to the comprehension of these works, as Cage wove these studies into the very foundation of his own evolving aesthetic, shaping the larger intellectual realm in which these works were written. At times, these studies provided him with a new terminology; at others, they supplied flexible notions that he could convert into confirmation for his own ultra-modernist agenda, despite the anti-modernist proclivities of their original source. Ultimately, and perhaps most significantly, these studies served as aesthetic seed corn, and the thread of many of the concepts described in this essay remained with Cage throughout his life, as he cleverly extended and translated them into terminology derived from East Asian philosophy in the 1950s (e.g., Taoism, Buddhism and in particular, Zen), from social philosophy in the 1960s (e.g., Marshall McLuhan and Buckminster Fuller), and from Thoreau and anarchic theory in the 1970s.

Notes

1.   With the exception of a few childhood years spent in Michigan, a year spent traveling Europe (1930–31), and about eighteen months studying in New York (1933–34), Cage lived in California until 1938, when he went to Seattle to work at the Cornish School. For an excellent and historically corrective account of this California period, see Thomas S. Hines, "Then Not Yet 'Cage': The Los Angeles Years, 1912–38," in *John Cage: Composed in America,* ed. Marjorie Perloff and Charles Junkerman (Chicago: The University of Chicago Press, 1994), 65–99.

2.   Hines, 65.

3.   In this instance, Cage was Cowell's "pupil." In the 1940s, however, Cage occasionally served as a substitute lecturer for Cowell at the New School. See "At the New School . . .," *Silence: Lectures and Writings* (Middletown: Wesleyan Univ. Press, 1961), 93.

4.   Richard Lippold, telephone interview with the author, December 8, 1993.

5.   Cage's New York debut concert of percussion works at the Museum of Modern Art in February of 1943, for example, prompted several comparisons with the music of Bali. See N.S., "Percussion 'Music' Heard at Concert," *The New York Times,* Feb. 8, 1943. See also Paul Bowles, "Percussionists in Concert Led By John Cage," *New York Herald Tribune,* Feb. 8, 1943.

6.   It is difficult to convey the degree of originality with which Cage's percussion works were credited at the time. Suffice it to illustrate, in a 1943 *Time* magazine profile of Cage, the editors felt it necessary to include an uncharacteristic footnote to the text defining the curious term "percussion music" for its readers. See n.a., "Percussionist," *Time,* Feb. 22, 1943, 70. (The

definition read: "The type of music produced by instruments that are struck with sticks or hammers, e.g., drums, cymbals, gongs.")

Virgil Thomson was one of the most insightful of Cage's critics regarding his relation to Asian music, commenting in 1945, "The effect in general is slightly reminiscent, on first hearing, of Indonesian gamelan orchestras, though the interior structure of Mr. Cage's music is not Oriental at all. His work attaches itself, in fact, to two different traditions of Western modernism. One is the percussive experiments begun by Marinetti's Futurist noisemakers and continued in the music of Edgard Varèse, Henry Cowell, and George Antheil, all of which, though made in full awareness of Oriental methods, is thoroughly Western in its expression. The other is, curiously enough, the atonal music of Arnold Schoenberg." (Virgil Thomson, "Expressive Percussion" [January 22, 1945]), in *John Cage: An Anthology*, ed. Richard Kostelanetz (New York: Da Capo Press, 1991), 72.

7.   A.V.B., "Composers Forum: Jacob Avshalomoff Shares Program with John Cage," *New York Herald Tribune*, Jan. 26, 1948.

8.   Even those who take Cage's reminiscences at face value will find little to corroborate any claims of Asian musical influence. His only recollections on the subject of transcultural exchange cast him as the exporter, rather than the importer, of materials, as he described how a recording of his *Book of Music* (1944) for two prepared pianos was "used by the OWI [Office of War Information] during the war as Indonesian Supplement no. 1, which meant that when there was nothing urgent to do on the radio-beamed-to-the-South-Pacific this music was used, with the hope of convincing the natives that America loves the Orient." John Cage, "A Composer's Confessions" [or "Vassar Lecture," 1948], in *John Cage: Writer*, ed. Richard Kostelanetz (New York: Limelight Editions, 1993), 40.

9.   A promotional flyer indicates that on February 18, 1939, Cage served as a panelist on a symposium entitled "What Next in American Art?" sponsored by the Seattle Artists League. His presentation included "selected records of negro music—from 'primitive to boogie-woogie.'" Three years later, Cage described the rhythmic system of *Quartet*, his first percussion work, commenting, "I organized the composition on a rhythmic basis, indicating no instruments. Friends helped me perform it on kitchen utensils, pieces of wood, tire rims, brake drums, etc. I was unaware at the time that I was doing what many negro street musicians in New Orleans had done. I was sharing points of view of Schoenberg and hot jazz combined." Quoted in Peter Yates, "Organized Sound: Notes in the history of a new disagreement: between sound and tone," *California Arts and Architecture*, 1942.

10.   William ("Bill") Russell (1905–1992), is remembered today primarily for his contributions to jazz. During the late 1930s, he was an active participant in Cage's percussion "movement," contributing works to the repertory and serving as conductor in several percussion concerts.

11.   John Cage, "The Future of Music: Credo" (c. 1940), *Silence*, 5.

12.   John Cage, "Some Ideas About Music and Film" (1951), *John Cage: Writer*, 63.

13.   Cage, "A Composer's Confessions" (1948), *John Cage: Writer*, 36.

14.   John Cage, "Tokyo Lecture and Three Mesostics" (1986), *John Cage: Writer*, 178.

15.   John Cage, "Preface to Indeterminacy" (1958–59), *John Cage: Writer*, 78–79.

16.   Admittedly, many of Cage's earliest musical statements, which assumed the form of public lectures, are lost; however, the glimpses provided into these lectures through extant advertisements and subsequent reviews give no indication of the use of Asian-derived concepts or terminology. At the Annual Dinner of the Seattle Chapter of Pro Music, Inc. of October 10, 1938, for example, Cage was featured guest artist, presenting a lecture-recital entitled "Some Aspects of Modern Music." His talk, according to a promotional newspaper announcement, was "to reflect particularly his interests in percussion music, problems of rhythm, and in electrical music." Cage then played several works at the piano, including the premiere of his own *Metamorphosis*. On December 11, 1939, Cage, in another lecture-recital, spoke on "New Directions in Music," the featured lecturer on music for the Seattle Artists League's program of drama, music and painting which opened the League's 1939–40 season.

17.   John Cage, "Grace and Clarity" (1944), *Silence*, 90.

18.   Eckhart was greatly admired by Coomaraswamy, who claimed that this theologian " . . . with the possible exception of Dante, can be regarded from an Indian point of view as the greatest of all Europeans." Ananda Coomaraswamy, "Vedanta and Western Tradition" (1939), *Coomaraswamy: Selected Papers and Metaphysics*, ed. Roger Lipsey, Bollingen Series 89, vol. 2, (Princeton: Princeton University Press, 1977), 6. Buddhist scholar Daisetz Teitaro Suzuki also held Eckhart in high regard, and Cage would come across Eckhart again in Suzuki's public lectures and classes at Columbia University in the early 1950s.

19.   Mahendranath Gupta, *The Gospel of Sri Ramakrishna*, translated and with an introduction by Swami Nikhilananda (New York: Ramakrishna-Vivekananda Center, 1942).

20.   Cage typically recalled this text as his alternative for psychoanalysis during the latter 1940s. See, for example, "List No. 2" (1961), *John Cage: An Anthology*, 138.

21.   Cage, "A Composer's Confessions," 41.

22.   Coomaraswamy's "rediscovery" of Indian art represents just one manifestation of the growing anti-Imperialist, nationalist Indian movement of the time. His writings were appreciated, therefore, not just as lucid explications of Indian art, but as refutations of the predominant European attitude toward such art as senseless, ornamental, and non-functional.

23.   Joseph Campbell met Coomaraswamy in Boston on New Year's Eve of 1939. Cage never met Coomaraswamy, although he did strike up a friendship later with his widow, Dona Luisa, who was herself a Sanskrit scholar. Coomaraswamy did deliver at least one address at the Brooklyn Academy of Music on February 28, 1946, but it is unknown whether Cage attended.

24.   S. Chandrasekhar, *Ananda K. Coomaraswamy: A Critical Appreciation* (Bombay, India: Blackie and Son Publishers, 1977), 24.

25.   M. Sivaramkrishna, "Art and Nature in Ananda K. Coomaraswamy's Aesthetic," *Ananda Coomaraswamy: Centenary Essays*, ed. C.D. Narasimhaiah (Mysore, India: Univ. of Mysore, 1982), 130. Sivaramkrishna also identifies a fourth tenet essential to Coomaraswamy's aesthetic that deals with the role of the spectator, which is beyond the scope of this essay.

26.   Coomaraswamy's own terms for this concept are manifold. At times referred to as "God" this concept is also dubbed the "Supreme Identity," "the Divine Intellect," and a variety of other names. One can also draw rough analogies between these terms and the Taoist notion of "Tao," or the Buddhist concept of "Nothing." For the sake of clarity, Siviramkrishna's term "Ultimate Reality" will be employed consistently in this research, with open acknowledgement of the problematic nature of the term.

27.   Ananda Coomaraswamy, "The Vedic Doctrine of 'Silence'" (1937), in *Coomaraswamy: Selected Papers and Metaphysics*, ed. Roger Lipsey, Bollingen Series 89, vol. 2 (Princeton, NJ: Princeton University Press, 1977), 198.

28.   Ananda Coomaraswamy, "Meister Eckhart's View of Art," in *The Transformation of Nature in Art* (Cambridge, MA: Harvard University Press, 1934), 71.

29.   This state of "right-mindedness" will be discussed in detail in the pages that follow.

30.   Roger Lipsey, Introduction to *Coomaraswamy: Selected Papers*, ed. Roger Lipsey (Princeton, NJ: Bollingen Press, 1977), 6.

31.   *Philosophia perennis* is also the theme of Aldous Huxley's monograph, *The Perennial Philosophy* (New York: Harper & Bros., 1945). While Cage became familiar with this work as well during the 1940s, he never elevated Huxley to prominence in his private pantheon, as he did Coomaraswamy.

32.   Coomaraswamy, "Meister Eckhart's View of Art," 64–65.

33.   Ananda Coomaraswamy, "The Theory of Art in Asia," *The Transformation of Nature in Art*, 9.

34.   Ananda Coomaraswamy, "A Figure of Speech or a Figure of Thought?" *Studies in Comparative Religion* 6, no. 1 (Winter 1972): 45–46.

35.   Coomaraswamy, "The Theory of Art in Asia," 35.

36.   Coomaraswamy, "Meister Eckhart's View of Art," 64–65.

37.   Ibid.

38.   John Cage, "The East in the West," (1946), in *John Cage: Writer*, 24.

39.   John Cage, "Composition as Process" (1958), *Silence*, 44.

40.   One of the rare instances of Cage's use of the term "Ultimate Reality" appears in the Foreword to *A Year From Monday*, ix, where the concept is fused with rhetoric derived from Marshall McLuhan: "I then explained that I believe—and am acting upon—Marshall McLuhan's statement that we have through electronic technology produced an extension of our brains to the world formerly outside of us. To me that means that the disciplines, gradual and sudden (principally Oriental), formerly practiced by individuals to pacify their minds, bringing them into accord with ultimate reality, must now be practiced socially—that is, not just inside our heads, but outside of them, in the world, where our central nervous system effectively now is."

41. Ananda Coomaraswamy, "What is Common to Indian and Chinese Art?" *Studies in Comparative Religion* 7, no. 2 (Spring 1973): 77.

42. John Cage, "Lecture on Something" (c. 1951–52), *Silence*, 140.

43. John Cage, "Diary: How to Improve the World (You Will Only Make Matters Worse) 1965," *A Year From Monday*, 19.

44. John Cage, "Forerunners of Modern Music" (1949), originally published in *The Tiger's Eye* (March 1949), 52–56. Reprinted in *Silence*, 66.

45. Cage, "Lecture on Something" (c. 1951–52), *Silence*, 129.

46. John Cage, "More Satie" (1950), *John Cage: An Anthology*, 93.

47. Cage, "Composition as Process" (1958), 44–45.

48. The greater portion of this cross-referencing occurs in the voluminous footnotes which typified Coomaraswamy's writings. This brand of methodical and copious citation seems itself to be atypical of the Indian tradition of scholarship; the greater portion of scholarship from South Asia on Coomaraswamy consulted for this research, for example, quotes liberally from his writings, but seldom identifies original sources in the copious Western style.

49. Coomaraswamy, "What is Common to Indian and Chinese Art?," 77–78.

In this regard, Coomaraswamy's impact on Joseph Campbell's mode of scholarship is quite evident; Campbell himself noted that following his own early exchanges with Coomaraswamy, "I saw that my final object must be the substantial human Norm over which play the historical styles like so many passing moods. From the historical, perhaps too much was thereby subtracted; yet my study of mythology became simplified, clarified, and marvellously enriched." [Joseph Campbell, *The War Diary*, (n.d.) quoted in Stephen and Robin Larsen, *A Fire in the Mind: The Life of Joseph Campbell* (New York: Anchor Books, 1991), 287.]

50. Coomaraswamy, "The Theory of Art in Asia," 18.

51. Coomaraswamy, "What is Common to Indian and Chinese Art?", 77.

52. Betty Heimann, "Indian Art—and its Transcendence," *Ananda Coomaraswamy: Remembering and Remembering Again and Again*, ed. S. Durai Raja Singam (Petaling Jaya, Malaysia: Raja Singam, 1974), 24–25.

53. To date, there is no full-scale biography of Coomaraswamy, in large part due to his own insistence that one not be written.

54. Coomaraswamy, "Meister Eckhart's View of Art," 69.

55. Ananda Coomaraswamy, as quoted in Asok K. Bhattacharya's "Coomaraswamy's Approach to Art," in *Ananda Coomaraswamy: A Centenary Volume*, ed. Kalyan Kumar Dasgupta (Calcutta: Centre of Advanced Study in Ancient Indian History and Culture, Calcutta University, 1981), 9.

56. Coomaraswamy, "Meister Eckhart's View of Art," 91.

57. P. S. Sastri, *Ananda K. Coomaraswamy* (New Delhi: Arnold-Heinemann Publishers, 1974), 115.

58. John Cage, "Diary: How to Improve the World (You Will Only Make Matters Worse) 1965," *A Year From Monday*, 3.

59. Cage, "A Composer's Confessions," 40. Providing a definition for another term that would become quite prominent in his own rhetoric, Cage

goes on in this lecture to explain that the composer who makes music "without concern for money or fame but simple for the love of making it," is working, "as the Orient would say, *disinterestedly*." ("A Composer's Confessions," 42).

60.   Cage, "Lecture on Something" (c. 1951–52), *Silence*, 129. This last sentence may at first seem somewhat cryptic. However, it is simply Cage's appeal to reconfigure the Western mode of artistic creation and appreciation in a way which will restore an awareness of Ultimate Reality. "Nothing," a stock term in Buddhist literature, is roughly akin to Coomaraswamy's Ultimate Reality—a great state of undifferentiation, i.e., one in which distinctions and definitions are non-operative, and are thereby unable to cleave objects or ideas either from their common origin or from each other.

61.   Cage, "Forerunners of Modern Music," 63.

62.   John Cage, "Diary: How To Improve the World (You Will Only Make Matters Worse) Continued 1967," *A Year From Monday*, 151.

63.   Cage, "Diary: How To Improve the World (You Will Only Make Matters Worse) 1965," 7–8.

64.   Coomaraswamy, "The Theory of Art in Asia," 14.

65.   Ananda Coomaraswamy, "Akimcanna: Self-Naughting" (1940), *Coomaraswamy: Selected Papers and Metaphysics*, 88.

66.   Coomaraswamy, "Akimcanna: Self-Naughting," 101–102.

67.   Coomaraswamy also refers to the state of dementation as "the Eternal Mystery." See Ananda Coomaraswamy, "Manas" (1940), *Coomaraswamy: Selected Papers and Metaphysics*, 213–214.

68.   Coomaraswamy, "Manas," 215–216.

69.   "Arhat" is a Hindu term indicating an ascetic who has achieved an advanced spiritual state and is therefore entitled to material support and public reverence. Buddhism adopted this term, using it to designate an enlightened (and consequently, liberated) being.

70.   Coomaraswamy, "Akimcanna: Self-Naughting," 104.

71.   Coomaraswamy, "Manas," 212.

72.   John Cage, "Juilliard Lecture" (1952), *A Year From Monday*, 97.

73.   John Cage, "The History of Experimental Music in the United States" (1959), *Silence*, 69.

74.   John Cage, *45' For a Speaker* (1954), *Silence*, 155.

75.   Ibid., 170.

76.   John Cage, "Contemporary Music Festivals are Held in Italy," *Musical America* (June 1949). Reprinted in *John Cage: Writer*, 47.

77.   Cage, "Composition as Process," 37.

78.   Philip Guston, quoted in Philip Pavia and Irving Sandler, eds., "The Philadelphia Panel," *It Is* 5 (Spring 1960): 37, in Robert Storr, *Philip Guston* (New York: Abbeville Press, 1986), 62–4.

79.   This statement makes several appearances in Cage's prose, and may be found in "On Robert Rauschenberg, Artist and his Work" (1961), *Silence*, 100.

80.   "Ars imitatur naturam in sua operatione." See *Summa Theologica of St. Thomas Aquinas*, 22 vols., literally translated by Fathers of the English Dominican Province (London, 1913–1942), I.117.I.

81. Coomaraswamy, "A Figure of Speech or a Figure of Thought?," 50.

82. Coomaraswamy, "Why Exhibit Works of Art?," 181.

83. Coomaraswamy, "A Figure of Speech or a Figure of Thought?," 50.

84. Coomaraswamy, "The Theory of Art in Asia," 10–11.

85. Sastri, *Ananda K. Coomaraswamy*, 114–15.

86. Ananda Coomaraswamy, quoted in Sastri, *Ananda K. Coomaraswamy*, 114–15.

87. Ananda Coomaraswamy, "Christian and Oriental," 18, quoted in P. S. Sastri, "Coomaraswamy's Concept of Beauty," *Ananda Coomaraswamy: Centenary Essays*, 103.

88. Coomaraswamy, "The Theory of Art in Asia," 14–15.

89. Ananda Coomaraswamy, "The Philosophy of Mediaeval and Oriental Art" (1938), in *Coomaraswamy: Selected Papers: Traditional Art and Symbolism*, ed. Roger Lipsey, Bollingen Series 89, vol. 1 (Princeton: Princeton University Press, 1977), 54.

90. Coomaraswamy, "Why Exhibit Works of Art?," 175.

91. Ananda Coomaraswamy, "Reactions to Art in India," *The Transformation of Nature in Art*, 100.

92. Coomaraswamy, "Meister Eckhart's View of Art," 83–84.

93. Ibid.

94. Coomaraswamy, "Why Exhibit Works of Art?," 179.

95. Coomaraswamy, "Why Exhibit Works of Art?," 179.

96. Cage, "A Composer's Confessions," 42.

97. Cage, "Juilliard Lecture," 101.

98. John Cage, "In This Day . . . " (1956), *Silence*, 95.

99. John Cage, "Experimental Music" (1957), *Silence*, 10. Eventually, though much later, Cage would deny even the communicative properties of language, explaining the necessity of "no-communication" in society: see, for example, "The Future of Music" (1974), in *Empty Words* (Middletown, CT: Wesleyan University Press, 1979), 184. "Since words, when they communicate, have no effect, it dawns on us that we need a society in which communication is not practiced, in which words become nonsense as they do between lovers, in which words become what they originally were: trees and stars and the rest of primeval environment. The demilitarization of language: a serious musical concern."

100. Coomaraswamy, "The Theory of Art in Asia," 39.

101. Ibid., 23–24.

102. Coomaraswamy, "What is Common to Indian and Chinese Art?," 77.

103. Coomaraswamy, "Reactions to Art in India," 108–109. In a few instances, Coomaraswamy did admit the possibility of "perfection" in a work that had been created from an unorthodox position; however, such a phenomenon was merely freakish—an accidental abnormality that succeeded not "because of a neglect of or emancipation from rules, but only in spite of such a taking of liberties." (Coomaraswamy, "What is Common to Indian and Chinese Art?," 89.)

104. Coomaraswamy, "Why Exhibit Works of Art?," 177.

105. Ibid.

106.   S. Durai Raja Singam, *Ananda Coomaraswamy: Remembering and Remembering Again and Again*, xxxi.

107.   Coomaraswamy, "The Philosophy of Mediaeval and Oriental Art" (1938), *Coomaraswamy: Selected Papers: Traditional Art and Symbolism*, 53–54.

108.   Coomaraswamy, "Why Exhibit Works of Art?," 177.

109.   Coomaraswamy, "The Philosophy of Mediaeval and Oriental Art," 53–54.

110.   Ibid.

111.   Coomaraswamy, "The Theory of Art in Asia," 22–23.

112.   Coomaraswamy, "A Figure of Speech or a Figure of Thought? (Part II)," *Studies in Comparative Religion* 6, no. 2 (Spring 1972): 111.

113.   Coomaraswamy, "A Figure of Speech or a Figure of Thought?," 57.

114.   Coomaraswamy, "The Philosophy of Mediaeval and Oriental Art," 43–44.

115.   Coomaraswamy, "The Theory of Art in Asia," 46–47.

116.   Cage, "Lecture on Something," 144.

117.   n.a., "Percussionist," *Time*, Feb. 22, 1943, 70.

118.   D.F., "Shahn, Cage Deal with Reasons and Ends of Modern Creativity," *Vassar Chronicle*, March 6, 1948, 4, 6. [A review related to events of the National Inter-Collegiate Arts Conference, Vassar College, Feb. 27–29, 1948.]

119.   Cage, "A Composer's Confessions," 41–42.

120.   John Cage, "Listening to Music" (1937), *John Cage: Writer*, 17.

121.   John Cage, "The History of Experimental Music in the United States" (1959), *Silence*, 75.

122.   Ibid.

123.   Ibid.

124.   Coomaraswamy, "What is Common to Indian and Chinese Art?," 86.

125.   Cage, "A Composer's Confessions," 38, 44.

126.   John Cage, "A Few Ideas about Music and Film" (1951), *John Cage: Writer*, 64.

127.   Lou Harrison, notes to *Party Pieces* (New York: C.F. Peters Corp., 1982).

128.   John Cage, "On Earlier Pieces" (1958), *John Cage: An Anthology*, 129.

129.   Preceding the *Sonatas and Interludes*, the two prepared piano movements of the four-movement *Amores* (1943), Cage explained in the 1960s, was meant "to express in combination the erotic and the tranquil, two of the permanent emotions of Indian tradition." (John Cage, "Notes on Compositions," *John Cage: Writer*, 9.) This description, however, seems to be an afterthought of years later, as little mention is made of Indian concepts in any of Cage's statements of the 1940s.

130.   Anahid Ajemian and George Avakian, interview with the author, July 13, 1993.

131.   The compositional procedures for *Sixteen Dances* is closely related to that for the *Concerto for Prepared Piano and Chamber Orchestra* (1950–1951). For an excellent description of these procedures, see James

Pritchett's, "From Choice to Chance: John Cage's *Concerto for Prepared Piano*," *Perspectives of New Music* 26 (Fall 1988): 50–81.

132.   Another of Cunningham's dances from this period based on an Indian subject is the 1948 *A Diversion*, which, its program notes explain, "may be taken as referring to the legend of Krishna and the Gopis." The music for the dance was Cage's *Suite for Toy Piano* (1948). The story of Krishna and the Gopis is summarized in *The Gospel of Sri Ramakrishna*. See Gupta, 226.

133.   John Cage, "On Earlier Pieces," 129.

134.   Program notes, New York Ballet Society (John Cage Archives, Northwestern University, Evanston, IL "1947" file).

135.   John Cage, "Notes on Compositions," C. F. Peters Catalog (New York: C.F. Peters), 1962. Reprinted in *John Cage: Writer*, 11.

136.   Cage, "Notes on Compositions," 51.

137.   Cage, "A Composer's Confessions," 44.

138.   " . . . discussing the summer with John and Merce last night, including plans for the collaboration on an opera for the coming year . . . " Richard Lippold, letter to Josef Albers, May 24–27, 1948, Black Mountain College Papers III, Faculty Files, Box 1, "Former Faculty—Summer" File, North Carolina State Archives, Raleigh.

139.   The author extends a special thanks to Jean Erdman, who graciously consented to share these materials.

7. An Imaginary Grid: Rhythmic Structure in Cage's Music Up to circa 1950

Paul van Emmerik

For Johanne Rivest

I. Structure

The compositional technique which Cage now called "rhythmic structure,"[1] now "structural rhythm"[2] and which he defined as "a division of actual time by conventional metrical means, meter taken as simply the measurement of quantity,"[3] was conceived under the influence of, as well as in a hidden polemic with, Arnold Schoenberg. And as such, there are historical links connecting the technique to integral serialism, as this essay will try to prove. Schoenberg's notion that musical form should be founded on pitch relationships, regardless of their appearance in tonal harmony, free atonality or in twelve-tone technique, was of particularly decisive importance to the development of Cage's technique. Schoenberg's influence is evident from Cage's terminology, in which "structure" indicates what is otherwise commonly known as "form." This is supported by Reinhard Kapp's assumption that Cage became acquainted with the foundations of Schoenberg's future *Structural Functions of Harmony* during his studies with him.[4] The hidden polemic with Schoenberg comes to the fore in Cage's descriptions of musical forms that are based exclusively on durational relationships. These are descriptions in which, without exception, he seems to make a counterattack against Schoenberg: "In contrast to a structure based on the frequency aspect of sound, tonality, that is, this rhythmic structure was as hospitable to non-musical sounds, noises, as it was to those of the conventional scales and instruments."[5] From this definition it becomes clear that "rhythm" means "duration." Although the term "structure" focuses attention on musical details, not on form, Cage's term "rhythmic structure" is used in this essay, since structure is more associated with abstract components of music than with concrete musical forms and more with the process of creation of a work than with the result.[6] In addition, the two latter associations—the abstract components as well as the emphasis on the process of creation—are more prominent in Cage's composition using rhythmic structures than the former.

To Cage, composing a rhythmic structure meant as a rule—albeit a rule with exceptions—creating a musical form based on numerical relationships between the durations of sections and of groups of measures of a composition in such a way that the durations of both levels were governed by a single series of proportions. Section lengths were counted in periods, marked in the score by double barlines or by rehearsal numbers or letters, and groups of measures were counted in measures. *First Construction (in Metal)* (1939),[7] the first large work having such a form based on durations, consists of sixteen periods of sixteen measures each, which are grouped into five large sections comprised of 4, 3, 2, 3, and 4 periods—or 64, 48, 32, 48, and 64 measures—respectively. Similarly, each individual period is subdivided into five groups of 4, 3, 2, 3, and 4 measures respectively, or the formula 16 x (4 + 3 + 2 + 3 + 4) measures. The piece ends with a nine-measure coda that falls outside of this formal order. The units in such durational series are often natural numbers, and they are sometimes arranged symmetrically, as is the case in the series of *First Construction*, in which the number 2 constitutes the axis of symmetry. More frequently, the organization of durations is asymmetric, as in the duration series for *Music for Marcel Duchamp* (1947), 2 + 1 + 1 + 3 + 1 + 2 + 1.[8]

In many respects, *First Construction (in Metal)* is a model of composition using rhythmic structures. Cage himself wrote that the work was composed "with the single objective of making the rhythmic structure [. . .] clear."[9] This firm tone, however, is somewhat misleading, for a comparison of Cage's many comments about this compositional technique with the works themselves suggests that he theoretically idealized the technique in his prose. The discrepancies between Cage's compositional theories and practices will be considered below, in the light of three fundamental characteristics of rhythmic structures: first, the proportional correspondences between groups of measures and sections; second, the regularity of the periodic form; and third, the arithmetical proportions between the units of the series themselves.

1.

The rhythmic structures described so far may be termed "divisive." This term draws attention to the fact that structurally, the compositional emphasis was on the division of the form of a work into a number of smaller units. In this case, the number of periods in a work corresponds to the number of measures in a period; the ratio between the number of measures of the work and the number of measures of each period is quadratic. It would be incorrect, however, to let oneself be enticed by the elegance of this principle and to ignore the numerous exceptions to this rule.

Many of Cage's works from the 1940s did not employ "divisive" structures; they employed structures that could be described as "additive." In most cases, additive rhythmic structures were used in incidental music for the dance, film, stage or radio play. In these situations, rhythmic structures were not determined by Cage but by the structure of the medium that the music was accompanying. This is the case in *Bacchanale* (1940), *Fads and Fancies in the Academy* (1940), *The City Wears a Slouch Hat* (1942), *Credo in Us* (1942), *Forever and Sunsmell* (1942), *Totem Ancestor* (1942), *And the Earth Shall Bear Again* (1942), *Primitive* (1942), *In the Name of the Holocaust* (1942), *Four Dances* (1943), *Ad Lib* (1943), *Our Spring Will Come* (1943), *Triple-Paced No. 1* (1943), *Triple-Paced No. 2* (1944), *Daughters of the Lonesome Isle* (1945), *Ophelia* (1946), *Works of Calder* (1949–1950) and possibly in *Jazz Study* (c. 1942).[10] "In writing music for the modern dance," Cage explained in a lecture in 1948, "I generally did so after the dance was completed. This means that I wrote music to the counts given me by the dancer. These counts were nearly always, from a musical point of view, totally lacking in organization [. . .]. I believe this disorder led me to the inception of structural rhythm."[11] In additive structures, the rhythmic sequences, unlike periods in divisive structures, are not necessarily of equal length; equivalent to periods, they are situated on the structural level between groups of measures and sections. Although it cannot be denied that Cage created divisive structures in collaboration with choreographers more than once (most notably with Merce Cunningham), his suggestion above that his discomfort led him to the exclusive use of divisive structures must be challenged.

Various irregularities in those works based on divisive structures prove that whenever he deemed it necessary, Cage readily undermined these structures. (This assertion excludes the numerous works having an extension of a single measure containing the final sound of the composition.) Thus *First Construction (in Metal)*, for example, has a coda of nine measures, which is subdivided like the final three units of the rhythmic structure: 2 + 3 + 4. *Imaginary Landscape No. 2* (1942),[12] having the rhythmic structure 3 + 4 + 2 + 3 + 5, does not run the expected 289 measures, or 17 squared, but is instead only 252 measures long. This can be explained by a note in the manuscript showing that the final section, beginning at measure 205, abandons periodic structure in favor of an additive structure, consisting of the cumulative addition of the units of the structure, as follows: 3, 3 + 4, 3 + 4 + 2, 3 + 4 + 2 + 3, and 3 + 4 + 2 + 3 + 5 measures; the sum is 48 measures instead of 85. More important than the occurrence of such irregularities in divisive structures is the observation that Cage's use of additive structures was not restricted to incidental music. In concert music composed before *First Construction*, such as *Five Songs for Contralto* (1938) and *Metamorphosis* (1938),[13] Cage used additive rhythmic structures, as James Pritchett has shown.[14] In *Imaginary Landscape No. 1* (1939),[15] a work composed of 70 measures, the sequences marked in the score by rehearsal letters can be grouped into four fifteen-measure sections, separated from one another by three contrasting interludes, one, two, and three measures long respectively, followed by a four-measure coda.[16] *Imaginary Landscape No. 2* of 1940,[17] which was withdrawn by Cage after its first performance, and which should not be confused with the work of 1942 of the same title, also has an additive structure, as do several works having additive-periodic rhythmic structures to be discussed below.

The division of Cage's output of the 1930s and 1940s into incidental and concert music, then, does not coincide with the division into additive and divisive structures. (Implicitly this could be concluded from Silke Hilger's survey of forms of collaboration between Cage and various choreographers.[18]) Both divisive and additive tendencies occur in works composed more or less concurrently. In actual compositional practice, Cage frequently compromised with himself over a precompositionally defined rhythmic structure, or he reached agreements with others about a structure mandated by the choreography, stage play, radio play or film. These findings illustrate a basic characteristic of Cage's total output, namely that the introduction of a new compositional technique—in this essay, the use of divisive rhythmic structures—in no way excludes the preservation of a technique used previously, such as the use of additive structures.

2.

In divisive structures the lengths of sections are counted in periods. However, periodicity is not an exclusive characteristic of divisive structures, nor are divisive structures necessarily periodic. These observations demand identification of further variants of rhythmic structures.

If one considers periodicity to be an exclusive characteristic of divisive structures, one will search in vain for an explanation of phenomena such as the strict structure of twelve periods of three measures each in *Composition for Three Voices* (1934) or of the similarly strict twenty-two movement structure of twelve measures each in *Chess Pieces* (1943).[19] According to the definition given above, these should be considered additive structures, since the number of measures per period (or movement) does not correspond to the number of periods or movements in the work as a whole. Notes in the draft of *Quartet* (1935) testify to the additive-periodic structure of its fourth movement.[20] Each of the four parts in this movement consists of periods of thirty-eight beats, grouped into the rhythmic structure 4 + 2 + 5 + 2 + 6 + 7 + 5 + 7 for players one, two and three and its retrograde for player four, respectively. However, the number of periods does not add up to thirty-eight, nor do the periods coincide. The four players start their first periods on the fourth, first, eighteenth and ninth beat of the movement, respectively. Additive-periodic structures in no way prevent the formation of sections, as is shown by the structure having four sections of 4 + 1 + 7 + 1 eight-measure periods in the fair copy of *The Unavailable Memory of* (1944);[21] such structures do not prevent the creation of different movements, as is evident in the second and third movements of *A Valentine Out of Season* (1944),[22] both having a structure of 2 x 17 measures. And just as he did in divisive structures, Cage introduced irregularities into additive-periodic structures, specifically by extending a period by a quarter or half its length, as in the identical structures of *Experiences No. 1* (1945) and *Experiences No. 2* (1948), in the five movements of *Mysterious Adventure* (1945) and in the three movements of *Encounter* (1946).[23] In *Four Walls* (1944)[24] Cage compensated for such irregularities. The structure of the ninth movement is a fair example, designed in a structure of 60 + 60 + 60 + 49 + 60 + 60 + 11; in this case, the eleven measures lacking in the fourth period were added at the end of the movement. Finally, hybrid periodic structures appear in the six-movement suite *The Perilous Night* (1943–1944).[25] The rhythmic structures of this work are divisive in the first four movements and additive in the final two. Similarly, in *Root of an Unfocus* (1944),[26] the first of the work's three sections is divisive, apportioned into units of 7 × (4 + 2 + 1) measures, while the remaining two sections are additive. The whole is followed by a four-measure coda.

On the other hand, divisive structures are not necessarily periodic. (James Pritchett, who wrote previously about these divisive-aperiodic structures, simply termed them "divisive."[27]) Cage's first use of a divisive-aperiodic structure appears in *A Flower* (1950).[28] The fifty measures of this composition are divided according to two superimposed rhythmic structures. The first of these is a divisive-periodic structure having four units, $7 \times (1 + 3 + 1 + 2)$ measures of $\frac{5}{4}$, the third section of which is extended by one measure. The second structure, which is divisive-aperiodic, is an extension of the first by one unit, but its values are halved, $\frac{1}{2} + 1\frac{1}{2} + \frac{1}{2} + 1 + 1\frac{1}{2}$. Cage, according to the preface in the score, counted the length of the sections in units of measures of $\frac{10}{4}$. In accordance with this structure, the fifty measures of the work were divided into five sections of 5, 15, 5, 10, and 15 measures respectively. This is as far as the analogy to periodic structure goes, for rather than each period, each of the five sections is subdivided according to the proportions of the rhythmic structure, which may be reduced to the formula $n + 3n + n + 2n + 3n$, where the factor n always represents one measure. (This results, for instance, in a structure of $1\frac{1}{2}$, $4\frac{1}{2}$, $1\frac{1}{2}$, 3, and $4\frac{1}{2}$ measures in the first section.) Cage determined the durations within each individual section by multiplying the given formula by the terms of the rhythmic structure, obtaining $\frac{1}{2}$, $1\frac{1}{2}$, $\frac{1}{2}$, 1, and $1\frac{1}{2}$ respectively. As described by James Pritchett,[29] Cage divided the thirty-six measures of *Waiting* (1952)[30] in a similar fashion, with six sections of 3, 9, 3, 12, 6, and 3 measures respectively, this time according to a single rhythmic structure, $\frac{1}{4} + \frac{3}{4} + \frac{1}{4} + 1 + \frac{1}{2} + \frac{1}{4}$, counted in units of twelve measures of $\frac{8}{8}$. The sections, for their part, were subdivided by multiplying the formula $n + 3n + n + 4n + 2n + n$ for each section by the successive terms of the rhythmic structure. In this specific category of rhythmic structures, sections are not counted by the number of periods, and no quadratic ratio exists between the number of measures of the work as a whole and the number of measures within a period. The basic principle of the rhythmic structure, however, that of the corresponding ratios of a series of durations on two levels, is preserved. The principle of the aperiodic-divisive structure readily lends itself for use with other units of measurement; in fact, Cage began to employ aperiodic-divisive structures in connection with proportional notation in the early 1950s.

3.

In several multi-movement works, Cage provided each movement with its individual, usually divisive structure, as is the case in *Living Room Music* (1940), *Amores* (1943), *The Perilous Night* (1943–1944), *Sonatas and Interludes* (1946–1948), and *Sixteen Dances* (1950–1951).[31] In other works, he distributed the terms of a single rhythmic structure among the movements. In both cases, the tempos usually differ from movement to movement. For the latter group of works, Cage devised a method that would maintain real–time proportions despite the fact that the tempo was changing. This method was first employed in *She Is Asleep* (1943). While originally conceived as a nine-movement suite, only four movements of this work were completed. Two of these were published as *She Is Asleep*, one as a work in its own right under the title *A Room* (1943), and one movement remains unpublished.[32] The original nine-movement plan can be deduced from the rhythmic structure of the first movement, a structure that was also the point of departure for the work as a whole, four periods of 4 + 7 + 2 + 5 + 4 + 7 + 2 + 3 + 5 measures. From the number of periods in the remaining movements it appears that they constitute the second, third, and eighth section of the rhythmic structure, since there are seven periods in the second movement, two in the third, *A Room*, and three in the unpublished eighth movement. (The instructions for performance of *A Room* explicitly state that this work forms the third section of the suite, not the seventh, which also would have had two periods; this makes a reasonable case for the assumption that the movements having four and seven periods respectively form the first and second sections, not the fifth and sixth.) In the first movement the length of a period is thirty-nine measures of $\frac{2}{2}$ or, at an average tempo of seventy-three half notes per minute, sixty-four seconds in round figures. (Although no tempo indication is given in *A Room*, the same tempo as in the first movement may be assumed on the basis of the identical period length.) In the slower second movement—given measures of the same length and the tempo of 104 quarter notes per minute—Cage shortened the period length to twenty-eight measures by omitting the fifth and sixth groups of measures of the original rhythmic structure, in order that the duration of the periods counted in seconds would approximate that of the first movement, sixty-five seconds in round figures.[33]

For the eighth movement, Cage found a method enabling him to change the tempo without affecting the duration of each period in seconds and the proportions of the structural units. Not only did he compensate for the shorter duration of the periods at a tempo of eighty-four beats per minute—given measures of equal length and the beat being a half note—by increasing the period length to forty-four measures lasting sixty-three seconds, but he also multiplied each of the terms of the original structure by the quotient of the new and the original tempos, $84/73$, which, expressed to the nearest integer or fraction of $1/2$, became 4 $1/2$ + 8 + 2 $1/2$ + 5 + 4 $1/2$ + 8 + 2 $1/2$ + 3 + 6 measures. Cage employed analogous procedures in some of the sections of the second movement of *A Book of Music* (1944); in the first, seventh and ninth movements of *The Seasons* (1947); and in the third and fourth movements of the *Suite for Toy Piano* (1948), although in these works the durations of the original structural units were changed while preserving the period length.[34] Seemingly, Cage used the same technique in *Three Dances* (1945),[35] apportioning the nine sections of the work as three movements of three sections each, corresponding to the three symmetrical groups of three structural units in the first movement: 2 + 5 + 2, 2 + 6 + 2, and 2 + 7 + 2. However, in the second movement the composer added one measure to each unit of the original structure, and in the third movement he added two more measures to the length of the structural units that had resulted in the second movement, and conversely to the method described so far, he adapted the tempo to the increased period length.

In *Four Walls* (1944)[36] neither the period length was adapted to the tempo, nor the tempo to the period length, but both elements adapted to a third factor, as Martin Erdmann explains:[37] *Four Walls* was written as music to a choreography lasting one hour.[38] Taking into account the compensations in this work as described in the above, the first act consists of thirty-five periods, each having a length of forty-four measures, a half note equaling eighty-eight beats per minute in a time signature of $\frac{2}{2}$; the second act consists of twenty-four periods—not twenty-five, as was Erdmann's assumption—having a period length of sixty measures at a tempo of one hundred and twenty half notes per minute while the meter remains unchanged. Both the tempo and the number of measures per period were chosen by Cage in such a way that in either act of the choreography, a period would always last sixty seconds, the work as a whole lasting fifty-nine minutes. The choice of tempo for the second act avowedly conforms to the intended duration in real time; not only does each period last one minute, but every measure also lasts one second. This connection between tempo and clock time was preserved by the composer for obvious reasons in his film scores of the 1940s: one hundred and twenty beats per minute in *Music for Marcel Duchamp* (1947) and sixty beats per minute in *Works of Calder* (1949–1950).

It is hardly surprising that Cage drew an audacious, if cautious, conclusion from the equalization of the beat of a piece of music to clock time. In his works of the 1950s, the chronometer gradually replaced the metronome, and metric notation gave way to proportional notation. Consequently, rhythmic structures, now notated directly in clock time, eventually became true temporal structures. In spite of the relative simplicity of notation in clock time—at least in comparison to the complicated calculations that had to be made for music in metric notation having tempo changes—the number of works using such temporal structures is limited. In all probability, the reason is that Cage, in the meantime, had discovered far-reaching possibilities in composition using clock time. These were possibilities he would continue to explore until his death.

II. Functions

The functions of rhythmic structures differ. Their structural units may—to mention the most prominent categories—first, regulate the use of motifs; second, dictate correspondences and differences of density; or third, determine differentiations of musical texture by means of rests or silences. They may even combine any or all of these musical purposes. Moreover, the overt governing function of one rhythmic structure in operation in one piece may well remain in the background or be omitted altogether in another. It is therefore impossible to reduce the functions of a rhythmic structure to the universal application of invariable principles.

1.

Motivically speaking, in the additive structure that Cage used in his percussion music of the 1930s, the concept of "variation" does not refer to the changing character of any individual motif but to its recasting within a varying musical texture, as Deborah Campana wrote about *Quartet* (1935)[39]:

> Once stated, a theme remains intact or constant, maintaining its original identity throughout the movement. Variation is most importantly understood as occurring not on the level of the theme, motivically, or within a single voice, but on the level of textural change, as patterns in all four voices are repeated and combined. Development unfolds then as the texture evolves through pattern repetition within individual voices and pattern coincidence with other voices.[40]

The organization of unvaried motifs in the first three movements of this work is, however, rather different from the motivic organization in the fourth and final movement. In the final movement, rhythmic motifs are made to fit within the units of a rhythmic structure, and the motivic lengths correspond to those of the units in which they are placed. In Example 7-1 (beats 132 through 176 of the movement), the structural units, 4 + 2 + 5 + 2 + 6 + 7 + 5 + 7 for players one, two, and three, as well as its retrograde for player four, are indicated by arabic numerals below each part. This example reveals a conflict between the audible musical continuity and the abstract structural units, for the boundaries of the individual structural units are occasionally veiled or concealed, since several motifs begin or end with a rest or a tie. Such is the case in the motifs having a length of seven quarter notes (beats 137–143 of the part for player one and beats 146–152 of the part for player two).

In explaining the sometimes deliberate conflict between rhythmic motifs and the larger rhythmic structure, Cage, in a short essay published in 1944, introduced the twin concepts of "grace" and "clarity." "Grace," he defined, "is not here used to mean prettiness; it is used to mean the play with and against the clarity of the rhythmic structure."[41] Time and again this play causes, as Martin Erdmann has observed, "discrepancies between the given time frame and the course of the actual music as it was composed. This can easily be seen by the fact that in many pieces the double barlines, marking the temporal frame, are frequently ignored by the musical shapes, as if in enjambment."[42]

Example 7-1. John Cage, *Quartet* (1935), beats 132–176. Used by permission of C.F. Peters Corporation on behalf of Henmar Press Inc.

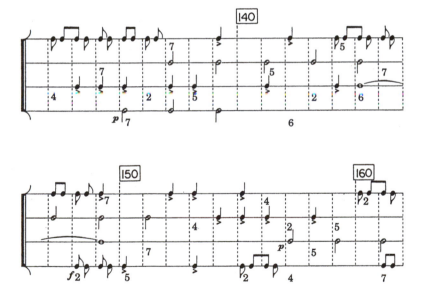

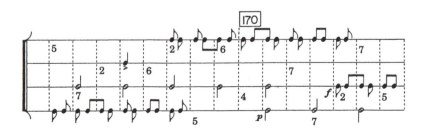

In *Second Construction* (1940),[43] having the structure 4 + 3 + 4 + 5, this principle of conflict is aptly expressed in the rhythmic fugue with which the work concludes. In this fugue, which starts one period before the final section, the subject always starts at the first and third units of structure (apportioned into equal units of four measures each), while in contrast, its answer begins at the second and fourth units of the structure, apportioned into three and five measures respectively. In addition, the answer appears one measure early in each successive period, causing a *stretto* that leads to a subject left unanswered in the penultimate period of the work.

The relations of motifs to rhythmic structure embrace even deeper nuances. The boundaries of a motif and a structural unit may coincide; in such cases, motifs actually articulate the rhythmic structure. Or, in contrast, motivic continuity may veil structural units or even deliberately conflict with them. Also, however, the motifs may neither articulate structural units nor conflict with them. This ambiguous situation exists, for instance, in the percussion quartet *Double Music* (1941), composed by Cage in collaboration with Lou Harrison.[44] (The present discussion is confined to Cage's contribution to this collaborative effort, i.e., the parts for players one and three.) On the basis of textural changes, it is a relatively easy task to ascertain the division of Cage's portion of this 200-measure work into fourteen periods having fourteen measures each (grouped into three sections of 2 + 5 + 7 periods for player one and of 7 + 2 + 5 periods for player three) and a four-measure coda. It is just as easy to determine the analogous subdivision of each period in the part for player three into three groups of 7 + 2 + 5 measures respectively, since it is usually articulated very clearly by two Japanese temple bells (or "kin") and tam–tam. The subdivision of periods in the part for player one, however, cannot be ascertained unequivocally on the basis of the score. (By analogy with the division of the work into sections, a succession of 2 + 5 + 7 measures might be assumed.) This ambiguity derives from the fact that the motifs to a large extent consist of ostinatos, moving almost continuously in eighth notes. (A similar situation appears in Example 7-1, in beats 167 through 174 of the part for player one.) If one did not know better, one would be inclined to think that "the rhythmic motifs seem to be freely composed, combined and varied," as David Nicholls wrote, and that this apparent independence of motifs and rhythmic structure, which is actually a constant interplay of both, is the rule rather than the exception in Cage's music of the 1940s.[45]

2.

In several works of the 1940s the rhythmic structure acts as a regulating factor that determines shifts in "density," a term defined here as the number of sounds or attacks per structural unit. In the first movement of *The Perilous Night* (1943–1944), for example, the number of attacks in the seventh measure of each of the ten ten-measure periods is zero (see Example 7-2). This measure of rest divides all of the periods in this movement into two groups, each with four different levels of density. The first six measures of each period—in themselves apparently restricted to four numbers, 11, 21, 30, and 36—have 21, 21, 36, 21, 11, 30, 21, 21, 21, and 21 attacks respective to each period. Likewise, the final three measures are based on four numbers, 11, 12, 20, and 24; they are comprised of 20, 20, 24, 12, 11, 11, 12, 12, 12, and 20 attacks respective to each period. The number of attacks per period, or the sum of the corresponding terms of both number series, again results in a row having four different levels of density, namely 41, 41, 60, 33, 22, 41, 33, 33, 33, 41 (21 plus 20 equals 41, 36 plus 24 equals 60, etc.). As can be seen, in none of these three "density rows" do the different numbers of attacks turn out to be in the same order. Cage first described this compositional technique in 1959, explaining how he used it in *She Is Asleep* of 1943.[46] In the first movement of this work, a movement comprising a percussion quartet, Cage assigned a specific level of density not only to each group of measures but also to each of the four parts, using density rows having the length of a period. In the second movement, a duet for voice and prepared piano, he used the technique now in the piano, now in the vocal part. As James Pritchett has shown, Cage had used this technique previously in the second movement of *Amores* (1943) as well.[47] The variation techniques affecting density in these compositions include the exchange of density rows among the parts themselves, retrograde movement of density rows, moving a density row up to a later measure within a period and continuing it into the next, rotating a density row begun in a later measure by returning to the beginning of the same period and continuing from there to the measure in which the row was begun.

According to Cage, he used these techniques in order to create correspondences and differences among the units of the rhythmic structure.[48] These techniques are highly abstract and purely numerical; they not only dictate the flow of such correspondences and differences, but they also determine the formation of the rhythmic motifs themselves. In fact, this numerical basis for composition appears to have incited Cage's rhythmic imagination, as is evident from the fact that in any work almost every level of density is continuously varied at the rhythmic level. Thus each of the identical terms, in the algebraic sense, in the density rows of the first movement of *The Perilous Night*, 21, 20, 41, and 11, manifests itself in a different musical shape (see Example 7-2).

3.

Cage's assertion that each of his rhythmic structures "was conceived, in fact, so that it could be as well expressed by the absence of [. . .] materials as by their presence" justifies an examination of the function of rests or silences in compositions using rhythmic structures.[49] The quotation may lead one to believe that in Cage's music, sound and silence are considered equal. Quite the contrary is the case. The rests in the fourth movement of the *Quartet*, discussed above, are integrated components of the collection of motifs with which the length of a given group of measures can be expressed. This is evident from the parts for player one, beats 156–159 and 162–166; player two, beats 159–163 and 166–171; and player four, 142–147 and 157–160 in Example 7-1. The two-beat motive in the example, for instance, is expressed as quarter rest plus quarter note, half note, four eighth notes, or half rest. In addition, not all rests are audible as such, since they belong to parts in a polyphonic complex, the density of which they help differentiate. However, silences of lengths equal to those of the rhythmic motifs that Cage employed in *Music for Wind Instruments* (1938), for instance, actually coincide, yielding general pauses.[50] Such actual silences or, as in ensemble pieces, general pauses, manifest themselves on all levels in works such as *Credo in Us* (1942), *Experiences No. 1* (1945), *A Book of Music* (1944), *Two Pieces for Piano* (1946), *Experiences No. 2* (1948) and *Sixteen Dances* (1950–1951).[51] In these works, the silences are equal to the length of groups of measures. In *Four Walls* (1944), they are equal to the length of groups of measures and of periods. In *Waiting* (1952), they are equal to the length of sections (no less than four out of six), and in *4'33"* (1952) they are even equal to the length of each of the three movements of the piece.[52] (In incidental music, for that matter, part of the general pauses can be explained functionally; the music is silent, for instance, during passages of spoken word, as occurs in *Credo in Us*.) The silent units that appear consecutively in numerous works abstract the rhythmic structure to the point of inaudibility. As paradoxical as it may seem, these units are indeed soundless enjambments.

Beginning with *4'33"* Cage's idiosyncratic interpretation of the aesthetic function of silence made its entry into his music, an interpretation expressed in his description of the work as "a piece in three movements during all three of which no sounds are intentionally

Example 7-2. John Cage, *The Perilous Night* (1943–44), mm. 1–25.
Used by permission of C. F. Peters Corporation on behalf of Henmar Press Inc.

produced."[53] This proclaimed non-intentionality was caused by an experience that proved to the composer that:

> . . . silence becomes something else—not silence at all, but sounds, the ambient sounds. [. . .] These sounds (which are called silence only because they do not form part of a musical intention) may be depended upon to exist. The world teems with them, and is, in fact, at no point free of them. He who has entered an anechoic chamber, a room made as silent as technologically possible, has heard there two sounds, one high, one low—the high the listener's nervous system in operation, the low his blood in circulation.[54]

During a seminar that Cage gave when he held the 1988–1989 Charles Eliot Norton chair of poetry at Harvard University, he told his audience that the rhythmic structure of 4'33" was originally conceived and written in metric notation, as had been the case in *Music of Changes* (1951):[55] "I actually used the same method of working, and I built up the silence of each movement—and the three movements add up to 4'33"—I built up each movement by means of short silences put together. It seems idiotic, but that's what I did."[56] The pianist who gave the work its first performance, David Tudor, in conversation with William Fetterman was able to remember a manuscript—now apparently lost—in which the work indeed is written in metric notation. Unlike *Music of Changes*, however, the groups of measures in 4'33" only know a single tempo, sixty beats per minute.[57] This structure is not only inaudible but it is also invisible, since in the fair copy now published in facsimile, Cage indicated only the resulting durations of each movement, 30, 143, and 100 seconds respectively, through the use of proportional notation. In a subsequent version of the work, Cage notated the silences in a way that cannot but be called conventional, namely by using the word "tacet," while a footnote states that the movements of the first version lasted 33, 160, and 80 seconds respectively. Presumably, Cage's memory was letting him down while writing this footnote; it cannot be considered a serious error, since—while preserving the three-movement structure—the determination of the duration of the performance in the second version is left to the performer.

*

As is being pointed out more and more frequently, Cage did not work in a vacuum, and his use of rhythmic structures must be interpreted in the historical context that Cage and his contemporaries in Europe shared—that of twelve-tone technique. The fact that Cage's technique of rhythmic structures is based on axioms similar to those of "integral" serialism can be corroborated by considering two closely interrelated compositional principles of twelve-tone technique: the definition of certain materials or methods prior to the principal act of composition; and the technique of composition using abstractions, such as independent manipulation and synthesis of individual parameters, both of which were extended by Cage as well as by various postwar composers of serial music.

1.

From the postwar perspective of music history, Schoenberg's emphatic resistance against what Carl Dahlhaus characterized as the tendency "to exhibit skill and artificial devices rather than keeping them concealed," proved to be in vain.[58] In music since World War II, whether in Cage's music or serial works, attention to the completed work of art diminished in favor of a focus on its process of creation. Composers were "plainly obsessed by the idea that fixing a creation would be a kind of betrayal of the possible," as Dahlhaus put it,[59] and by trying to keep possibilities open, they consciously or unconsciously emphasized the materials and methods they used, not the resulting products. Consequently, the various "plans and decisions a composer makes prior to the principal act of composition," as the definition of what was to be called "precomposition" reads, acquired considerable significance.[60] The irony of history has decreed that the term "precomposition" originated with the establishment of a theory of twelve-tone technique. Thus Schoenberg, by creating this technique, also indirectly spawned a term reflecting an aesthetic notion for which he did not have the slightest affinity. Even so, it is taken for granted that any serial work presupposes a precompositional ordering of pitch and interval classes. And although precomposition and composition are part of the same creative process, both potentially simultaneous and indivisibly present, the intensely systematic nature of the compositional techniques under discussion justifies an arrangement into phases in which the precompositional is "chronologically" distinguished from the simply "compositional."

In most of Cage's works, including those using rhythmic structures, a precompositional phase is involved in the creative process. In her study of three of Cage's works of the 1930s, Deborah Campana judges precomposition to be the essential common denominator on either side of 1950, not only providing the foundation for the techniques Cage used in the early works employing rhythmic structures, but also prescribing those techniques associated with chance composition:

> At the heart of Cage's composing process, and indeed the feature which is most appropriately associated with his eventual use of chance operations, are those precompositional decisions. Such

conventions [. . .] functioned as the means by which Cage could make decisions with regard to the work's evolution before he actually applied pencil to paper to compose. [. . .] By defining procedures or processes apart from the actual compositional act, Cage realized that he could compose music and relinquish what could be considered a composer's autonomous control over the work.[61]

In a similar manner, composers of serial music determined the musical elements to be used as well as the rules on the basis of which these elements could be subjected to a serial mechanism prior to the principal act of composition.

In compositions using either rhythmic structures or serial techniques, then, the compositional phase included the organization of musical elements by means of a preconceived structure or mechanism. The resulting unforeseen possibilities seem to explain the fascination that Cage and the composers of serial music held for using such compositional techniques. Inherently, it seemed, preconceived structures or mechanisms surpassed individual musical imagination, achieving musical results which, as sound heard or imagined only, would have remained impervious, as Carl Dahlhaus has argued before.[62]

2.

As Dahlhaus claims, a twelve-tone row is a sequence of pitches and intervals abstracted from audible reality:

It consists of nothing but the relationship linking basic set, inversion, retrograde and retrograde inversion. [. . .] The basic set is just one form of the row among others. What can be notated is a particular interval, a major third, for instance. The concept of a row, however, refers to the abstract factor which is common to the major third, the minor sixth and the major tenth, both upwards and downwards—to a feature for which there is neither a name nor a sign.[63]

The abstract character of a tone row also reveals itself in the fact that the sequence of pitches it produces is conceived independently of any rhythm, dynamic or timbre, and without these elements, a sequence of pitches is not part of audible reality.

In serial music and in the music of John Cage, the manipulation of such abstract phenomena manifests itself in similar compositional techniques. In serial music, the consequence one drew from these abstractions was an analogous ordering into a series of independently composed pitches, durations, degrees of loudness and timbres. In Cage's music the abstract nature of independently composed parameters manifests itself in the separation of rhythmic structure on the one hand from the sound materials that were to occur on the other. This compositional technique was conceived by Cage under the influence of as well as in a hidden polemic with Schoenberg's notion that musical form should be founded on pitch relationships. In her dissertation, Deborah Campana concludes that:

> . . . inspiration for Cage's creative process arises initially from an idea, which in itself may not necessarily have any relation to the sound eventually realized. The manner in which Cage develops this idea can be described as cultivating an environment within which the idea becomes an aurally-significant expression. To Cage, this environment is defined by considering the dimensions of the composition in terms of formal outline and structural organization.[64]

In his contention that a twelve-tone row, strictly speaking, cannot be notated, Dahlhaus was referring to conventional notation. In developing twelve-tone theory, various attempts have been made to express the nameless and signless abstraction to which Dahlhaus refers through the use of numbers. Both Cage and the composers of serial music also made use of numbers in order to notate the parameters abstracted from audible reality, at least in the precompositional phase. In a composition like Boulez's *Structures Ia*, durations, dynamics and nuances of timbre originate from a numerical order exclusively deduced from the order of tones in a twelve-tone row, rather than from the proportions of the tones among themselves. In composition using rhythmic structures, Cage used numbers not only in the process of conceiving the structures themselves, but also in designating the density rows he employed to vary the number of sounds per structural unit.

In spite of the numerous and drastic metamorphoses that composition using rhythmic structures underwent in the course of time, especially after the 1940s, its basic principle—the manipulation of temporal units and subsequent affixing of musical functions to them—is a constant factor in Cage's music. Were one to name the most essential characteristic of composition in rhythmic structure, it would be Cage's insistence that structure and sound material can be composed separately. He phrased this idea in its most radical way in 1958 when he wrote that "nothing about the structure was determined by the materials which were to occur in it."[65] Cage's notion lends composition using rhythmic structures a highly abstract nature, and it frequently results in certain discrepancies between the musical continuity as it was composed and as it can be perceived. As Campana wrote, "it is apparent that Cage considered template units to be an indication of the time-span available for musical composition. [. . .] They function as compositional guidelines and are not intended to be aurally perceived."[66] Even so, rhythmic structures affected the audible musical continuity in such a way that, as Morton Feldman has argued convincingly, "an imaginary grid seemed always in operation."[67]

Notes

1. John Cage, "Composition as Process" (1958), in *Silence: Lectures and Writings* (Middletown, CT: Wesleyan University Press, 1961), 19.
2. John Cage, "A Composers Confessions=Bekenntnisse eines Komponisten," trans. Gisela Gronemeyer, *Musiktexte* 40–41 (August 1991): 60.
3. Cage, "Composition as Process," 19.
4. Reinhard Kapp, "Cage, John," in *Metzler Komponisten-Lexikon: 340 werkgeschichtliche Porträts*, ed. Horst Weber (Stuttgart [etc.]: Metzler, 1992), 123.
5. Cage, "Composition as Process," 19.
6. Carl Dahlhaus, *Schoenberg and the New Music: Essays*, trans. Derrick Puffett and Alfred Clayton (Cambridge: Cambridge University Press, 1987), 261.
7. John Cage, *First Construction (in Metal)* (New York: Henmar Press of C. F. Peters, 1962).
8. John Cage, *Music for Marcel Duchamp* (New York: Henmar Press of C. F. Peters, 1961).
9. John Cage, [Untitled], liner notes for records KO8Y 1499–1504, on separate double leaves (New York: George Avakian, 1959), unpaginated.
10. The following were published by the Henmar Press of C. F. Peters in New York: *Bacchanale, Forever and Sunsmell, Totem Ancestor* (in both facsimile and engraved editions), *And the Earth Shall Bear Again* in 1960; *Credo in Us* in 1962; *Primitive, In the Name of the Holocaust, Our Spring Will Come, Daughters of the Lonesome Isle, Ophelia* in 1977; *Four Dances* in 1991. The following are held by the New York Public Library, under the call number JPB 94–24: *Fads and Fancies in the Academy*, folder 49 (fair copy); *Totem Ancestor*, folder 88 (draft); *Ad Lib*, folder 92 (sketch and draft) and folder 93 (fair copy); *Triple-Paced No. 1*, folder 106 (fair copy); *Triple-Paced No. 2*, folder 108 (fair copy); *Works of Calder*, folder 159 (draft); *Jazz Study*, folder 934 (photocopy of fair copy, allograph). *The City Wears a Slouch Hat* is in the New York Public Library, call number JPB 88–70 (revised version, fair copy).
11. Cage, "A Composers Confessions=Bekenntnisse eines Komponisten," 60.
12. Held by the New York Public Library, under the call number JPB 94–24 in folder 73 (fair copy). Both *Imaginary Landscape No. 1* and *No. 2* were also published in New York by the Henmar Press of C. F. Peters in 1960.
13. *Five Songs for Contralto* was published by the Henmar Press of C. F. Peters in New York in 1960. *Metamorphosis* was published by the same press in 1961.
14. James Pritchett, *The Music of John Cage* (Cambridge: Cambridge University Press, 1993), 14–15.

15.   Published by the Henmar Press of C. F. Peters in New York in 1960.

16.   John Cage, [Untitled], in *John Cage*, ed. Robert Dunn (New York: Henmar Press, 1962), 35–36.

17.   Held by the New York Public Library, under the call number JPB 94–24 in folder 50 (fair copy).

18.   Silke Hilger, "Cage und Cunningham: Von 'Rhythmic Structures' zu Zufallsoperationen," in *John Cage II*, ed. Heinz-Klaus Metzger and Rainer Riehn (München: Text + Kritik, 1990), 35.

19.   *Composition for Three Voices* was published by the Henmar Press of C. F. Peters in New York in 1974. *Chess Pieces* is held by the New York Public Library under the call number JPB 94–24, folder 99 (sketches and draft).

20.   Held by the New York Public Library under the call number JPB 94–24, folder 13 (draft).

21.   Held by the New York Public Library under the call number JPB 94–24, folder 120 (fair copy).

22.   Published by the Henmar Press of C. F. Peters in New York, 1960.

23.   *Experiences No. 1* and *No. 2* were published by the Henmar Press of C. F. Peters in New York, 1962 and *Mysterious Adventure* was published by the same press in 1982. *Encounter* is held by the New York Public Library under the call number JPB 94–24, folder 127 (sketches).

24.   Published by the Henmar Press of C. F. Peters in New York in 1982.

25.   Published by the Henmar Press of C. F. Peters in New York in 1960.

26.   Published by the Henmar Press of C. F. Peters in New York in 1960.

27.   James Pritchett, "The Development of Chance Techniques in the Music of John Cage, 1950–1956" (Ph.D. diss., New York University, 1988), 183.

28.   Published by the Henmar Press of C. F. Peters in New York in 1960.

29.   Pritchett, "The Development of Chance Techniques in the Music of John Cage, 1950–1956," 185–189.

30.   Published by the Henmar Press of C. F. Peters in New York in 1960.

31.   *Amores, The Perilous Night, Sonatas and Interludes* and *Sixteen Dances* were published by the Henmar Press of C. F. Peters in New York in 1960. *Living Room Music* was published by the same press in 1976.

32.   The first and second movements of *She Is Asleep* and *A Room* were published in 1960 by the Henmar Press of C. F. Peters in New York. The New York Public Library holds the eighth (unpublished) movement of this under the call-number JPB 94–24, folder 103 (draft).

33.   John Cage, [Untitled], 1959, unpaginated.

34.   All three of these pieces were published by the Henmar Press of C. F. Peters in New York in 1960. *The Seasons* was published as both an orchestral score and in piano reduction.

35.   The second version of *Three Dances* was published by the Henmar Press of C. F. Peters in New York in 1977.

36.   Published by the Henmar Press of C. F. Peters in New York in 1982.

37.   Martin Erdmann, "Untersuchungen zum Gesamtwerk von John Cage" (Ph.D. diss., Rheinische Friedrich-Wilhems-Universität, Bonn, 1993), 118.

38. Merce Cunningham, "A Collaborative Process between Music and Dance," *Triquarterly* 54 (Spring 1982): 174.

39. *Quartet* was published by the Henmar Press of C. F. Peters in New York in 1977.

40. Deborah Campana, "Form and Structure in the Music of John Cage" (Ph.D. diss., Northwestern University, Evanston, Illinois, 1985), 25.

41. John Cage, "Grace and Clarity," *Dance Observer* 11, no. 9 (Nov. 1944): 109.

42. Erdmann, 118.

43. Published by the Henmar Press of C. F. Peters in New York in 1978.

44. Published by C. F. Peters, New York, 1961.

45. David Nicholls, *American Experimental Music, 1890–1940* (Cambridge: Cambridge University Press, 1990), 215.

46. John Cage, [Untitled], 1959, unpaginated.

47. Pritchett, *The Music of John Cage*, 21–22.

48. John Cage, [Untitled], 1959, unpaginated.

49. John Cage, "Composition as Process," 19–20.

50. *Music for Wind Instruments* was published by the Henmar Press of C. F. Peters in New York in 1961. John Cage, [Untitled], 1962, 24.

51. All of these were published by the Henmar Press of C. F. Peters in New York: *A Book of Music* and *Sixteen Dances* in 1960; *Experiences No. 1* and *No. 2* in 1961; *Credo in Us* in 1962; *Two Pieces for Piano* in 1970.

52. *Waiting* was published by the Henmar Press of C. F. Peters in 1960. The second version of *4'33"* was published by the same press also in 1960, and the first version of the piece (fair copy) is in the possession of Irwin Kremen, Durham, North Carolina. It was published in facsimile in *Source* 1, no. 2 (July 1967): 46–54; reprinted New York: Henmar Press of C. F. Peters, 1993.

53. John Cage, [Untitled], 1962, 25.

54. Cage, "Composition as Process," 22–23.

55. Published by the Henmar Press of C. F. Peters in New York in 1961.

56. John Cage, I-VI: MethodStructureIntentionDisciplineNotation-IndeterminacyInterpenetrationImitationDevotionCircumstancesVariableStructureNonunderstandingContingencyInconsistencyPerformance (Cambridge, MA: Cambridge University Press, 1990), 20–21.

57. William Fetterman, "John Cage's Theatre Pieces: Notations and Performances" (Ph.D. diss., New York University, 1992), 139.

58. Carl Dahlhaus, "Die Krise des Experiments," in *Komponieren heute: Ästhetische, soziologische und pädagogische Fragen: Sieben Beiträge,* (Institute for New Music and Music Education publication 23 [Darmstadt], ed. Ekkehard Jost (Mainz: Schott, 1983), 90.

59. Ibid.

60. John Vinton, ed., *Dictionary of Twentieth-Century Music* (London: Thames and Hudson, 1974), 591.

61. Campana, 239.

62. Dahlhaus, "Die Krise des Experiments," 87.

63. Dahlhaus, *Schoenberg and the New Music*, 257.

64. Campana, 134.

65. Cage, "Composition as Process," 19.

66. Campana, 64–65.
67. Morton Feldman, "Crippled Symmetry," *Res* 2 (Fall 1981), 98.

8. Structure vs. Form in *The Sonatas and Interludes for Prepared Piano*

Chadwick Jenkins

The writings of John Cage are replete with references to "Structure" and "Form" and like much of Cage's terminology, these concepts continued to evolve through subtle alterations in connotation until they encompassed such a wide scope of meaning as to defy any single definition. Seemingly, the concept of "Structure" as demonstrated in the early percussion works of the late 1930s and early 1940s has little to do with the "Structure" of *Music of Changes* from the early 1950s; yet Cage was able to expand and revise his definition of this term between these years without contradicting himself, ultimately circumscribing the procedures used in both pieces. In contrast to the fairly clear meanings of Structure, its companion term, Form, remains vague, making its line of development more difficult to trace. Because Cage's shifting view of "Structure" and "Form" bore a significant impact upon his compositions, it is imperative for those interested in understanding the music itself to distill first the meaning of these terms at the time of any given composition with as much clarity as possible.

The concepts of Form and Structure developed directly out of another of Cage's favorite precepts: silence. In 1949, he wrote, "the opposite and necessary coexistent of sound is silence,"[1] out of his sense that musical organization should arise through the juxtaposition of these two elements. Composition, therefore, was the act of integrating sound and silence. In making these assertions, Cage found confirmation in the work of Erik Satie and Anton Webern as well as in the musical traditions of India and China. In surveying the development of Western art music, Cage stated that Beethoven had led music astray by basing his structures on functional tonality. Even

Schoenberg, he argued, relied on harmony, although clearly not functional harmony in the traditional sense as the structural determinant of his works. In contrast, Cage's reliance on time as the fundamental organizational principle is expressed directly in his aesthetic prose, in which the keywords Structure, Form, Method and Materials emerged. From this essential concept, Cage derived many other corollaries concerning the organization of music, the most important being the dichotomy and interdependence of "Form" and "Structure."

For Cage, the terms Structure, Form, Method and Materials ultimately defined the four aspects of his compositional approach, and he relied on them for the explication of his style throughout his career. However, his definitions and uses of these concepts gradually changed to fit his developing aesthetic. This is particularly clear in relation to Structure, which is perhaps the most easily defined of these terms. Over the course of Cage's lifetime, the meaning of Structure shifted from indicating the tightly controlled, carefully delineated planning of his early works to describing an open, indeterminate duration in his later works, a situation in which Structure still serves to impose an order but does so regardless of the composer's intentions.

As Cage postulated from the outset, sound has four components: pitch, timbre, loudness and duration, whereas silence involves only duration. And since duration is the only mutual characteristic between these dual phenomena, it seemed logical to Cage that time lengths be the basis for the organization of music rather than harmonic structure. This understanding was the essence of his approach to Structure, dividing any work into temporal sections. For the greater part of Cage's early career, the composer realized Structure by what he termed micro-macrocosmic, or square-root, form. This meant that the large-scale divisions of the piece reflected the divisions on the local level through the application of the same ratios. In the *First Construction (In Metal)* (1939), the organization of the local phrases is: 4, 3, 2, 3, 4, designated by their respective number of measures. Each pass through this series could be considered a cycle of sorts. The overall (macrocosmic) design of the piece mimics this local (microcosmic) pattern, as the first large section consists of four cycles of the microcosmic series, followed by a section made up of three such cycles, followed by three more large sections made up of two, three and four microcosmic cycles respectively. Consequently, the sixteen-measure pattern that makes up the initial phrase structure is itself repeated sixteen times, yielding a structure of 16 x 16 (hence the term square-root form). The formal demarcations in *First Construction* are especially clear, both in the score and to the ear, as distinct instrumentation characterizes each individual phrase on the microcosmic level, while changes in tempo distinguish sections on the macrocosmic level.

Within this method, Form becomes the necessary counterpart to Structure. While Structure dictates the exact temporal divisions of a piece, Form can work both with and against that rigid outline, providing an overarching continuity of sound. In *First Construction*, the Form consists of various motives that carry over from one phrase into the next, lending the music its sense of cohesion and development. However, the fluidity of the Form in this particular composition never goes so far as to obscure the divisions of the Structure, for Cage made these divisions consistently clear through his instrumentation. Yet as his aesthetic developed, his concepts of Form and Structure changed, and this pristine aural clarity fell into obsolescence. Although he continued to use micro-macrocosmic form in later compositions, the definitions and musical realizations of Structure and Form became increasingly ambiguous.

The tense dynamic between Structure and Form is especially well documented in the *Sonatas and Interludes for Prepared Piano* (1946–48), perhaps Cage's most widely performed and appreciated piece, as well as the magnum opus of the composer's work for his "invented"instrument. More important for the purposes of this essay, this work constitutes a compendium of Cage's various applications and interrelations of Form and Structure up to that point. It also anticipates Form and Structure as they would be manifested in later compositions. Indeed, each of these twenty short movements could well be considered an essay in the manipulation of rigidly controlled Structure and, in at least one case, they demonstrate the ultimate futility of the composer's attempt to impose this strict order. Cage seems to have recognized that these pieces confirmed that Structure occurs regardless of one's attempts to impose it. On the other hand, as he still concerned himself with dictating Structure during this period, the *Sonatas and Interludes* provide a clear example of the "poetry" of Form working "with and against the clarity of the rhythmic structure."[2]

The relationships that Cage posited between Structure and Form in his music and aesthetic can be approached from three primary vantage points. First, a comparison of Cage's changing interpretations of the terms Structure, Form, Materials and Methods both before and after the completion of *Sonatas and Interludes* documents a subtly shifting emphasis away from the comparatively simple aspects of musical organization towards the much more complex manifestations of his burgeoning aesthetic. Specifically, the essays "Grace and Clarity" (1944), "Defense of Satie" (1948), "Forerunners of Modern Music" (1949), the infamous "Lecture on Nothing" (c. 1949–1950) and

"Composition as Process" (1958) all concern various aspects of Structure and Form, documenting the gradual changes in meaning that these terms underwent. Second, an overview of Cage's various expressions of Structure within *Sonatas and Interludes* indicates not only a surprising amount of flexibility in what would seem like a fairly straightforward and strict system of organization, but also an ever-increasing tendency towards the loosening of compositional control. Finally, a study of the *Sonatas and Interludes* facilitates a crucial comprehension of the circumstances by which the interplay between Form and Structure occurs. As Cage himself asserted, this constant interplay created the "poetry" in his music. In this particular composition, Structure and Form found what is perhaps their finest vehicle in Cage's entire oeuvre. Many of the pieces provide clear illustrations of the rigidity of Structure in contrast to the mutability of Form. On the other hand, certain pieces undoubtedly demonstrate the inevitability of Structure arising on its own regardless of the composer's intention, especially in those instances where Cage seems less intent on demarcating the divisions of his Structures.

Immediately after completing the *Sonatas and Interludes*, Cage explained in his lecture "A Composer's Confessions" (1948) that this work was the result of a passing remark made by Edwin Denby, who asserted that, "short pieces can have just as much in them as long pieces." Through an examination of his writings up through 1958, it is clear that Cage found in these short pieces the materials that would in large part fuel the remainder of his creative output. The significance of the *Sonatas and Interludes* is not self-expression but rather a means of testing the limits of the juxtaposition of Structure and Form. As Cage himself explained, "composing in this way changes me, rather than expresses me."[3]

Cage wrote "Grace and Clarity" two years before beginning the *Sonatas and Interludes*, and in many ways this essay represents the conceptual inception of Structure and Form. The overarching contention in this essay suggested that modern dance was no longer accessible to the public because it had lost its sense of "clarity," and in the context of Cage's remarks, the notion of "Clarity" is an obvious precursor to that of Structure. In ballet, he explained, the phrase structure is always self-evident: "Phrases begin and end in such a way that anyone in the audience knows when they begin and end, and breathes accordingly." Furthermore, dance, like music, is an art form that reveals itself in time, and therefore a temporal structure is of the utmost importance not only to the composer but also to the choreographer. Modern dance—and perhaps through inference, modern music—has alienated its audience by refusing to supply a clear phrase structure. Similarly, the counterpart of Clarity, "Grace," is an early manifestation of Cage's concept of Form, and he explains their relationship directly:

> Together they have a relation like that of body and soul. Clarity is cold, mathematical, inhuman, but basic and earthy. Grace is warm, incalculable, human, opposed to clarity, and like the air. Grace is not here used to mean prettiness; it is used to mean the play with and against the clarity of the rhythmic structure.[4]

While hoping that the proper balance between Grace and Clarity will increase accessibility to and comprehension of the dance, Cage is not suggesting a creative simplification or pandering. On the contrary, the duality of Grace and Clarity demands a highly sophisticated approach in which Grace (i.e., Form) is set in "perpetual conflict" with Clarity (Structure). Cage likens this phenomenon to the improvisational art of the jazz musician who sometimes plays ahead of or behind the beat, but nonetheless plays in constant reference to the beat.[5]

Cage first introduced the terms Structure, Form, Materials and Method in his lecture, "Defense of Satie,"which he delivered in the summer of 1948 to a group of students and faculty at Black Mountain College. In this lecture Cage loosely defined these concepts, asking his audience: "What kinds of things in art (music in particular) can be agreed upon?" The answer that Cage offered was Structure, "otherwise chaos," he warned: "Sameness in this field is reassuring. We call whatever diverges from sameness of structure monstrous." In an effort to present difficult music to an audience in a way that they could follow it, Cage relied upon the clarity of its organization. He felt that even the most complex music would be accepted if listeners could follow its mode of presentation. However, he qualifies this with the observation that a wide variety of structures are tenable; quite possibly this remark refers to his own recent investigations into the various permutations of micro-macrocosmic form in the *Sonatas and Interludes*, which had been completed just a few months before.

Cage's essay "Forerunners of Modern Music" was published in the journal *The Tiger's Eye* in March of 1949, a date suggesting that its writing took place near or immediately after the completion of *Sonatas and Interludes*. This essay demonstrates the impact that his work on these pieces had upon his aesthetic outlook, and towards the very beginning, Cage provides the first concise definitions of his four essential terms:

> Structure in music is its divisibility into successive parts from phrases to long sections. Form is content, the continuity. Method is the means of controlling the continuity from note to note. The

material of music is sound and silence. Integrating these is composing.[6]

Cage elaborates further, claiming Structure to be "mind-con-
trolled," delighting in "precision, clarity and the observance of rules."
Form, on the other hand, is "heart-controlled" and therefore follows
either no rules, or as Cage qualifies, rules that have "never been and
never will be written." One must remember that what Cage terms
Structure was commonly the definition of Form, (e.g., the structure
known as "sonata-form"), and even Cage at times confused the issue
by referring to his Structure as micro-macrocosmic *form*. However,
form in the traditional sense is harmonically driven; in the context of
Cage's music, Form constitutes "content" and therefore may still contain elements of harmony presented within a Structure which is based
solely upon lengths of time.

Up to this point in his career, Cage used these four terms solely as
a description of the parameters of his compositional technique.
However, beginning with "Forerunners of Modern Music," he also
infused these terms with an aesthetic value, making them resonate
with his developing interest in a spiritual justification for art, and in
particular as exemplified by specific themes culled from Indian aesthetics. The essay is replete with references to Indian philosophy as
well as to the western mystic, Meister Eckhart, opening with a reference to Eckhart's concept of the soul as "the gatherer-together of disparate elements." These "disparate elements," musically organized
through the Form of a piece, are gathered together and understood
only through the efforts of the mind which perceives Structure. Set
against this determined background of Structure, the disparate,
uncontrolled elements proceed in a manner through which "we shall
be informed by the divine unconsciousness and in that our ignorance
will be ennobled and adorned with supernatural knowledge." When
the composer maintains Structure, Form can "express nature in her
manner of operation thus making the soul susceptible to divine influences." Cage, clearly inspired by Eckhart, also put it another way: "If
the mind is disciplined, the heart turns from fear towards love."
Heart-controlled Form is free to expand and exist uninhibited but
within a defined space, Structure.

Cage also hints towards his own compositional and aesthetic
future in this essay:

> In the case of a year, rhythmic structure is a matter of seasons,
> months, weeks, and days. Other time lengths such as that taken
> by a fire or the playing of a piece of music occur accidentally or
> freely without explicit recognition of an all-embracing order, but
> nevertheless, necessarily within that order.[7]

Clearly, Cage's aesthetic was already moving towards his use of open form and indeterminacy, perceiving random events as occurring within the structure of time; and while the mind demands Structure, Form moves freely within it.

The "Lecture on Nothing" (c. 1949–50) is a speech that is itself written in micro-macrocosmic form, and as such, it is an ingenious introduction to Cage's use of that structure. The lecture presents Cage's four elemental terms in much the same manner as found in "Forerunners of Modern Music," their meanings further enhanced by references to his new aesthetic terminology based on his borrowings from Eastern thought. For example, Structure becomes:

> . . . a discipline which, accepted, in return accepts whatever. Structure without Life is dead. But Life without Structure is unseen. Pure life expresses itself within and through structure.[8]

At this point, Cage had discerned that while he was correct in contending that Structure is necessary in order for one to comprehend Art/Life, it is also an inherent element of existence itself, and therefore it is unnecessary for the composer to impose that structure consciously. That is, life itself is structured, and one cannot write a piece of music that occurs outside of that natural Structure. Consequently, in the final analysis, "structure has no point." Likewise, Cage significantly altered his interpretation of Form, describing it as the "demonstration of disinterestedness—a proof that our delight lies not in possessing anything. Each moment presents what happens." This definition of Form now sounds conspicuously similar to the concept behind Cage's "silent" piece, *4'33"*, in which the sounds arise of themselves. Again Cage seems to imply that the actual manifestation of Form may occur without the guiding hand of the composer's intention, a reinterpretation of this definition that complements his recent fascination with the "now moment."

The greatest significance of "Lecture on Nothing" with regard to Form and Structure lies in Cage's intriguing illustration of this dichotomy, as he reflexively traces the flow of the micro-macrocosmic form of the speech itself as he delivers it. From the aspect of Structure, the forty-minute lecture is divided into five large sections whose lengths are determined by the ratio: 7, 6, 14, 14, 7. From the point of view of Form, the first large section itself is a discussion of the idea of Form, while the second considers Structure. Up to this point, by changing the themes of his discussion from one section to the next (i.e., by altering its Formal content), Cage's Structure is as clear as the divisions in the *First Construction*. However, an interesting moment arises at the opening of the third section, and Cage describes the conflict as it occurs within the talk itself:

> We are now at the beginning of the third part and that part is not
> the part devoted to structure. It's the part about material. But I am
> still talking about structure. It must be clear from this that struc-
> ture has no point, and, as we have seen, form has no point either.
> Clearly, we are beginning to get nowhere.[9]

As Cage describes within the Structure of the lecture itself, the second macrocosmic unit of the lecture constitutes a discussion of
Structure, while the third macrocosmic unit is reserved for the subject
of Materials, and within each unit, ideas and words (i.e., the Form)
unfold. Ideally, within the macrocosmic unit set aside for a discussion
of Structure, ideas embellishing this specific concept would occur. As
these ideas regarding Structure continue to flow into the next macrocosmic unit—a unit ostensibly devoted to ideas about Materials—
Cage achieves a verbal illustration of the manner in which Form may
work both with and against Structure.

A much later essay, "Composition as Process" (1958) uses *Sonatas
and Interludes* as a springboard for a discussion of Form and
Structure. In discussing the conceptual development of Form and
Structure, Cage notes that the micro-macrocosmic structure of the
Sonatas and Interludes features the added parameter of an overall
binary or ternary form for each sonata; the realization of Form
involved making the "progress from the end of a section to its beginning seem inevitable." In this formidable essay, Cage describes his
development of chance procedures as the next step in a progression
towards an ego-less representation of nature in her manner of operation, and he re-evaluates the *Sonatas and Interludes* as a major step in
that direction.

Cage's definition of Form as the "morphology of a continuity" is
perhaps even more significant. Morphology, "the biological study of
the *form* and *structure* of living organisms" (italics mine) is, in
essence, the analysis of Form (i.e., the shape or outline of an object) in
contrast to its structure (the division of the whole into parts).
According to Cage, the study of Form observes nothing less than the
development and evolution of an unending, living flow; it traces the
outward shape and character of an organic entity as it moves through
a Structure. While more speculative, the linguistic application of the
term "morphology" ("the study of word formations in a language
including inflection, derivation and the formation of compounds")
may also shed light on Cage's concept of Form as it is a flow of sound
(a musical continuity) that reveals itself through manipulations of
melodic figures, timbral effects and the formation of pitch aggregates.

While Cage's writings document the gradual change that his conceptions of Structure and Form underwent, these evolutions were

themselves direct results of the lessons that he learned through the act of composition. In *Sonatas and Interludes*, he manipulated the micro-macrocosmic Structure in such a wide variety of ways that he began to perceive Structure as ubiquitous, arising as much out of the listener's natural inclination to organize the sounds being heard as from the intentional designs of the composer. A closer look at the means of Structural organization employed in the composition of *Sonatas and Interludes* reveals the implications of Cage's experiments.

Structure

From the late 1930s, Structure manifested itself in Cage's music through micro-macrocosmic form. His early use of this method remained relatively straightforward. As already illustrated in *First Construction*, the reliance on a cycle based on whole numbers (16 x 16) facilitated a lucid overarching plan, and it was not difficult to repeat or subdivide this basic pattern. In *Sonatas and Interludes*, however, Cage's Structures include fractions (e.g., Sonata VI, in which the basic six-measure unit is apportioned as {2 ⅔, 2 ⅔, ⅓, ⅓}), and it is not such a simple matter to repeat or divide such a cycle systematically. Often, there were no easy solutions to such dilemmas, and as the *Sonata and Interludes* demonstrate, Cage ultimately arrived at a multiplicity of intriguing solutions, reinforcing his assertion in "Defense of Satie" that there are a variety of feasible Structures. Through his inclusion of fractions in his rhythmic cycles, Cage created for himself an obstacle which gave rise to a high level of complexity in a seemingly constrictive system.

In *First Construction*, changes in timbre, tempi and rhythm from section to section made the Structure of the piece audible and even visible in performance. In contrast, Cage did not resort to changes of tempi to delineate overall sections in the *Sonatas and Interludes*, and unlike the percussion ensemble works, these pieces for solo instrument do not provide blatant visual cues as to their Structures. In addition, the extent of preparation rendered the instrument so rich in unique sounds that the discernment of Structure through the manipulation of timbre is futile.

Cage resolved these problems through a variety of means, and the *Sonatas and Interludes* are a virtual textbook on his techniques in the manipulation of Structure. Since each individual sonata and interlude maintains a consistent tempo, Cage demarcated his Structures audibly through rhythm. Consequently, the phrases of these pieces serve dual roles:

1) defining the beginnings and endings of divisions in the micro-macrocosmic form, as dictated by the parameters of a given piece's Structure;

2) working alternately with and against the micro-macrocosmic Structure, as dictated by the freedom of Form. Cage often presents two melodies simultaneously, one defining the Structure while the other, following the dictates of Form, blurs the distinctions of that Structure.

Of the sixteen sonatas, thirteen are in binary form with each section repeated, much like the pre-Classical era sonatas of Scarlatti. The remaining three, however, are in ternary form with two of the three sections repeated and the other stated only once (one may think of this as binary form with an interpolated extra section). The placement of this extra section varies for each of the three sonatas: Sonata IX has a Structure of ‖:A ‖:B:‖ ‖:C:‖; Sonata X, ‖:A:‖ ‖:B:‖ C ‖; and Sonata XI, ‖:A:‖ B ‖:C:‖. Of the four interludes, two are through-composed, while the other two are in four-part form, in which each section is repeated (‖:A:‖ ‖:B:‖ ‖:C:‖ ‖:D:‖). Within these relatively clear frameworks, Cage infused his assorted micro-macrocosmic rhythmic Structures. As James Pritchett points out, the use of binary and ternary forms bears a direct impact upon the proportions that comprise the Structures, as the repeated numbers of rhythmic cycles are the result of the sectional repetitions of the forms. In Sonata VII, for example, the rhythmic structure is {2, 2, 1, 1}; on the macrocosmic level of this ‖:A:‖ ‖:B:‖ design, therefore, the first statement of the A section contains two presentations of the full microcosmic cycle to fulfill the first macrocosmic unit (consisting of two cycles), while its repetition satisfies the second macrocosmic unit of equal length. Likewise, the B section consists of one run-through of the cycle, satisfying the third section of the macro-level, while the fourth section is the result of the repeat of B. This can be graphically represented as follows:

Binary divisions/ Macrocosmic units	A	A (repeated)	B	B (repeated)
# of microcosmic units within each Macrocosmic unit	2	2	1	1
Microcosmic breakdown of each Macrocosmic unit (in measures)	[2, 2, 1, 1] [2, 2, 1, 1]	[2, 2, 1, 1] [2, 2, 1, 1]	[2, 2, 1, 1]	[2, 2, 1, 1]

The ternary forms follow a similar pattern, the difference being that the non-repeated number within the cycle represents the non-repeated section of the overarching form. In Sonata IX, the rhythmic structure {1, 2, 2, 1 ½, 1 ½} signifies that the A section, consisting of one presentation of the cycle, is not repeated, whereas both the B and C sections are repeated, consisting of two presentations of the cycle and one and a half presentations, respectively.

Of course, the intricacies of manipulating rhythmic structures that use fractions transcend these mere formal outlines, and the *Sonatas and Interludes* present a staggering range of structurally complex realizations. Overall, Cage's approaches to Structure in these instances can be grouped into four main categories: 1) the direct presentation provided by the exclusive use of whole numbers within the cycles; 2) halving the structure by eliminating the repeats of sections; 3) maintaining the ratio of the parts in structures that use fractions by dividing the musical material according to the proportions inherent in the structure; and 4) reducing sections though diminution to accommodate the fractions in the rhythmic structure.[10] There is a subtle difference in Cage's handling of the macrocosmic as opposed to the microcosmic. The macro-level of organization is always the more obvious of the two, in that it largely requires no more than the counting of measures, or sometimes beats, to determine. The macro-level, therefore, consists of nothing but fixed divisions of empty space in which "one may accept anything." Sonata XIII, for example is based on the cycle {1 ½, 1 ½, 3 ½, 3 ½}. One microcosmic unit equals one measure of $\frac{4}{4}$. Ten measures of $\frac{4}{4}$ is the space required for one complete presentation of the microcosmic cycle. At the macrocosmic level, the A section, based on the number 1 ½, must constitute 1.5 microcosmic cycles; it comprises ten measures (one full cycle) plus five measures (one half cycle), for a total of fifteen measures. Similarly, the B section, based on 3 ½, contains thirty measures (three full cycles) plus five measures (one half cycle), or thirty-five measures. Within the complete macrocosmic structure, the microcosmic level comprises repetitions of the cycle of proportions, and it is at this level that devices such as "halving the structure," "maintaining the ratio" and "diminution" are applied.

The simplest of Structures in the *Sonatas and Interludes* appear in Sonatas IV, VII, X, XIV and XV, which rely solely on the use of whole numbers within their cycles, thereby yielding a structure similar to that of *First Construction*. In Sonatas XIV and XV, for instance, both have the rhythmic structure {2, 2, 3, 3}; the overall structural plan presents itself as follows:

Binary divisions/Macrocosmic units	A	A (repeated)	B	B (repeated
# of Microcosmic units within each Macrocosmic unit	2	2	3	3
Microcosmic breakdown of each Macrocosmic unit (in measures)	[2, 2, 3, 3] [2, 2, 3, 3]	[2, 2, 3, 3] [2, 2, 3, 3]	[2, 2, 3, 3] [2, 2, 3, 3] [2, 2, 3, 3]	[2, 2, 3, 3] [2, 2, 3, 3] [2, 2, 3, 3]

Typically, even when rhythmic structures became extremely complex through the use of fractions, Cage maintained his divisions with intense mathematical precision. Yet there are exceptions; in Sonata VII a unique and curious anomaly occurs when, three measures before the end of the A section, Cage inserts an extra half-measure that stands entirely outside the parameters of the rhythmic structure, as though he suspended his structure to accommodate the sonata's melodic implications in an almost Beethovenian moment of motivic development.[11] Perhaps this is a loosening of the constraints of Structure, a glaring contradiction to Cage's own vehement insistence that the rhythmic Structure be maintained. However, it seems more likely that this is an extreme example of Form working against Structure, even to the point of overcoming and momentarily suspending that Structure.

The inclusion of whole numbers, even in rhythmic cycles which incorporate fractions, facilitated a handling of Structure similar to that outlined above. For instance, in Sonata III, the rhythmic structure $\{1, 1, 3\ 1/4, 3\ 1/4\}$ mandates that the A section consist of a single presentation of the cycle. The unit of measurement on the micro-level is one measure of $\frac{4}{4}$; in order to achieve the fractional proportions in this cycle, Cage interpolates measures of $\frac{5}{4}$ into the A section.[12]

Several of the sonatas containing the fraction $1/2$ within their rhythmic structure demonstrate Cage's second method of realizing structure, as he accommodates this $1/2$ unit on the micro-level by eliminating the repeats inherent in its rhythmic structure. Again turning to Sonata XIII, we see that at the macrocosmic level, the A section requires one full (ten-measure) statement of the cycle and one half (five-measure) presentation. On the micro-level, Cage fits his rhythmic structure into this reduced amount of space by presenting only one unit of $1\ 1/2$ and one unit of $3\ 1/2$. An outline of this structural design follows:

Sonata XIII: A section only (basic cycle: 1 $\frac{1}{2}$, 1 $\frac{1}{2}$, 3 $\frac{1}{2}$, 3 $\frac{1}{2}$)

# of Microcosmic units within each Macrocosmic unit	1	+	$\frac{1}{2}$
Microcosmic breakdown of each Macrocosmic unit (in measures)	[1, 1 $\frac{1}{2}$, 3 $\frac{1}{2}$, 3 $\frac{1}{2}$]		[1 $\frac{1}{2}$, 3 $\frac{1}{2}$]

Since Cage simply omits half of the cycle, I refer to this technique as "halving the structure."[13]

In several sonatas, the structural divisions of the phrases are so blurred that they are nearly impossible to discern; this is possibly the result of Cage's note-to-note method that he described as "considered improvisation."[14] In these instances, one method Cage employed was that of maintaining the ratio between the first half of the cycle and the second half. For instance, in Sonata V, a cycle of nine measures is divided into the proportions {2, 2, 2 $\frac{1}{2}$, 2 $\frac{1}{2}$}; this creates the ratio of 4:5 between the first and second halves of this cycle. Since one unit of the cycle equals a single measure of $\frac{2}{2}$, the macro-level of the B section requires two full cycles (nine measures each) as well as one half-cycle (four and a half measures long). In this case, Cage accommodates this four-and-a-half measure partial cycle through three measures of $\frac{2}{2}$ and one of $\frac{3}{2}$, the equivalent to one full measure plus a half-measure of $\frac{2}{2}$. On the micro-level, Cage maintains the ratio of 4:5 within the final four and a half measures but does not attempt to distinguish the smaller divisions at all, preferring instead to use long note values. This gives the piece a fine sense of closure but does little to emphasize the divisions of the phrase. Remarkably, Cage signifies the division of the ratio through the release of the notes D and B, identifying the progression from one section of the Structure to the next by moving from the tension of the tonal cluster (B, C and D) to the relative serenity of the single note C. In the hands of a pianist sensitive to the strictures of Cage's Structure, this is indeed a striking moment. Employing the same method, the B section of Sonata II presents a more complex instance arising from the problematic inclusion of the fraction $\frac{3}{8}$. The complete rhythmic cycle in Sonata II is seven and three-quarters measures in length, subdivided into the series {1 $\frac{1}{2}$, 1 $\frac{1}{2}$, 2 $\frac{3}{8}$, 2 $\frac{3}{8}$}, the two halves of this series yielding the ratio 3:4. On the macro-level, the B section therefore requires two and three-eighths presentations of the cycle. At the conclusion of this section, the space provided for the three-eighths presentation of the cycle consists of a large group of 23 eighth notes, divided into three measures of $\frac{3}{8}$ followed by two measures of $\frac{7}{8}$. From another perspective, each $\frac{7}{8}$ measure is equivalent to two measures of $\frac{3}{8}$ plus an extra eighth note; therefore, this portion of the cycle consists of seven measures of $\frac{3}{8}$ plus two extra eighth notes. As seven measures of $\frac{3}{8}$ constitutes three-eighths of seven measures of $\frac{4}{4}$ (the predominant meter), this leaves the remaining space of a quarter note (two eighth notes) for the reduction of three-fourths of a measure (the original cycle consisting of 7 $\frac{3}{4}$ measures) to three-eighths of its original length, or $\frac{9}{32}$ of a measure. This is approximately equal to the fraction $\frac{8}{32}$, or $\frac{1}{4}$, the musical equivalent of the two remaining eighth notes. A summary of this process follows:

The cycle = 7 $\frac{3}{4}$ measures = 7 + $\frac{3}{4}$.

7 x $\frac{3}{8}$ = 7 measures of $\frac{3}{8}$ (since the unit one = a measure of $\frac{4}{4}$, three-eighths of one is a measure of $\frac{3}{8}$).

$\frac{3}{4}$ x $\frac{3}{8}$ = $\frac{9}{32}$, which is approximately equal to $\frac{8}{32}$.

$\frac{8}{32}$ = $\frac{1}{4}$ = $\frac{2}{8}$ (or two eighth notes).

Obviously, the complexity of this section precluded the clarity of structural divisions possible in other sonatas. Therefore, Cage maintained the ratio of 3:4, $\frac{3}{4}$ through the use of three measures of $\frac{3}{8}$ and two measures of $\frac{7}{8}$, which equals four measures of $\frac{3}{8}$ plus Cage's approximation of three-eighths of three-quarters of a measure. This may seem a hasty approximation to some, but one must remember that Cage had a limited amount of actual, not theoretical, space with which to work. Therefore, the inclusion of that missing thirty-second note, which incidentally would theoretically be divided between two measures, making each $\frac{7}{8}+\frac{1}{64}$, would have needlessly complicated matters for the performer and remained inaudible to the audience.[15]

The fourth main structural strategy that Cage employed was diminution of the rhythmic structures. In other words, he reduced the number of beats per measure to fit the fractions on the macro-level. The rhythmic structure—{1 $\frac{1}{4}$, $\frac{3}{4}$, 1 $\frac{1}{4}$, $\frac{3}{4}$, 1 $\frac{1}{2}$, 1 $\frac{1}{2}$} of Sonata I, for example—mandates that the B section consist of one and one-half presentations of the seven-measure cycle, the equivalent of ten and a half measures. However, Cage approaches the problem by changing the meter from $\frac{2}{2}$ to $\frac{2}{4}$, writing seven measures in this new meter. Therefore, instead of dividing the total number of the cycle's measures in half, he reduces the length of each measure by half. The music on the micro-level continues to reflect the structural divisions of {1 $\frac{1}{4}$, $\frac{3}{4}$, 1 $\frac{1}{4}$, $\frac{3}{4}$, 1 $\frac{1}{2}$, 1 $\frac{1}{2}$} but reduces the scale by fifty percent at the appropriate points.[16]

There are five sonatas that require separate discussion due to their use of unusual structural procedures. These sonatas defy any of the four main categories, revealing some of the more interesting aspects of Cage's manipulation of Structure.

The eight and a half measure cycle of Sonata III, divided into the proportions {1, 1, 3 $\frac{1}{4}$, 3 $\frac{1}{4}$} with one unit equaling one measure of $\frac{4}{4}$, requires three and a half presentations of the cycle in the B section. Surprisingly, Cage did not resort to any of the methods outlined above but instead used two full presentations of the cycle, then one full presentation of the cycle with the unit of measurement enhanced momentarily to a measure of $\frac{5}{4}$, thus increasing the cycle by the necessary one-fourth and fulfilling the 3 $\frac{1}{4}$ run-through on the macro-level. On the microcosmic level, Cage accommodates the 3 $\frac{1}{4}$ proportion by using two measures of $\frac{5}{4}$ followed by one of $\frac{5}{16} + \frac{5}{4}$, deriving $\frac{5}{16}$ as one fourth of a measure of $\frac{5}{4}$.

The First Interlude is a special case in that it contains an added dimension to its simple design. The cycle in this piece is ten measures long and is repeated ten times, as the micro-macrocosmic structure mandates. However, the rhythmic subdivision of this cycle is {1 $\frac{1}{2}$, 1 $\frac{1}{2}$, 2, 1 $\frac{1}{2}$, 1 $\frac{1}{2}$, 2}. The second presentation of the cycle on the micro-level is cut in half by the macro-level division, thus bringing the two levels momentarily out of synch. The latter half of this presentation is used to satisfy the second proportion on the macro-level, realigning the micro- and macro-levels. The micro-level continues to spin itself out regardless of the sections as delineated by the macro-level. We can refer to this phenomenon as "micro-elision." The relative simplicity of this technique as employed in the First Interlude, largely as a result of its uncomplicated rhythmic cycle, belies the extreme complexity that Cage achieved through "micro-elision" in Sonatas I and VI. Sonata I has the rhythmic structure {1 $\frac{1}{4}$, $\frac{3}{4}$, 1 $\frac{1}{4}$, $\frac{3}{4}$, 1 $\frac{1}{2}$, 1 $\frac{1}{2}$}, which Cage divides into binary form by grouping the 1 $\frac{1}{4}$ and $\frac{3}{4}$ sections together on the macro-level to set the space requirement of the A section. He presents one full presentation of the cycle (seven measures of $\frac{4}{4}$) followed by a measure of $\frac{7}{4}$ (one-fourth of seven measures of $\frac{4}{4}$) to produce the 1 $\frac{1}{4}$ division. The $\frac{3}{4}$ division contains two measures of $\frac{6}{4}$ and two of $\frac{9}{8}$, equaling twenty-one quarter notes (three-fourths of seven measures of $\frac{4}{4}$). Furthermore, the measure of $\frac{7}{4}$ contains a large, sustained aggregate on the fifth beat, thereby dividing the measure into a group of four beats followed by a group of three beats, emphasizing the operative ratio of 4:3 in the rhythmic structure. Likewise, on the macrocosmic level, the $\frac{3}{4}$ section, from its division into two measures of $\frac{6}{4}$ and two of $\frac{9}{8}$, maintains the proportion of twenty-four eighth notes (contained within two measures of $\frac{6}{4}$) to eighteen eighth notes (contained in two measures of $\frac{9}{8}$) respectively, which again reduces to the ratio of 4:3. Starting again at the measure of $\frac{7}{4}$, we can trace the entire cycle {1 $\frac{1}{4}$, $\frac{3}{4}$, 1 $\frac{1}{4}$, $\frac{3}{4}$, 1 $\frac{1}{2}$, 1 $\frac{1}{2}$} through to the double bar. Therefore, through this technique of "micro-elision," Sonata I: A maintains the ratio within the individual sections while allowing the cycle to continue uninterrupted on the microcosmic level.

Unlike the majority of the sonatas that rely on a single measure of $\frac{4}{4}$ as the unit of measurement, Sonata VI uses a measure of $\frac{3}{4}$ for its rhythmic structure of {2 $\frac{2}{3}$, 2 $\frac{2}{3}$, $\frac{1}{3}$, $\frac{1}{3}$}. Hence the macrocosmic level of the A section contains two full presentations of the cycle followed by a two–third's presentation, idiosyncratically arranged as a measure of $\frac{4}{4}$ followed by one of $\frac{3}{4}$, and completed by a measure of $\frac{2}{4}$. The B section consists solely of two measures of $\frac{3}{4}$ (one-third of six measures of $\frac{3}{4}$). On the micro-level, the cycle elides the divisions of the macro-level by continuing to scroll through its rhythmic structure. Therefore, the first phrase of 2 $\frac{2}{3}$ divides the measure of $\frac{2}{4}$ in half, the second division of 2 $\frac{2}{3}$ uses the second beat of the $\frac{2}{4}$ measure through the first beat of the final measure, and each section of $\frac{1}{3}$ occupies one beat of the final measure. This is the unique example of the micro-elision actually crossing the divisions of the binary form.

Perhaps the most perplexing sonata with regard to Structure is Sonata XII, which Pritchett describes as having a nine-measure rhythmic structure divided into the proportions {2, 2, 2 $\frac{1}{2}$, 2 $\frac{1}{2}$}. However, even a cursory glance at the score reveals the difficulty arising from this assertion. The meter is in constant flux, shifting from $\frac{6}{4}$ to $\frac{4}{4}$ to $\frac{7}{4}$ and eventually to $\frac{5}{4}$, $\frac{2}{4}$ and even $\frac{9}{4}$ and $\frac{8}{4}$. Deciding which meter serves as the unit of measurement is immediately problematic and indeed, none of the above time signatures suffice. Furthermore, the varying meters of the A section are arranged in two groups: the first contains three measures of $\frac{6}{4}$ on either side of a measure of $\frac{4}{4}$, while the second group has a repeated pattern of three measures of $\frac{6}{4}$ rounded off by a measure of $\frac{7}{4}$. The first group contains forty beats, while the second is comprised of fifty, confirming the ratio implicit in Pritchett's assessment of the rhythmic structure, 4:5. However, the B section is more complex in that the first ending is a measure of $\frac{8}{4}$, whereas the second ending is a measure of $\frac{7}{4}$. Thus, the first presentation of the B section consists of one-hundred and thirteen beats, whereas the second presentation only contains one-hundred and twelve. The mean of these totals is one-hundred and twelve and one-half beats. As is demonstrated below this provides the ratio of 4:5 between the A and B sections.

A Section   B Section

90 beats   113 beats (1st time)
                 112 beats (2nd time)
                 225 beats (total)

                 $\div 2 =$
                 112.5 beats (average B section)

Ratio between A & B sections: 90:112.5 = 4:5

The proportions of the rhythmic structure of this sonata function almost exclusively on the macro-level, maintaining the ratio of 4:5 within and between the two large sections of the binary form. Cage made no attempt to structure this particular work on any more than the most basic level; the Form of Sonata XII, therefore, seems especially unhindered by the constraints of micro-macrocosmic structure, yet the sonata maintains its outward characteristics of carefully delineated measurements of time. This is perhaps a direct demonstration of Cage's waning interest in defining structure with the meticulous attention he had paid it previously, documenting his shift towards a Structure which "accepted, accepts whatever."[17] That is, from the conceptual rejection of Structure as a consciously controlled parameter towards Structure as it arises, it is no longer dependent upon the designs of the composer but rather on the listener's inherent tendency to organize the sounds around him.

The following chart outlines the methods Cage employed for each section of the *Sonatas and Interludes*:[18]

Whole Number	Halving	Ratio	Dimunition	Micro-Elision	Special
		Sonata I: A	Sonata I: B	Sonata I: A	
	Sonata II: A	Sonata II: B			
Sonata III: A					Sonata III: B
Sonata IV					
1st Interlude				1st Interlude	
Sonata V: A		Sonata V: B			
				Sonata VI	
Sonata VII					
Sonata VIII: A	Sonata VIII: B				
		3rd Interlude			
Sonata IX: A,B			Sonata IX: C		
Sonata X					

Whole Number	Halving	Ratio	Dimunition	Micro-Elision	Special
Sonata XI: A,B		Sonata XI: C			
		Sonata XII			Sonata XII
	Sonata XIII				
4th Interlude: A,B,C		4th Interlude: D			
Sonata XIV					
Sonata XV					
	Sonata XVI				

Form

Cage defined Form as the "morphology of a continuity," the element of a composition which embodies the chaotic, living aspects of existence. Whereas he postulated that "analysis is at home" in the study of Structure, Form "only wants the freedom to be." Paradoxically, these elements share a deeply symbiotic relationship, each incapable of expression without the other. As has been demonstrated, Structure may be regarded as a carefully apportioned frame of empty space, but it is Form—the actual musical material—that ultimately elucidates structural boundaries, thereby producing what Cage termed the "poetry" of his music.

Cage's stated purpose with regard to Form in the *Sonatas and Interludes* was to make the repetitions of each binary section as well as the transition from one to the next seem inevitable. Sonata V, a case in point, opens with an A section that contains the simultaneous exposition of two parts: the upper part, consisting of a two-measure melodic figure beginning on an E-flat dotted quarter note; and a one-measure ostinato figure, constituting the lower part. Each of these figures is manipulated in ways that reflect the overarching rhythmic structure of the sonata. In particular, the left hand figure remains unchanged for thirteen measures; at measure 14, it is extended by two eighth notes to encompass one and one-fourth measures of time. This extended figure is immediately repeated and followed by two presentations of the original ostinato, which is now rhythmically displaced by half a measure. From measures 14–18, therefore, the altered ostinato pattern is 1 $\frac{1}{4}$, 1 $\frac{1}{4}$, 1, 1, which reflects the ratio of 5:4, the very reverse of the ratio established by the sonata's rhythmic cycle—Form acting with and against Structure. The conclusion of the A section essentially falls on beat three of measure 18 when the ostinato pattern closes on a B, the same note with which it began. The A section is then repeated after a beat of silence, taking up the ostinato figure precisely where it left off. The transition to the B section (mm. 17-18) is also notable in its blurring of distinctions between the two halves of the sonata. Starting on beat 3 of measure 17, the final presentation of the ostinato within the A section is accompanied by an extended C in the right hand. The B section then opens with another C in the right hand suspended above a slightly altered version of the left-hand ostinato. The B section continues the process of rhythmically manipulating the ostinato, now using the closing figure of the A section, by alternately extending it by four eighth notes, ending it on a half note B or presenting it as a one-measure figure followed by a half note B and a half rest. Additional half rests satisfy the latter part of the rhythmic cycle. Through an ever-evolving manipulation of the sonata's ostinato, Cage effectively elides the boundaries of the Structure, as the Form flows freely from one section to the next.

The Fourth Interlude offers another intriguing example of Cage's manipulation of transitions from one section to another in subtle and exciting ways. The penultimate measure of the A section (m. 8) features a rising figure ending on the F—a whole step below the G with which the piece opens. However, before the repeat of the A section, Cage interposes a silent measure of $\frac{4}{8}$. The second ending, however, replaces this silent measure with a chord that first appeared on the last eighth note of measure 4, containing the same G as its uppermost note. The immediate resolution to the high G that was denied in the initial statement of the A section is now achieved. The B section also opens with the high G, transforming the lower notes of the previously heard chord as an ostinato, motivically linking this moment with the previous section. The melodic content in the right hand uses much of the same pitch ordering as the A section but with elongated note values. Like the A section, the B section concludes with a $\frac{4}{8}$ measure of rest. The C section further expands upon the melodic fragments of the B section beginning with a figure drawn from measure 14 and ending with the resumption in its penultimate measure of the opening ostinato of the B section. The high G is once again the highest point of the piece's tessitura, and the section concludes with a $\frac{4}{8}$ measure of rest. The recurring ostinato, the consistent use of an empty measure of $\frac{4}{8}$ as a closing gesture, and the emphasis of the high G tend to blur the divisions between the sections. Hence the D section, at first, seems unrelated to the earlier music of the interlude, even transcending the upper barrier previously established by the high G; however, on the last beat of its fourth measure (m. 31) the G returns, trilled above a rising figure in the left hand. The piece ends on the G with which it commenced, closing the interlude by returning the listener to its most characteristic sound. Thus Cage has designed the transitions of this piece to move the listener through four distinct sections with such subtlety as to make it appear almost through-composed.

Whereas Form follows no set procedure and is indeed created anew for each of the pieces within *Sonatas and Interludes*, it is more instructive to engage two pieces closely rather than attempt to construct what would be empty generalizations about the entire collection. Sonata IV is remarkable in the amount of variety that it cultivates from a considerably limited amount of material, turning its sparseness into one of the most eloquent expressions of Form to be found within the set. Structurally, the piece is rather simplistic, based on the rhythmic structure {3, 3, 2, 2}. The first microcosmic presentation of the cycle opens with a five-note phrase (B-C-A-E-B) that serves as the germinal motive for the entire first half of the binary form. This figure is repeated to satisfy the next proportion of the rhythmic cycle, except for the initial B, which is merely tied over from the ending of the last phrase, subtly offsetting the balance of the three-measure phrases. Each of the following two-measure phrases presents short melodic gestures to mark its beginning, while the remainder of the phrases consist of silence. At measure 7, the two-bar phrase expands its initial four-note gesture to include a high G; the following phrase states all five pitches in an ascending scalar passage that foreshadows the figure that can be labeled motive A as it appears in both the A and B sections. In the second microcosmic cycle (mm. 11–20), the right-hand melodic material is limited to the pitches E, C and B. The first phrase (mm. 11–13) presents these pitches in descending order followed by the figure C, E, C. The next phrase (mm. 14–16) sets this figure as a mordent and then reverses the mordent (E, C, E); the final two phrases (mm. 17–20) present the single pitch, B. The move from the E to the B in measures 16-20 is an elongation of this gesture as presented in measure 2 and measure 5. The return to the beginning of the A section is almost indistinct due to the sustained B which leads back to the piece's opening phrase; in the second ending of the A section, the transition to the B section satisfies an urgent need for movement within this almost static piece. The opening of the B section is comprised of two elements: in the right hand, three sustained notes (all of which are outside of the A section's pitch set) establish the divisions of the rhythmic structure; the five-beat ostinato in the left hand, however, works against that structure which is based on four-beat units (note that the two and a half measures of rest are equivalent to two groups of five beats).

Cage underscores the textural sparseness by strategically arranging the placement of attacks. The majority of the notes of the first and third microcosmic cycles of the A section are performed on beat 1 while in the second cycle more weight is given to beat 3. However, both cycles of the B section demonstrate an almost even distribution of the attacks among all four beats. Perhaps this is an example of Cage's representation of the tendency of the nine permanent emotions towards tranquillity, in that the stress placed upon traditionally strong beats resolves itself in the B section by leveling the aural landscape.

A Section

	Beat 1	Beat 2	Beat 3	Beat 4
Cycle 1	11	3	2	0
Cycle 2	5	4	9	3
Cycle 3	6	2	3	2

B Section

	Beat 1	Beat 2	Beat 3	Beat 4
Cycle 1	8	7	8	8
Cycle 2	3	3	3	2

Finally, the cadences of the A and B sections are almost identical. The A section's third and final cycle is signaled by an ascending motive that fills the entire first three-measure phrase (mm. 21–23). This is followed by a brief three-note gesture and two measures of silence, while a four-measure cadential figure occupies the latter half of the cycle. This figure consists of a suspended B punctuated by a dyad (the D flat/A unit) on beats 1 and 4 of the first measure and a solitary D flat on beat 3 of the succeeding measure. Therefore, the punctuating notes reflect the ratio 3:2 of the rhythmic structure. Conversely, the final microcosmic cycle in the B section (mm. 41–50) commences with three measures of silence, followed by the return of the opening motive of the A section. Cage reverses the order of the presentation within the B section of music heard earlier in the A section, allowing the climactic opening motive to lead directly into the cadential figure. Significantly, the cadential figure itself is subtly altered, as the punctuating dyad on beats 1 and 4 (m. 47) becomes a three-note chord though the inclusion of an additional A♭ below the D♭. This D♭/A♭ unit appears on beat 3 of the next measure, and the A♭ is performed alone on the second beat of the following measure. This gradual elimination of tones in these final four measures creates a profound sense of closure, while the added A♭ and repositioning of the ascending opening motive (mm. 44–46) lend increased weight to a cadential figure which must serve to close both sections of the binary form.

As the analyses above demonstrate, Cage constructed much of the excitement and power of the *Sonatas and Interludes for Prepared Piano* out of the tension inherent in his conceptions of Structure and Form. From his earliest reference to Structure and Form in his essay "Grace and Clarity," Cage maintained that these concepts were necessary to the production of a music which communicates with an audience. Structure allows the listener to breathe with the musical phrases, demarcating the temporal divisions of the piece, while Form imbues the composition with life; the interplay of these elements, properly balanced, promotes a vital and urgent art form. Although each of these pieces relies upon Cage's micro-macrocosmic form, the composer achieved that specific Structure through several discrete methods, creating the variety of manifestations of Structure that he had suggested in his 1948 lecture, "Defense of Satie." Through the inclusion of fractions within the rhythmic cycles of many of the sonatas, Cage posed a compositional dilemma, forcing himself to transcend the limitations of what could easily have become an overly simplistic and constrictive system. Form is, as Cage intended, inimical towards generalizations and straightforward analysis, and varies considerably from piece to piece. Together, perhaps more significantly in the *Sonatas and Interludes* than in any of Cage's remaining works, Structure and Form combine to produce a symbiotic relationship in which one is inextricable from the other. Indeed, it is nearly impossible to represent the composer's realization of one concept without reference to the other. In this work, Cage developed strategies, far outdistancing his previous works, that fully explored the interdependence of these concepts and established in concrete musical form the theories of his lectures and prose. On the other hand, the extreme complexity of some of the pieces, paired with the absolute obfuscation of the Structure of others, suggested to Cage the possibility of permitting Structure to arise regardless of the composer's attempts to impose it; this is a concept which would reach fruition in his later chance-derived pieces. Ultimately, these works invite the listener to continually return to them, to engage them anew, and indeed, each confrontation with such seemingly unassuming and direct music reveals deeper levels of intricacy and beauty.

Notes

1.   John Cage, "Forerunners of Modern Music" (1949), in *Silence: Lectures and Writings* (Middletown, CT: Wesleyan University Press, 1961), 63.

2.   John Cage, "Grace and Clarity" (1946), in *Silence: Lectures and Writings* (Middletown, CT: Wesleyan University Press, 1961), 91–92.

3.   John Cage and Joan Retallack, *Musicage: Cage Muses on Words Art Music* (Middletown, CT: Wesleyan University Press, 1996).

4.   Cage, "Grace and Clarity," 91–92.

5.   Ibid., 92.

6.   Cage, "Forerunners of Modern Music," 62.

7.   Ibid., 65.

8.   John Cage, "Lecture on Nothing" (c. 1950), in *Silence*, 113.

9.   Ibid., 114.

10.   There are also five sonatas in which Cage employed special means to fulfill their structural plans; these will be discussed separately at the end of this section.

11.   By half-measure I mean the insertion of a measure of $\frac{2}{4}$ in a piece based on the time signature of $\frac{4}{4}$.

12.   Other pieces which contain sections following similar procedures include: Sonata V: A; Sonata VIII: A; Sonata IX: A and B; Sonata XI: A and B; and the A, B and C sections of the 4th Interlude.

13.   Other sonatas that conform to this design are: Sonata II: A; VIII: B; XIII: A and B; and XVI: A and B.

14.   John Cage, "Composition as Process" (1958), in *Silence* (Middletown, CT: Wesleyan University Press, 1961), 19.

15.   The sonatas that use this technique of maintaining the ratio are: Sonata I: A; II: B; V: B, the Third Interlude; Sonata XI; XII; and the Fourth Interlude.

16.   Cage used a similar procedure in the A section of this same sonata. When, on the macro-level, he required the space of one-fourth of the seven measure cycle he used a measure of $\frac{7}{4}$, seven beats (that is one-fourth of each measure) being the equivalent of one-fourth of the cycle. The other sonata that uses diminution as a structural procedure is Sonata IX: C.

17.   Cage, "Lecture on Nothing," 110.

18.   The Second Interlude divides into cycles of eight measures. However, as Pritchett demonstrates, Cage's conception of its further subdivision is unclear.

Contributors

DAVID W. BERNSTEIN is Professor of Music at Mills College. In 1995 he organized an international festival/conference entitled "Here Comes Everybody: The Music, Poetry, and Art of John Cage" at Mills College. His publications on Cage include *Writings through John Cage's Music, Poetry, and Art* (University of Chicago Press, 2001) co-edited with Christopher Hatch, "Techniques of Appropriation in Music of John Cage" (forthcoming in the *Contemporary Music Review*), and "John Cage and the Aesthetic of Indifference" (forthcoming in a collection of essays edited by Steven Johnson and published by Routledge). He is also a contributor to the forthcoming Cambridge University Press Cage Companion edited by David Nicholls.

PAUL VAN EMMERIK received his Ph.D. in 1996 from the University of Amsterdam, where he studied musicology, library science and American studies. He is faculty member at Utrecht University, where he currently teaches music history, with emphasis on twentieth-century art music.

CHARLES HAMM, the Arthur R. Virgin Professor of Music Emeritus at Dartmouth College and past president of the American Musicological Society, has published books, articles and reviews on American music, popular music, the music of southern Africa, musical theater, and the avant-garde. A colleague of John Cage's at the University of Illinois for several years, he wrote the entry on Cage for the *New Grove Dictionary of Music and Musicians*. He was involved in performances of Cage's music from time to time, conducting the *Concert for Piano and Orchestra* at Illinois in 1965.

CHADWICK JENKINS is a Ph.D. candidate at Columbia University. His interests include the music of John Cage and the New York School and the operas of Giuseppe Verdi.

BRANDEN W. JOSEPH received his Ph.D. from the Department of History of Art and Architecture at Harvard University. Among other articles, he is the author of "John Cage and the Architecture of Silence" (*October*), "Hitchhiker in an Omni-directional Transport: The Spatial Politics of John Cage and Buckminster Fuller" (*ANY Magazine*), and "Blanc sur blanc" (*Les Cahiers du Musée national d'art moderne*). He is also a founding editor of *Grey Room*, a journal of architecture, art, media and politics (MIT Press).

SUSAN KEY is a musicologist specializing in American music, with emphasis on the interactions of music, technology, and society. She recieved her Ph.D in musicology from the Univeristy of Maryland at College Park and has taught at the College of William and Mary and Stanford University. Currently she works on special projects for the San Francisco Symphony.

LETA E. MILLER, professor of music at the University of California, Santa Cruz, is a musicologist and flutist whose most recent work has focused on twentieth-century America. In 1998 Oxford University Press published her book *Lou Harrison: Composing a World* (co-authored with ethnomusicologist Fred Lieberman), and her critical edition of Harrison's chamber music appeared in the series *Music in the United States of America*. In press are three articles on Harrison and Cage and a new compact disc recording of music by Henry Cowell. Miller's previous work also includes books, articles, and critical editions on the sixteenth-century chanson and madrigal, music and science in the baroque, and the flute music of C.P.E. Bach, as well as more than a dozen solo recordings on renaissance, baroque, and modern flute.

DAVID W. PATTERSON is an assistant professor of music history at the University of Illinois at Urbana-Champaign. To date, his research on Cage has appeared in *Perspectives of New Music*, *MusikTexte*, *Musicworks* and *repercussions*. His dissertation on Cage's rhetorical borrowings from South and East Asia was awarded the Dissertation Prize from the Sonneck Society for American Music in 1996.

CHRISTOPHER SHULTIS is Professor of Music at the University of New Mexico where he teaches composition, music history, and interdisciplinary studies. His book, *Silencing the Sounded Self: John Cage and the American Experimental Tradition*, is published by Northeastern University Press.

Index